WHITE KIDS

CRITICAL PERSPECTIVES ON YOUTH

General Editors: Amy L. Best, Lorena Garcia, and Jessica K. Taft

This series aims to elaborate a set of theoretical and methodological tenets for a distinctive critical youth studies approach rooted in empirical inquiry. The series draws on the following as some of the key theoretical elements of critical approaches: the socially constructed nature of childhood and adolescence over and against the universalizing and naturalizing propensities of early developmental theory; the centering of young people's social worlds and social locations as the starting point for analysis; exploration of how the meaning and experience of youth is shaped by other important axes of social difference, including but not limited to race, class, gender, place, nation, and sexuality; the recognition that youths' worlds are constituted through multiple processes, institutions, and discourses and that central to understanding youth identity and experience is understanding social inequalities; engagement with the dynamics of global transformation in the experience of childhood and youth; and the relevance of these elements for policy and practice.

Books in the series:

Fast-Food Kids: French Fries, Lunch Lines, and Social Ties
Amy L. Best

White Kids: Growing Up with Privilege in a Racially Divided America
Margaret A. Hagerman

White Kids

Growing Up with Privilege in a
Racially Divided America

Margaret A. Hagerman

NEW YORK UNIVERSITY PRESS

New York

NEW YORK UNIVERSITY PRESS
New York
www.nyupress.org

References to Internet websites (URLs) were accurate at the time of writing. Neither the author nor New York University Press is responsible for URLs that may have expired or changed since the manuscript was prepared.

ISBN: 978-1-4798-0368-2

For Library of Congress Cataloging-in-Publication data, please contact the Library of Congress.

New York University Press books are printed on acid-free paper, and their binding materials are chosen for strength and durability. We strive to use environmentally responsible suppliers and materials to the greatest extent possible in publishing our books.

Manufactured in the United States of America

10 9 8 7 6 5 4 3 2 1

Also available as an ebook

CONTENTS

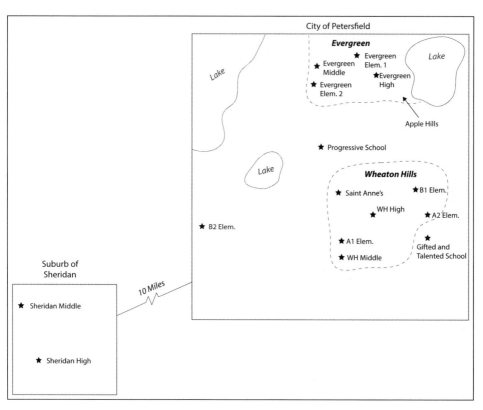

Map of Petersfield and Sheridan

Introduction

Racism is not a problem anymore. . . . Racism was a problem when all those slaves were around and that, like, bus thing and the water fountain. I mean, everything was crazy back in the olden days. . . . But now, I mean, since Martin Luther King and, like, Eleanor Roosevelt, and how she went on the bus. And she was African American and sat on the white part. . . . After the 1920s and all that, things changed.
—Natalie (11, Sheridan)

I think [racism] is a *way* bigger problem than people realize. It's nowhere near what it used to be. . . . It's just different, and white people don't realize it. . . . I think it's still there. It's just not as present, and people want to hide it. Because they are scared to talk about it.
—Conor (11, Evergreen)

I think that the white kids, since they have more power in general in society, . . . disciplinary actions aren't brought down as hard upon them. But when it's, you know, a black kid getting in trouble with the police, . . . I think people are going to be tougher with them, because, you know, [black kids] can't really fight back as well.
—Chris (11, Wheaton Hills)

Natalie, Conor, and Chris are all growing up in the same midwestern metropolitan area.[1] They are 11-years-old and in middle school. They all participate in a variety of sports and extracurricular activities, and they have busy social lives with their friends. These kids often travel with their families across the country, sometimes even across the globe. All three attend expensive summer camps and enrichment programs, most play instruments and take private music lessons, and many of them have attended private school or have received private tutoring, at least once in their lives. Like most kids, they are interested in popular culture, though their favorite celebrities vary, especially with respect to Justin Bieber. Every single one loves animals.

Overall, the children in this book are growing up with upper-middle-class privilege in a society where private wealth shapes the experiences, opportunities, and outcomes that follow such childhoods of privilege. These kids have parents with some of the highest levels of educational attainment possible, being alumni of world-class law schools, medical schools, graduate schools, and business schools. These children's parents work in highly prestigious and influential professions and earn lucrative incomes. These parents also all experience heterosexual privilege. While a small number of the mothers in this study do not work outside the home, these women are heavily involved in their children's schools, their local churches and synagogues, and charitable and volunteer organizations. They all have college educations, the majority holding advanced degrees. The fathers all work outside the home, and some are highly involved in the daily lives of their children and coach sports teams or lead clubs. These children are growing up in valuable, well-maintained single-family homes that their parents own, and some families even have vacation homes in different parts of the country.

But these children are not only privileged in that they benefit from the wealth of their parents: these kids are also growing up white and with racial privilege—or as founding figure of American sociology W. E. B. Du Bois wrote, with a "public and psychological wage": the wages of whiteness.[2] Although many Americans may not believe that race shapes experiences, opportunities, and outcomes in the United States, social science research indicates otherwise. The United States is a racialized society, or a society that "allocates differential economic, political, social, and even psychological rewards to groups along racial lines; lines that are socially constructed."[3] This means that though the racial categories that we have today are meaningful to us, at their core, they are categories crafted by human beings.[4]

Evidence that we live in a society in which race shapes the lived experiences, opportunities, and outcomes of people can be seen across a range of institutions.[5] When it comes to children specifically, race structures the education they receive and experiences they have both inside and between schools,[6] race structures youth exposure to and treatment with law enforcement and within the juvenile (in)justice system,[7] and race structures the bonds children have (or do not have) with family members as a result of racialized mass incarceration and the War on Drugs.[8] Race structures kids' experiences in foster care and the child welfare system.[9] Race structures children's access to health care[10] and even pain medication,[11] and race structures the knowledge children receive through sex education about their own body and sexuality.[12] Race structures where kids live and play,[13] the availability of welfare benefits,[14] and, as mentioned, family private wealth holdings that offer children profoundly different lived experiences and opportunities.[15] The list goes on and on. To put it in simple terms, then, all children growing up in the United States have lives that are structured by race—and this includes the affluent, white kids in this book.

As the epigraphs to this chapter make clear, however, not all white kids think about race in the same way. Despite the similarities in structural privileges that these children have, despite the fact that sociologists often tend to assume these kids think alike, despite these kids' shared interests, and despite the fact that they all live within one metropolitan area, these white, affluent kids have *different* understandings of race and racism in America today.

I spent two years studying these white children and their families and can show that these kids talk about and interpret race differently. Their subtle behaviors reflect that they think about race and class inequality differently, and the experiences they have with their families and in their day-to-day interactions are substantively different from one another. For example, while some of the 36 children in this study believe racism is present in today's society, some do not. While some of these children believe that the police racially profile and abuse black and Latinx youth, some believe that black and Latinx youth are "bad kids" because their parents "do not care about them." Some of these children are close friends with children of color, and some of these children rarely even see a person of color. Similarly, while some think that all schools in the United States provide kids with the same education, others speak passionately about how unequal schools in the United States are "a big problem." Some children believe that the impact of slavery on the black community with regard to wealth holdings can still be seen today, yet other children believe that slavery and the civil rights movement era were one and the same. Some of these kids believe that talking about race "makes you racist," while other children think white people need to talk and think carefully about race much more often. Some children think that black people have "extra muscles" that make them jump higher, while other children think this is absurd. While some of these children believe people get rich because they work hard, some have other ideas about the causes of social stratification. And while some of the children in this study thought the shooting of Trayvon Martin was a grave violation of human rights and evidence of continued racial violence and racism in the United States, other children did not even know Trayvon's name.

How can this be? How can these white, affluent children have so much in common yet think about race in the United States in such different ways? And how do these kids form these different ideas in the first place? How do white kids learn race? What role do parents play in shaping children's racial views? How do kids growing up in families that do not talk openly about race or acknowledge its impact learn about race? And what about children growing up in families with parents who consider themselves to be "antiracist"? What lessons are these children learning about race, and what is the outcome? Finally, how can children's agency and their own participation in their production of ideas be accounted for within this broader process of racial socialization or racial learning? Do kids simply parrot the ideas of their parents, or is there a more complex process under way? In what ways do kids challenge their parents' perspectives on race, perhaps even influencing parents' views in the process? Answering these questions will allow us to understand the role white kids and their families play in the reproduction, reworking, or maybe challenging of existing forms of racism.

Before providing answers to these questions, I think it is important to address a few key considerations about both what I have written and what I have not. First, this book is *not* about centering whiteness in a way that detracts from the critical scholarship on race as did much family-based ethnographic research of the past.[16] Traditionally, family research and early developmental psychology assumed white families and children to be "the norm" to which families and children of color were compared and often found to be inferior. Rather than putting white families back at the center of family research, this book seeks to examine white families with the intention of addressing critically the role that white families play in the production and reproduction of white racial power.[17]

Second, I have *not* written a book about middle-class or working-class white families. I believe that class plays a role in the process of racial learning—that what is at stake for working-class families when it comes to interpretations of race in the United States may be very different than it is for those with both race and class privilege. For families where economic struggles are not a concern, where power and privilege and security are well-rooted features of everyday life, and where parents and children do not feel any sort of real threat to their status and well-being, the messages about race sent to children may not be the same as those messages received by children growing up in families that are struggling to get by. Research shows that some working-class whites exhibit resentment toward people of color because of a perceived threat to their whiteness, white privilege, and economic interests.[18] As the sociologist Maria Kefalas writes, "While the true victims of race in America were, of course, African Americans, working-class whites could legitimately claim that upper-class whites could more easily avoid the costs of racial change."[19] Other studies challenge this view and find evidence that working-class whites, particularly young white women, are *more* likely to be racially progressive.[20] While this debate continues, it is certainly the case that very little research critically examines racial socialization processes in affluent white families. As such, I chose to study comprehensive racial learning in these kinds of families *deliberately*. The parents in this book have access to nearly unlimited resources that allow them to make almost any decision they desire for their children—choices that are accessible only to those with economic privilege, such as tuition costs for private schools or vacations to China or Mozambique or the capability to remove a child from a situation (e.g., switching to a new school) at a moment's notice if deemed necessary. As such, I can show how ideas about race inform the decisions parents make since their choices are less about availability of resources, or what they can afford, and more about what parents truly think is important or "best" for their child. As I will demonstrate, these views about what is important or "best" are shaped in part by racial ideologies and, in turn, send powerful messages to kids about race, privilege, and power. This is true whether parents realize this is the case or not and regardless of what parents actually say out loud to their children about race.

This book is also *not* about early childhood racial socialization processes, though that decision is not because I think early childhood is irrelevant to this discussion: certainly, it is, as the sociologists Debra Van Ausdale and Joe R. Feagin document in their research on how children as young as three years old learn race and racism at a day-care center.[21] Rather, I made the deliberate choice to explore children as they make their way through *middle childhood*. Middle childhood is a developmental stage during which children begin thinking in ideological terms, looking at patterns around them, and considering the experiences of others in new ways. This is also often when children spend increasing amounts of time outside the home and have more daily interactions with more people.[22]

This book is also *not* about gender socialization or how children learn about sexuality but not because I think these learning processes are unimportant. I absolutely believe that these processes are entwined with racial learning processes, and more intersectional and critical race research needs to be conducted in this area. However, it is beyond the scope of this book to explore fully these complexities, though I do periodically draw attention to moments when kids articulate ideas about gender and sexuality alongside race.[23]

Finally, studying *young people* rather than exclusively adults is also a deliberate choice. Kids growing up in affluent families are likely to experience the world through a lens of interrelated race and class privilege. Listening to kids and understanding how affluent, white children think about, make sense of, justify, and perhaps even challenge existing notions about race in the United States is important for at least three reasons—each tied to inequality and injustice in the country.

First, sociologists know very little about how the ideas that support racial inequality are actually reproduced from one generation to the next. Scholars have offered theories about how this process works, but very little empirical evidence has been gathered to support or challenge these theories. As the leading sociologist and race scholar Eduardo Bonilla-Silva argues, racial ideologies are "mechanisms responsible for the reproduction of racial privilege in a society."[24] Thus, uncovering patterns in how ideologies that uphold racial inequality (i.e., racism) are produced and reproduced by white kids is key to understanding the role that white childhood plays in the perpetuation of the racial status quo.

A second reason to study these kids is because through the intergenerational transfer of wealth and as a consequence of the wages of whiteness, these children will likely grow up to hold powerful positions within US society themselves. As such, this work can enhance our understanding of the future of race relations in the United States and how the ideas of future powerful people take hold during childhood.

The third and perhaps more pressing reason to study this particular group of young people has to do with race and class in the United States right now, in the present moment, in an applied sense. American children are growing up in a world with ongoing public debates about race—a world that has seen two completed terms of the first black president of the United States, fervid political and racialized arguments about immigration and criminal justice system reform, recent acts of overt white nationalism and violence such as that in Charlottesville, Virginia, unprecedented youth access to other people through social media, and growing youth activism and protest, such as the emergence of #BlackLivesMatter and many other groups working for racial justice across the country (many with youth leaders and participants). These are children growing up in a world that has seen white peers chanting "Trump" and "Build the Wall!" at basketball games against predominantly Latinx schools, kids who attend schools that have teachers reporting increased bullying along racial lines in classrooms, increased media coverage of the racial disproportionality in who is subjected to violence and torture at the hands of the police, and seemingly heightened discourse about inequality in the United States at large.

In addition to the current events that are marking this contemporary moment as significant in the long history of racism in the United States, social science research shows that white children receive the wages of whiteness from very early ages and well into young adulthood. For instance, one of the driving forces behind increased residential segregation involves patterned decisions made by parents concerning where their white kids will go to school. Research also finds that white kids are more likely to be considered "innocent" in comparison to black and brown peers in the juvenile injustice context or in the context of school discipline.[25] When white young adults commit crimes—as in 2015, when a 21-year-old white man murdered nine black parishioners in the Emanuel African Methodist Episcopal Church in Charleston, South Carolina, or when in 2014 when a 22-year-old white man shot a BB gun at police officers in Concord, New Hampshire—their lives remained intact. Young black people are murdered in seconds by the police even when they are simply suspected of criminal behavior, such as 12-year-old Tamir Rice playing with a toy gun in a public park or 14-year-old Cameron Tillman, who entered an abandoned house with a BB gun. Research shows that even though white youth are more likely to use illegal drugs, arrest rates do not reflect this reality.[26] Studies also show that teachers are more likely to designate white children as "gifted and talented" and perceive them as smarter and more capable than peers of color.[27] When doctors think black children need less pain medication, they demonstrate their belief that white children need more, suggesting white children are more fragile, more innocent, and more important to protect from physical pain. These are the privileges of whiteness.[28]

I believe that it is important to examine empirically how white children, such as those in this book, not only are going to have power in their futures as white adults but also already have power and influence in the present moment, as young white people, in their families and communities. Pushing back against the notion that children lack agency or free will or power to shape adults around them, this book explores the power of white kids in their families, their schools, their peer groups, their extracurricular spaces, and public discourse about who is "innocent" and who is not, who is "special" and who is not, and who is "deserving" and who is not. White childhood is a place where power and privilege take on not only ideological significance but also material significance for white youth, which is why it ought to be studied.

Of course, the children in this book are not at personal fault for their unearned advantages—certainly, their power is tied directly to the social structure of the society into which they are born and to their position within the structural hierarchies that they neither asked for nor can control. I am not interested in demonizing these kids or their parents, and I am not suggesting that they are individually at fault for racial inequality in the United States. However, I am interested in confronting honestly what is going on beneath the surface within affluent, white families and communities that serves to perpetuate racism and racial inequality in the United States.

1

"Race Really Doesn't Matter Anymore"

Growing Up with Privilege

One wintery afternoon, I drive 12-year-old Edward home from basketball practice. He is sitting in the backseat, sweaty despite the frigid temperatures outside. Snowflakes are just starting to fall from the sky, and I turn on my windshield wipers to brush them away. Edward leans forward and asks if we can stop at McDonalds for a snack. I reluctantly agree and think about where the nearest McDonalds is located. As we approach the restaurant, Edward looks out the window and says, "Hey, this isn't where we usually go. We usually go to the one over by the mall!" Not thinking much about his comment, I tell him nicely that this is the most convenient location and that this is where we are going. He does not respond, so I glance in the rearview mirror to check his expression. Edward is looking out the window.

Because it is snowing, I opt to go to the drive-thru. I place his order and fumble around in my purse for some cash as we wait to pull forward. As I do so, Edward continues to look out the window. He watches a group of seven children walk across the parking lot in front of us. The kids all look to be the same age as Edward, likely in seventh or eighth grade. They are wearing clothes like Edward typically wears—winter coats, hats, jeans, boots, and gloves—and they are black. The kids are laughing, joking around, and carrying their school backpacks. As we wait for his milkshake, one of the girls makes a snowball and throws it at one of the boys, all of the kids laughing when the snowball hits the back of the boy's coat. Watching the kids goof around, much as I had seen Edward goof around with his own friends on previous occasions, Edward states definitively, "This neighborhood really isn't all that good, is it?"

"What do you mean?" I ask, wondering what he will say.

"I dunno," he replies. "It just seems like there are a lot of poor people around here. We don't usually stop here. My mom says it's dangerous."

"Oh," I say nonchalantly. "Why do you think she says it's dangerous?"

"Well, I don't think she would say it unless it was true," Edward tells me matter-of-factly.

It is our turn to pull up to the window. As soon as I pass back the milkshake to Edward, his attention shifts, and he starts talking about his snowmobile. But even as I listen to him chatter on and on, I am reminded of something Edward told me—not this day at McDonalds in the drive-thru but another day a few weeks prior. "We are all the same," he had said. "Race doesn't really matter anymore." We continue on into the snow.

* * *

I often hear my students, my friends, and even my own family members talk about how they "were socialized" or about "how kids are social-ized these days." This word, "socialization," is one that social scientists use to refer to the process of how new members of society learn about the social world. Traditionally, this term refers to the role that families play in transforming children into social actors who know the norms of a society and are able to interact with other members of that society. At the core of these understandings of socialization—both my students' understandings and many social scientists'—is an assumption that kids will become members of society as the adults around them see fit. And yet anyone who has spent any time with children knows that kids do not simply take the ideas of adults and make them their own; kids constantly break rules, challenge adult authority, disagree with parents, form their own opinions, create their own make-believe games, build their own youth culture, produce their own imaginative artwork, disregard social norms, and so forth. Given this reality, scholars adhering to what is called the "New Sociology of Childhood" argue that this term "socialization" does not adequately take into account children's active participation, or agency, in social learning processes.[1] The word "socialization" removes the active role children play in their own lives. "Socialization" implies that children are passive, blank slates to be written on by adults in a determin-istic fashion, empty vessels to be filled with whatever adults determine, or "sponges," rather than, as the childhood sociologist William Corsaro argues, "active, creative social agents who produce their own unique chil-dren's cultures while simultaneously contributing to the production of adult societies."[2]

This same terminology of "racial socialization" is used to explain how children make sense of race. And this term carries with it the same problems just described involving limits to children's agency, or free will. As the African American studies scholar Erin Winkler argues, the term "racial socialization" "refers exclusively to how *parents* teach their children about race and racism, . . . indicating something that happens *to* children."[3] Not only does this term reflect a lack of recognition of the role that children themselves play in forming ideas about race and racism, but it also assumes that parents are the sole providers of these racial lessons. In fact, common definitions of "racial socialization" are typically limited to "*parents'* race-related communications to children"[4] or "an adaptive strategy *parents* use to prepare children to negotiate experiences associated with social position."[5] These definitions are adult-centric and ignore children's participation in this process altogether. For instance, many studies of racial socialization focus on the kinds of approaches parents take to conveying messages to their children, such as counts of how many times particular topics are brought up in conversation. As a result, much of what we know about how children learn about race does not come from children themselves but rather from the adults in their lives. This quantitative work is much different from ethnographic work that uncovers the interpretive processes involved in how kids make sense of the messages conveyed to them in their everyday lives. While of course we can learn much from existing research, children's active participation in racial socialization processes needs further empirical analysis if we truly want to understand how commonsense ideas about race are formed by the newest generation themselves.[6]

In order to take account of the richer and more complex ways that kids learn about race, Winkler argues for the use of a new framework that she calls "comprehensive racial learning." This is a term that refers to "the process through which children negotiate, interpret, and make meaning of the various and conflicting messages they receive about race, ultimately forming their own understandings of how race works in society and their lives."[7] This framework moves beyond simply what happens within the family and includes all aspects of a child's life, such as neighborhood, school, peers, activities, travel, and media. This framework also embraces the theory that children learn through their interactions with and interpretations of the surrounding social environment. Rather than passively "being socialized," children actively engage their own interpretive process of learning and making sense of the social world around them. I embrace Winkler's theory of comprehensive racial learning in the pages to come, using this framework as a starting place from which to develop further theoretical work on how this process operates for children who are *white* and *affluent*—children such as Edward and the 35 other kids in this book.

Growing Up in a Racialized Social System

US society is and always has been structured by race.[8] Race shapes the lives of everyone in the United States, whether people believe this to be true or not. Race organizes society, race influences how people think about themselves and others, and race is tied to power and inequality. More than just a country with a few bigoted individuals, the United States is what Bonilla-Silva refers to as a "racialized social system."[9] "This term refers to societies in which economic, political, social, and ideological levels are partially structured by the placement of actors in racial categories or races."[10] In a racialized social system, people are classified into different groups based on a set of socially defined physical characteristics, such as skin color. While it is commonplace to think of race as biological, race is "an invented political grouping" that "has been disguised as a biological one."[11] As the legal scholar Dorothy Roberts explains,

> We know race is a political grouping because it has political roots in slavery and colonialism, it has served a political function over the four hundred years since its inception, and its boundary lines—how many races there are and who belongs to each one—have shifted over time and across nations to suit those political purposes. Who counts as white, black, and Indian has been the matter of countless rule changes and judicial decisions. These racial reclassifications did not occur in response to scientific advances in human biology, but in response to sociopolitical imperatives. They reveal that what is being defined, organized, and interpreted is a political relationship and not an innate classification.[12]

In other words, race is a political category created by human beings and state practices and does not have a genetic basis. This process of racialization, or "the extension of racial meaning to a previously racially unclassified relationship, social practice or group," has occurred throughout the history of the United States.[13] The classification process, or the process by which racial categories are socially constructed, happens when people fill out their census forms or when children are born and their race is marked down on birth certificates. Historical examples of racialization include the prerequisite cases of immigrants such as Takao Ozawa, born in Japan in 1875, who petitioned the US government to be classified as "white" so that he could gain citizenship rights.[14] Antimiscegenation laws, Jim Crow laws, and immigration laws—all of these laws draw on some collective and/or legal understanding of what race is despite the reality that these definitions are created by people, that they change over time or across different contexts, and that power is often connected to them.[15] So too are privileges and punishments, such as the right to own land or being targeted by the police, distributed along the lines of this racial order.[16] Though race is socially constructed, it is very real in its consequences.

The process of racialization in the United States is rooted deeply in history. From the genocide of American Indians to the stealing of their land to the enslavement and exploitation of African people, the United States of America was established from its colonial roots as a racialized society, or a society structured by a racial hierarchy.[17] This structure was perpetuated by the exploited labor of Chinese and Japanese immigrants and the military acquisition of half of Mexico's land, among other innumerable acts of racial violence over time. Indeed, the concept of race itself and the desire to establish this way of politically grouping human beings is the very product of racism, rather than racism emerging from the creation of race.[18] Although this history of European colonial domination and the emergence of US white supremacy may seem part of the distant past, the legacy of this history—that is, the continued subordination of members of racial groups defined legally and socially as not *white*—continues to shape the most basic of institutions in US society.

In order to make these structural roots seem natural, and in order to justify the continuation of this racialized distribution of privileges and

punishments, particular frameworks, or ideologies, that serve to ratio-
nalize one's own privilege are produced and reproduced, beginning in
childhood. Ideologies serve a very particular purpose in a racialized and
class-stratified social system such as the United States. As the sociologist
Heather Beth Johnson writes, "Ideology is a critical component in the
contemporary United States because ideology—in how it helps to mask
and justify systems of inequality—contributes to the collective denial and
thus maintenance, of structural inequities."[19] For example, ideologies
such as that of meritocracy, or the American Dream, justify the superior
position of the wealthy by claiming that the rich worked harder than everyone else and therefore deserve their privilege and the social rewards
that accompany it. Similarly, as the sociologist Amanda Lewis writes,
"In a society riddled with social inequality, ideologies must naturalize a
system that ensures subordination for millions."[20] Religion, capitalism,
and science each played their own role in the formation of dominant
ideological explanations that justified the racial hierarchy, making it seem
"natural" that white people were in positions of dominance over all other
people. Forms of racism that have been used across time to justify the
mistreatment of people of color by whites have certainly mutated as times
have changed, but the material consequences of racism still exist alongside reworked racial ideology. Without understanding how people learn
dominant ideologies and how these ideologies are reproduced and reconstituted, we cannot entirely understand how racism (racial ideology) both
persists and mutates into new forms in the United States. Importantly,
these ideological discourses and practices are not simply expressions or
outcomes of a hierarchy; rather, they are central to "the constitution of
social and political life" in the first place.[21] In other words, how white,
affluent children make sense of race not only reflects but also reproduces
and reinforces the existing racial order.

Understanding how white children produce, reproduce, and sometimes even reinterpret racial ideologies is central to larger understandings of how structures of white supremacy endure in a society such as
ours. As the sociologist Tyrone Forman writes, "Clearly our efforts to
eradicate racial and ethnic inequality will not be successful until we better understand the precise mechanisms reproducing it."[22] We cannot
fully understand the reproduction of racism without considering the
active role that children play in this process.

Examining Privilege

Often researchers focus on the experiences and conditions of marginalized groups in order to understand inequality. Numerous important ethnographies, for instance, document the lived experiences of people of color, youth growing up in poverty, homeless women, gang members, street artists, the working poor, and so forth. This book is instead an ethnographic study of an aspect of inequality from the vantage point of the privileged, of families and children at the top of race and class hierarchies. This book focuses intently on questions related to how comprehensive racial learning operates for white children growing up in affluent families. But this discussion is rooted in a broader sociological question: how do ideologies get socially reproduced by children who benefit the most from the maintenance of these ideologies, and how do ideological positions themselves shape choices involved in raising a child?[23]

The study of racial socialization has focused on families of color and how parents of children of color raise their children in a racialized society. This body of research responds critically to early developmental theories that made problematic assumptions about what the "normal" American family constituted (i.e., white, middle-class, heterosexual married parents) and instead acknowledges how inequality in society fundamentally shapes children's lived experiences. Research on racial socialization examines the "messages and strategies used by black parents to teach their children about black American culture, prepare them for potential experiences with racism and prejudice, and promote healthy mistrust of non-blacks."[24] Although this area of research has been ongoing for the past 30 years, it continues to grow in new and urgent ways in the present moment and is generally conceptualized as a strategy of resilience that parents use when raising kids in a racist world. For instance, following the shooting of Trayvon Martin, researchers interviewed parents of black youth, exploring how this tragic event shaped the conversations parents had with their black children about racial violence and the police and how to keep themselves safe.[25] The bulk of this literature has examined how, where, and when messages about race and racism are communicated to kids,[26] what these messages include,[27] why parents choose to send the particular messages they do,[28] how social class impacts the process[29] as well as other socio-demographic factors,[30] how current racialized events such as shootings of young black and brown people shape these messages,[31] and, perhaps most commonly, what kinds of child outcomes can be linked to particular parental racial socialization practices, such as positive racial identity formation, increased self-esteem, strong mental health, resilience, cognitive development, and academic achievement.[32] Over the past two decades, studies of racial socialization have broadened in scope, documenting racial socialization as an important and "influential component of childrearing"[33] among black, Latinx, Asian American, and multiracial families.[34] In conjunction with previous work with black families, this new body of research shows that "minority socialization" usually includes direct and explicit messages conveyed from parents to children about race, particularly as parents prepare their children for living in a hostile racial environment.

The critical study of how white children learn about race and racism within the family is underdeveloped. This is largely due to the assumption or "the fallacy that only non-Whites 'have' race."[35] As the sociologist Linda Burton and her colleagues describe, "Our review of the decade's literature found that studies of racial socialization assumed that people of color will encounter racism but did not fully examine the socialization processes among Whites that lead them to discriminate."[36] Thus, it is not that white families should be placed at the center of family research as in the past; rather, the private worlds of white families should be studied critically as racialized places where ideas about race get reproduced and reworked by children with racial privilege. White families ought not to be disconnected from the study of race and racism. Indeed, white families are the first places where the newest generation of whites learn ideas about race, racism, privilege, and inequality in the United States. As such, how racial ideologies shape the private lives of white families in the United States and how white children reproduce these ideologies are important questions to interrogate if we hope to do the work of challenging the racial status quo.

The very few but important studies that have examined aspects of racial socialization within white families illustrate that some white parents do not even think about race when it comes to raising white children[37] and that white parents do not believe it is necessary to talk to their white children about race.[38] For instance, the sociologist Megan R. Underhill finds that during the protests in Ferguson, Missouri, following the police shooting of Michael Brown, white, middle-class parents generally reported not speaking with their kids about the racial tension in ways that addressed power and inequality.[39] As the sociologists Joe Feagin and Eileen O'Brien explain by drawing on elite white men's retrospective accounts of their own childhoods, "the way that whites think and feel about racial matters as adults is commonly shaped by family and school contexts in which they grow up."[40] While of course these accounts are important in that they explore how these men make sense of their privileged childhoods, observing how these processes unfold in the moment for children, rather than how they are remembered by adults 30–50 years later, tells us much more about the nuances and details of how white kids learn about race. Overall, there are no studies to my knowledge that examine white racial socialization as it happens, take seriously white children's own perspectives on race produced by kids in particular social contexts, or interrogate race privilege as it intersects with class privilege in the everyday racial meaning-making processes of children.

Over the past few decades, a handful of race scholars have suggested as part of broader theories of new forms of racism that whites' ideas about race form in childhood. For instance, drawing on Pierre Bourdieu's notion of "habitus,"[41] the sociologists Eduardo Bonilla-Silva, Carla Goar, and David Embrick theorize that white children experience a "racialized, uninterrupted socialization process that conditions and creates whites' racial tastes, perceptions, feelings, and emotions and their views on racial matters."[42] This socialization process is described as "comprehensive and begin[ning] early in life" and is understood to "normalize and legitimate social closure . . . justifying inequality and maintaining the existing racial hierarchy."[43] These scholars extend Bourdieu's notion of habitus in new and fruitful ways but disregard children's agency in this process.[44]

Whether social psychological models, social structural models, or political models, theories of contemporary racism offer mostly unexplained assertions about how white children "pick up" or "adopt" the racial ideas they discuss, ideas imagined to be shaped by the racialized social system into which they are born and "hard to reverse" once adopted or taken up. As the political scientists Donald Kinder and Lynn Sanders write, "Prejudice is an acquired taste. Children enter the world free of any such animosity, but their innocence is temporary, for they are born into a world in which socially significant distinctions are already in place."[45] Similarly, the social psychologists David Sears and P. J. Henry claim that "common cultural values [are] presumed to be acquired in the pre-adult years."[46] Here, the assumption is again made that children "acquire" commonsense ideas about race, yet no interrogation into how this process works is offered. In general, while scholars appear to be growing more interested in the topic of white racial socialization—and the role that it plays in the reproduction (and reworking) of dominant racial ideologies—very little empirical, ethnographic research examines the role that the white family plays in this process. Similarly, little work has been done to examine the mediation of factors such as social class in this process.

There are reasons to suspect that the content and process of comprehensive racial learning in white families is quite different from that documented in families of color. To begin with, many white people resist talking about race or racial socialization. In fact, research on contemporary whiteness shows that many whites talk about race in elusive and contradictory, roundabout ways, often avoiding the discussion or sometimes even refusing to engage with the subject.[47] This suggests that the intentional and deliberate strategies of racial socialization often at work in families of color—such as having an explicit conversation with a black child about interacting with authority figures—might look quite different in white families. In addition, given the group position of whites within the racial hierarchy that structures US society, the content of the messages conveyed to children, regardless of how they are conveyed, is likely different from the messages researchers have documented parents of children of color conveying to their kids. While some parents of black children are teaching their kids how to navigate racism to stay alive, some parents of white children are teaching their kids that race no longer matters in the United States.

There are also reasons to suspect that the content and process of comprehensive racial learning is different across white families, much as we know differences exist across families of color and mixed-race families.[48] As Amanda Lewis writes, "Whiteness works in distinct ways for and is embodied quite differently by homeless white men, golf-club-membership-owning executives, suburban soccer moms, urban hillbillies, antiracist skinheads, and/or union-card carrying factory workers."[49] In other words, though all whites benefit from their whiteness, whether they want to or not, whites act, think, or raise their children in different ways.[50] I show in the following pages that even within one class grouping, variations on a theme emerge.

Methods

For nearly two years, I conducted ethnographic research with white, affluent families in a metropolitan area in the Midwest. In addition to conducting in-depth interviews with 36 children between the ages of 10 and 13 and parents from 30 families, I also observed white families in their everyday lives, attempting to access the "'everydayness' of whiteness"[51] and the "distinctive interpretations of reality" of white children and their parents.[52] I observed public spaces and private spaces, drove children to sports practices, attended school and community events, and read the local newspaper. I spent countless hours watching video-game playing, preparing food and eating with kids, monitoring play dates, hearing phone calls with peers, listening to kids talk about friendships and fights at school, playing board games, playing backyard sports, painting nails, practicing the violin, and struggling through homework assignments. I sat on the sidelines, in gym bleachers, and in auditorium seats with parents, talking with them, listening to them talk with each other, and watching the children interact with their peers, coaches, music teachers, and other kids' parents. I spent a day at a private country club, many days at a private pool; I attended parties at families' homes; and I went to events with children, such as Little League practice, volleyball games, science fairs, and summer-camp celebrations. I listened to kids talk to each other in the backseat of my car as I drove them home from school, I hung around with the Boy Scout dads while they watched their sons play laser tag, and I accompanied children and their families to political protests.

Overall, by immersing myself into the communities in which these white, affluent children spent their time and by getting to know these kids and their families, I learned that these kids make sense of the world around them through the observations they make and the interactions they have within the confines of their everyday lives—what happens at school, soccer practice, birthday parties, clarinet lessons, and in the backseat of a car driving home from summer day camp shapes children's ideas about the social world. As Winkler argues, "Children develop their ideas about race in the context of systems, structures, institutions, government, and culture, all of which are racialized within the US context."[53] When thinking about white comprehensive racial learning, then, we ought to consider the particular racial context in which white children are growing up and how these contexts are racialized.[54]

Plan of the Book

This book is a story about how affluent, white kids interpret the racial context of childhood designed for them by their parents. A racial context of childhood is the social environment surrounding a child that shapes how that child make sense of race. This environment is designed by parents, and the design choices are often shaped by dominant racial ideologies. Racial contexts do not include the entire ecological system or the total "environment of nested structures" surrounding a child or arbitrary factors within a child's life.[55] Rather, my research shows that certain aspects of a child's local environment, especially one's neighborhood but also one's school, peers, siblings, travel, volunteering, and media, influence one's ideas about race. In this way, the choices their parents make about how to set up the racial context in the first place influence, though do not determine, the messages kids receive, interpret, and produce in everyday life. In order to show how this process works, important patterned variations in this process, and the outcomes of this process, this book is organized in the following way.

Chapter 2 lays the groundwork for understanding children's interpretive processes by focusing on choices made by these children's parents. Although this book intends to privilege the voices of the children rather than adults, the rationalizations for why parents set up their children's social environments in the ways that they do are central to understanding this process. Therefore, this chapter explores how and why affluent, white parents make particular choices about where to live and how these choices serve as the foundation to a racial context of childhood. Because parents in this study tend to make what I refer to as *bundled* decisions about their child's lives—that is, because neighborhood choice is so closely tied to school choice, which shapes peer interactions in extra-curricular spaces and so forth, neighborhoods are, in many ways, prox-ies for a child's racial context. Focusing on three different white, affluent neighborhoods within the Petersfield metropolitan area, I demonstrate how the perceptions that shape neighborhood choice are informed by shared, local ideas about race. Thick descriptions of the neighborhoods, their relation to segregation and public schools, notions about how com-munity demographics are changing, and the political identities of these neighborhoods are presented as well as the perspectives of what it means to live in these three distinct places, according to the people who live here.

Chapter 3 explores what it means to be a private school kid from the perspectives of private school children themselves. Here too I explore how private schooling, like neighborhoods, helps form a child's racial context. In addition to understanding various types of private schools and how children make sense of attending them, I also examine how and why affluent, white parents make these private schooling choices in the first place. Specifically, I consider why these decisions are made in the context of a community with strong public schools. I explore the justifi-cations that affluent, white parents give for why their child attends pri-vate school and the impact these justifications have on children's views of themselves as more special and deserving than other kids.

Chapter 4 describes how interactions with other kids shape how white children produce ideas about race. Here, I look not only at class-mates but at peers with whom the children in the study interact, such as best friends, enemies, classmates, and especially siblings. I describe how children talk about their peers, but I also provide observations of white children interacting with each other as they produce ideas about race and racism together. I also consider parents' role in facilitating and en-couraging friendships as well as examples of how kids push back against their parents, challenging rather than adopting the racial views of their parents.

Establishing yet another component of a young person's racial context of childhood, chapter 5 examines how these families interact with peo-ple of color through volunteering and traveling specifically. I show how children learn about who they are as well as how they are different from others from these interactions but also how some parents purposefully design these experiences to teach their children lessons about race and privilege. I interrogate the power dynamics between affluent whites and people of color in other parts of the world (travel) as well as locally (volunteer work).

By examining the role that media and extracurricular activities play in these families lives, chapter 6 documents how even families that do not see themselves as talking about race very often communicate about race all the time. I explore the subtle and explicit ways that children receive messages about race, and I illustrate differences in how parents understand the role of media in shaping their children's views as well as how these differences link to parents' racial ideological positions. This chapter also explores how these messages are often conveyed through watching the news, reading the newspaper, and watching television programs or films, as well as in spaces such as soccer fields, science and technology clubs, and so forth. Finally, this chapter examines the role parents play in these interactive spaces as leader or coaches, and it looks at how parents observe their children in these extracurricular spaces in order to assess aspects of their racial socialization.

Chapter 7 presents the children's actual views on race, racism, inequality, and privilege. I present the views of white kids on a range of topics related to race and racial inequality in the United States and show patterns across groups of these children. I examine the role of children's agency in racial socialization, documenting that while kids' perspectives may align in some important ways with their parents', their views are also uniquely their own. Finally, the relationship between children's agency and the broader social structure in which they live is considered.

Lastly, the conclusion to this book offers a brief look at the young people's perspectives as high school students, or approximately four years after the initial ethnography was completed. I discuss recent shifts in public dialogue about race in the United States and how these shifts matter for white comprehensive learning. I close with some final thoughts about how white families participate in the reproduction of racism and argue for the importance of rethinking "good" white parenting.

While this ethnographic account focuses on the everyday details and meaning-making processes of children and shares their unique perspectives, this book also offers some broader insights into how white kids may rework racial ideologies and transform them in new ways to fit new social conditions. Through this process, white kids participate in the reproduction of white supremacy but in new and unpredictable ways. As the sociologist and African American studies scholar Lawrence Bobo writes, "It is not enough to declare that race matters or that racism endures. The much more demanding challenge is to account for how and why such a social construction comes to be reconstituted, refreshed, and enacted anew in very different times and places."[56] This book embraces Bobo's challenge and endeavors to present new information about the role that white, affluent children and their families intentionally and unintentionally play in the social reproduction of racism.

2

"The Perfect Place to Live"

Choosing Schools and Neighborhoods

I think most people in my neighborhood are really fortunate. Most of them are really nice. And, like, I go trick-or-treating, and they are all smiling and happy. I don't really see my neighbors in bad moods. . . . I'd say all the kids who live near me have good parents with good heads on their shoulders, and they got good money for it. There's, like, a lot of medical people here. And there's probably a lot of other people too. They probably aren't all doctors [*laughing*]. Oh! There are also politicians and lawyers and that one famous guy.
—Rosie (10, Sheridan)

Neighborhoods are foundational to the concept of racial contexts of childhood for two major reasons. First, neighborhoods are a central part of the everyday lives of kids. This is where children play, interact with other families and adults, and spend leisure time. Neighborhoods often determine who become best friends with one another, who hang out together after school, and who are members of the same sports team. Not only are these places where kids interact with other kids, but they are also where children interact with adults. In this case, because these neighborhoods are where many other affluent, white people live, it is here that kids interact with adults in the community who are in positions of influence and power, such as local politicians. The kids in this book produce ideas about race in part on the basis of their lived experiences and the interactions with other kids and adults who live in the same neighborhood as they do. As this chapter examines, part of parents' decision of where to live is shaped by their perceptions of the *kinds of people* who live in these neighborhoods—the kinds of people they want their children growing up around.

But neighborhoods are also foundational to the concept of a racial context of childhood for a second reason. When parents make decisions about where to live, often they are simultaneously and strategically making decisions about *schools*. In turn, decisions about schools shape a range of other parenting decisions such as what extracurricular activities to participate in, which Little League team to join, what carpool makes the most sense, who the babysitters will be, and so forth. In this sense, parents are not only deciding where to live when they select a neighborhood but also making a larger set of decisions about the parameters of their child's life—parameters include a host of external forces that shape how kids form ideas about race, racism, inequality, and privilege.

Racial and Political Segregation in the Petersfield Metropolitan Area

Petersfield is a medium-sized midwestern city. Beautiful lakes and parks can be found throughout the city; depending on the season, sailboats graze across the top of the lake, or ice fisherman with their tents dig circular holes in the thick lake ice. A large public university and a community college are located in Petersfield, several industries are headquartered here, and the city is a hub for state politics. The city and its surrounding suburban communities are consistently ranked as some of the best places to live and visit in the country. The reason this city is so desirable to many people is in part due to the successful green initiatives, sidewalks and bike lanes, sustainable development programs, natural beauty of the landscape, large organic farmers' markets, popular sporting events, community events, museums, mainstream and boutique shopping, excellent local restaurants, countless bars and coffee shops, and a robust entertainment scene serving both the college campus community and the local community itself.

Almost all the white people I met living within the city limits told me they also like Petersfield because of the "progressive feel" of the city overall. The city has antidiscrimination policies that seek to protect nearly all classes of people, a newspaper written and sold by the homeless community discussing their concerns, a public transportation system that is widespread and heavily utilized, housing and food cooperatives located across the city, social justice organizations, community organizing around topics of interest, good public libraries, and a strong social support system for people facing poverty.

Despite these politically progressive programs and the white liberal attitudes, though, Petersfield has some serious social problems, particularly with respect to race. Many of the black people I met living in the city expressed concerns to me about racism and discrimination within the local community, and some cited recent reports analyzing data on racial outcomes in education, racial patterns of incarceration, and rates of black poverty. These reports document how Petersfield is indeed in many ways a terrible place to live if you are growing up black. As such, the city leadership is often criticized by the political Left as being "hypocritical" ("You say you care about racial inequality, but look at our criminal justice system!") and by the political Right as being "clueless" ("You invite criminals into this city through all your social programs and handouts and then complain when those people do bad things!").

Demographics

According to the 2010 US. Census, Petersfield was approximately 80% white, 7% black, 7% Asian, and 7% Latinx. The median household income in the city of Petersfield was around $50,000; the poverty rate was around 20%. The median home value was approximately $220,000.[1] In this study, I examine 10 families each living in three distinct neighborhoods. Two of these neighborhoods—Wheaton Hills and Evergreen—are located within the city of Petersfield. In contrast, the third neighborhood explored—Sheridan—is located in a nearby suburb. In 2010, Sheridan had a population of less than 20,000, was almost 96% white, 1.0% black, 1.2% Asian, and 2.2% Latinx. The median household income in Sheridan was closer to $90,000, the poverty rate was around 3%, and the median home value was nearly $310,000. In basic terms, not only is the suburban neighborhood of Sheridan whiter than Petersfield, but the people living here are on average far wealthier.

In the past 10 years, Petersfield County has grown by over 10%, and there has, in fact, been a demographic shift with respect to race in the local area. Despite the predominant perception that the influx of people of color is solely connected to a sizable impoverished black community moving to Petersfield, the shift has included an increase in the black, Asian, and

Latinx populations. Like the state overall, the largest increase has been in the Latinx population. As scholars have found in social psychological research on residential segregation, whites start moving out of neighborhoods or deeming neighborhoods undesirable after only a small number of black neighbors move in.[2] For a third of the families in this study, the perception that black people are moving into the city at large—and the city schools especially—causes them to engage in practices of white flight, which lead them to Sheridan, with some parents stating this bluntly.

While the demographics of Petersfield County have changed over time, the population remains nearly 85% white, which is a change in the order of around 4% between 2000 and 2010. Although changes have occurred, they are certainly not happening with the magnitude that whites in Sheridan ascribe to them—and there is no evidence to suggest that these changes are a crisis or that they have "ruined" the city as the people who have left for Sheridan suggest.

Racial and Political Residential Segregation

Residential segregation is and always has been high in the United States, even if modest declines have been noted in certain regions of the country over time. As the sociologists Kyle Crowder and Maria Krysan wrote in 2016, "Residential segregation by race remains a defining feature of most metropolitan areas and continues to exert strong and multifaceted impacts on the life chances of segregated populations."[3] Petersfield is by no means an exception. Researchers document how over the course of time, laws, public policies, and private practices have contributed to patterns of residential segregation. Discriminatory mortgage-lending practices, steering, redlining, physical violence, federal policies on public housing, suburbanization, restrictive covenants, and so forth restricted blacks from white neighborhoods.[4] Researchers also document the extreme racial differences in lived experiences as a result of patterns of segregation, including differential rates of infant mortality,[5] educational attainment,[6] exposure to pollution,[7] and so forth.[8] Indeed, residential segregation is understood to be "a 'structural linchpin' of racial inequality."[9]

While patterns of residential segregation are well documented, political scientists and social geographers also point to an increasing trend of residential segregation that is politically polarized, or the political polarization of neighborhoods.[10] And again, the Petersfield metropolitan area is no exception to these trends. Evidence of the segregation and polarization of neighborhoods in general can be observed using Twitter data, for instance, in which computer scientists have found that "neighborhood data can be comparable or better than user data at inferring a user's age and political orientation."[11] Further research demonstrates that most important to understanding "spatial variation in party support" between cities and suburbs "is the self-selection of supporters of political parties on the left into the inner city based on a conscious decision to link their political convictions to their lifestyle choices" and for purposes of having a "sense of community," while suburban home owners prefer "private space."[12] Similarly, a 2014 Pew Research Center study found that "conservatives would rather live in large houses in small towns and rural areas—ideally among people of the same religious faith—while liberals opt for smaller houses and walkable communities in cities, preferably with a mix of different races and ethnicities."[13]

As Erin Winkler argues in her research on how black children learn about race, "Research ignoring place in children's comprehensive racial learning misses a critical and profound piece of the puzzle."[14] Given what we know about the emerging trends of political polarization, alongside what we have known about residential segregation for a while now, it does not come as a surprise that these more conservatively minded, affluent, white families in this book choose to live—and, most importantly, to raise their children—in a place like Sheridan, while their progressively minded, affluent peers purposefully choose neighborhoods like Wheaton Hills and Evergreen. White comprehensive racial learning begins with the choices parents make about the place to raise their kids. And undergirding these perceptions of schools, people, and politics are parents' own ideas about race.

The Racial Context of Sheridan

Historically, the community where Sheridan is located was once a rural, white farming community. In the 1980s, a locally famous song was written about Sheridan, the central theme being that the snobby, out-of-touch undergraduate students attending the large university in Petersfield could not possibly understand the beer-drinking, deer-hunting, pickup-truck culture of Sheridan. And yet, between 2000 and 2010, according to census data, as well as residents' own perspectives, this community experienced massive growth and change. The median household income shot up, the population grew, and the values of homes increased tremendously. With these changes, in moved young families interested in purchasing big, newly constructed, custom homes outside the city of Petersfield. These families were almost all white. Unsurprisingly, today Sheridan is commonly understood as very conservative, very wealthy, and still very white. People from Petersfield largely ignore Sheridan, except for when it comes to high-stakes high school athletic competitions, but some do refer to those in Sheridan as "rich assholes" and denigrate the perceived conservative political attitudes of Sheridan residents. Meanwhile, people in Sheridan generally describe those living in the city of Petersfield as "out of touch," "naïve," and living within a liberal bubble "surrounded by reality." These perceptions held by members of both communities speak to the dramatic differences between these two places and the polarized nature of the political climate in the metropolitan area at large.

In addition to the poignant differences in political identification of these two places, miles of farmland and only one major road separate these two communities, creating a clear and distinct boundary between the two. Sheridan's much-higher average housing values and median household incomes alongside its almost-all-white population make it stand out as contextually different, even at first glance, from Petersfield. Despite their differences, though, both places are home to white, affluent, middle-school-aged children and their families.

The 10 families in this study who choose to live in Sheridan do so first and foremost because of the schools. While six of the families moved to Sheridan to escape the Petersfield schools, the other four moved here with their very young children's education in mind. In addition, these 10 families talked to me about how they appreciate the politics of their Sheridan neighbors and how they want to live in a community with people who are similar to them.

The Schultz Family

The Schultz family home was custom built in 2009 in a brand-new housing development in the suburban neighborhood of Sheridan. The stone-front, Tudor-style house has seven bedrooms, four bathrooms, a large, beautifully manicured lawn, and professional landscaping. Snowmobiles and bicycles line the outer edges of the garage along with tennis rackets and golf clubs for use at the local country club. All kinds of hula hoops, pom-poms, bicycles, ice skates, swim goggles, and other toys are neatly organized into labeled plastic containers along the back of the two-car garage. The Schultz family also owns a boat, which is docked at a lake in Petersfield in the neighborhood of Apple Hills. Natalie (11) and her sister, Erica (13), love to water-ski on the lake in the summer, as well as watch the Fourth of July fireworks from their boat.

Dean and Holly Schultz were both born in another midwestern state, which Holly described as "a lily-white community back then. . . . It was all lily-white Catholic everywhere." After meeting in college and getting married, Dean and Holly built a home in the exclusive neighborhood of Apple Hills in Petersfield, though eventually, they moved with their three children to Sheridan. Holly describes how these decisions unfolded:

> We initially chose Apple Hills. . . . We were very, very happy there. . . . But then it came time for our oldest to start high school, and we did not want to send her to Evergreen High School. So we looked for the best high school we could and decided that's where we would move to. That was the only decision. . . . We moved to benefit our children's education. We didn't need to leave. Loved it, we lived on the lake in a beautiful home. . . . I really didn't want to move, other than it was the high school that drove us out of there over to Sheridan.

Evergreen High, the public school to which kids in Apple Hills are assigned, is not understood as a "good" school in the minds of many Apple Hills parents. Though the close neighborly relationships, the lavish properties, and the easy access to an exclusive country club initially attracted the Schultz family and others to this Petersfield neighborhood, the Schulz family is part of a recent exodus from this community. The Schultz children, while living in Petersfield, attended a private school in town. However, high school is an entirely different matter in this city, as the private school options are more limited, especially for families who seek rich extracurricular opportunities, a full load of

Advanced Placement courses that will aid in more competitive college acceptance in their view, and what they perceive to be a "good" social environment.[15]

Current research on how white parents often choose schools suggests that parents rely on word-of-mouth information provided about a school's reputation from other parents or colleagues.[16] Affluent, white parents in the Petersfield metropolitan area too make choices about schools on the basis of word-of-mouth reputations and where these schools are located rather than test scores, college-placement rates, or other traditional measures of school quality. Both the schools' reputations and their locations are connected to locally shared understandings of race and class. The sociologists Thomas Shapiro and Heather Beth Johnson find similar trends in their research on race and patterns of school choice.[17] Johnson writes, "Parents tied a school's reputation directly to the race and class composition of its students. While claiming to be concerned about such things as safety and class size, the families . . . were ultimately seeking whiter—and in their view, inextricably wealthier—school districts for their children, regardless of any other of the school's characteristics."[18] Further, in her discussion of the social construction of a good school, Johnson explains that parents in her study understood that "a good school is in a good neighborhood, and a good neighborhood is a wealthier and whiter neighborhood."[19] This is precisely the case for Sheridan parents.

Holly describes her perceptions of Evergreen High, the public high school her children were slotted to attend:

> We had some concerns about the school because we had heard negative things about it, but we wanted to go check it out for ourselves. . . . My kids are good kids. . . . They're going to help out Evergreen High's grade point average! [Laughing] But, you know, we could not get in to [visit] Evergreen High. . . . There was no one who would make any arrangements for us to come and tour. . . . Finally one day, I just called the principal, and I said, "You know what? We're going to come. My husband and I are . . . just going to come in tomorrow. And we're just going to go walk through some classes." . . . We just forced our way in. It wasn't a welcome mat as it should have been. And I need a great high school that is going to work for my kids.

Holly is an engaged parent who desires a positive relationship between school administrators and her family, much like many other parents. She believes her children "are going to go places." For instance, she describes Joelle as "very, very, you know, smart, very wise, business-wise, and talented and driven." Like many parents, Holly has high expectations of the schools her children attend, and she expects those schools to cultivate the talents, interests, and educational potential of her children. Holly understands herself and her children as customers who are shopping for the right education among a range of options. And, because of her resources, she will get what she wants. From Holly's vantage point, the school's relationship with her family is transactional: by sending her child to this school, she will be providing the school with a high-achieving student who will then give back to the school community in the form of higher test scores and leadership activities and who will come with parents willing to contribute donations of time and money to various school-affiliated events and programs. This exchange includes the expectation that the school will operate in a way to advantage her child. As the sociologist Amanda Lewis and the education scholar John Diamond find in their study of a "good" school, "White middle-class parents are not just advocating for their own children. They are also advocating for the maintenance of the structures of inequality that facilitate their advantage."[20] Holly tells me, quite bluntly, that she was absolutely in search of a school that would "work" for her kids—a school that would function to provide her kids with what she wants for them.

In order for Holly to figure out if Evergreen High School was "a good fit" and wanting to be open-minded rather than following the advice of some of her other friends who urged her to move to Sheridan without second thought, she did tour the school to get her own sense of the quality of Evergreen High and how her children would be served by this institution. In this way, Holly is an exception to other parents in this study, as well as to affluent parents in other studies, in that she physically visited Evergreen High and tried to maintain an open mind despite knowledge of its reputation with her fellow affluent, white peers.[21] She describes her tour:

> We were out in a hallway talking to an English teacher. And an African American student came up to her and starts talking. . . . We just

mentioned that, "we're going to this Mr. Donald's class, the biology teacher." . . . And this African American student says, "You're going to that asshole's classroom? I can't stand that bastard." Well, the teacher's mortified, right? I mean, I can see the look of shock on her face. . . . And she's trying to shut this girl up, who's just talking and talking, really inappropriately, really loudly, to parents, prospective parents!

When describing this experience, Holly sits on the edge of her chair, clearly impassioned. She continues to describe the tour:

What stunned us was that it was obvious that the teacher did not have control of the situation. And that frightened us a little bit, you know? . . . We go to the biology classroom, and we're sitting through his biology class, which we enjoyed thoroughly. . . . After class, [the teacher] took us aside. . . . He said, "What other schools are you looking at?" And I said, ". . . I'll be touring Sheridan tomorrow." And he said, "I've been a summer school teacher in Sheridan for the past 17 years. . . . I know those families, I know that community, I know those students, and I will tell you right now, . . . if she were my granddaughter, she'd be going to Sheridan in a minute. That is an excellent school with excellent students and an excellent, excellent community. Get her out of Evergreen." This is their number-one teacher telling me this! I'm like, "Okay then."

The reputation of Evergreen High, especially in white, affluent circles, is that this is not a good school. This seems to be primarily because of the kids who attend it:

You know, Maggie, there were policemen on every single floor. . . . We were walking down halls, and kids would physically hit our bodies, . . . whereas, at Sheridan, . . . kids moved out of our way. One boy even held the door for us. They'd say, "Excuse me." It was a much more respectful environment. . . . I just felt like at any moment, things could explode at Evergreen . . . and become an unsafe situation. I don't want my kids to worry about safety. I want them to concentrate, focus, and direct their energies at school, nothing else. So I went to Sheridan the next day and thought, this school would fit for all of our kids because all our kids are very mature, focused children.

Holly's concerns about Evergreen High center on the behavior of the children who attend the school, particularly the behavior of one black student she encountered on her visit. In her view, some kids are too busy being disrespectful to learn, while her children are "very mature" and deserving of the best education available. Police are present in all of the schools in Petersfield as a matter of policy, and while some violence does occur in schools such as Evergreen High, the school is generally perceived as safe by those who attend the school and work within it.[22] While this discussion about public high school choice is not overtly about race or class, Evergreen High's demographics are undeniably different from those of Sheridan: many more students of color attend Evergreen, and many more kids there are living in poverty. However, when it comes to standardized test scores, paradoxically, despite what gets reported in informal social networks, between 2011 and 2012, Evergreen High and Sheridan High had very similar ACT scores and AP course offerings, and in some cases, Evergreen High actually had better results and offerings. The Schultz family, prioritizing a particular type of school and community experience for their children and viewing schools as commodities to be consumed, moved to Sheridan from their Apple Hills community. Erica and Natalie moved from their private K–8 school to the public Sheridan middle school, which is 96% white, and their older sister is enrolled at Sheridan High. I asked Holly if she thinks about the lack of people of color in her children's lives:

> HOLLY: [Sheridan] is lily-white, yeah.
> MAGGIE: Is that something that you and your husband talk about?
> HOLLY: No, we don't talk about it. It's, you know, it's a nonissue for us. I would welcome more people of color, but I just want everyone who's here to be on the same page as all the parents like me. I want to be in a community that all feels the same as we do, which is, we value education. And that is what this community is—we've found a community that really supports education.

While Holly's choice reflects supposed priorities of safety and "good" schooling, the choice is also connected to racialized understandings about who is smart, who values education, what kinds of people and communities support education, and how different groups of children behave. Her logic is nothing new; it is part of a long history of white parents securing a superior and segregated education for their own children. Her logic is also part of a long history of whites demonizing black students and parents, claiming that blacks do not value education, despite black parents' long-standing and continued fight for equal educational resources for their kids and empirical evidence that "black students are more committed to educational achievement and attainment than their white counterparts."[23] Her logic also maps onto long-standing white notions of integration—that if "they" could behave exactly like "us," we would welcome them. And the biology teacher's comments about the "excellent community" and "those families" in Sheridan in contrast to the black girl's words in the hallway serve to set up the dichotomy of "us" versus "them."

The Schultz parents and their neighbors have purposefully chosen to raise their children in what is essentially a racially sequestered community. The kids growing up here are surrounded by white country clubs, private dance lessons with white instructors, almost exclusively white classmates, predominantly white neighborhoods and soccer teams, exclusively white teachers and coaches, and exclusively white friends.

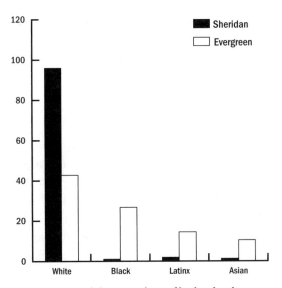

Figure 2.1. Racial demographics of high schools

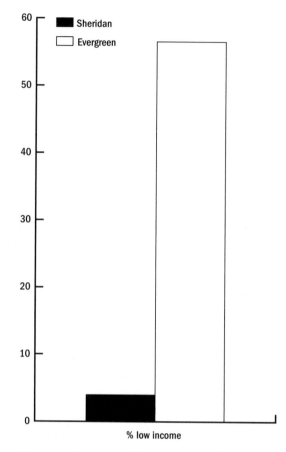

Figure 2.2. Percentage of low-income students across high schools

Through the interactions and lived experiences the Schultz children have with their own family, other families in Sheridan, and Sheridan teachers and administrators, as well as their interpretations of what they observe around them, embedded in this racial context of childhood, they develop their understanding of what race is and how it is relevant in their lives. And Holly and Dean's ideas about race are, in part, what guide the choices they make as they set up this particular social environment for their kids.

The Chablis Family

Victoria and Ryan Chablis own a large, newly constructed, four-bedroom, light-blue colonial in Sheridan. They chose this home for reasons similar to those of the Schultz family: so that their children could attend the local schools and so that they could be around people like themselves. In addition, the Chablis family also told me about two additional considerations shared by many Sheridan parents: *perceived demographic shifts* in the population and the *perceived political viewpoints* of many people who live in Petersfield. In many ways, Sheridan is the landing field for the white, conservative flight out of Petersfield.

Victoria and Ryan met in business school. They lived in the South for the first few years of their marriage, but due to Ryan's job, they moved to the Petersfield area. Ryan holds a high-power position within a major corporation. Victoria is a stay-at-home mom and is an avid exerciser. She constantly reminds her daughter, Meredith, to go running, which Meredith loudly resents. When the Chablis family moved to Sheridan, Meredith (now age 12) and Shane (now age 9) were in elementary and preschool, respectively. Their parents chose this community because of the word-of-mouth recommendations of friends and acquaintances.[24] Ryan's colleagues suggested that this would be a "great place to raise kids" and that it had "the best schools around," Victoria tells me. Unlike Holly, Victoria did not research school options widely; rather, she trusted the word of her husbands' colleagues, did a little looking around "here and there," but was very "trusting," which looking back, she feels was probably not the best way to make such a big decision. But she believes it is a decision in which they "really lucked out."

Because of the Chablises' choices about where to live, Meredith attends Sheridan Middle School and, like the Schultz children, has exclusively white friends, participates in activities within the borders of Sheridan, and is exposed primarily to people who hold very similar political views to those of her parents. Yet whiteness is invisible to parents such as Victoria, as is structural white privilege. As Victoria puts it, "Race isn't really part of my children's experience, so we don't really talk about it." She also tells me, "While some people try to play the race card, things are pretty much equal nowadays." "I guess there will always be those who want something for nothing!" she adds, laughing, unaware that she has just indicated one way that race continues to be meaningful to her. Victoria and Ryan strongly believe, and have no trouble articulating to me on a number of occasions, that current racial inequalities are the fault of people of color—specifically black people—and their supposed lack of motivation to work hard and to take advantage of the opportunities around them to achieve education, money, and success.

Here Victoria describes her thoughts on food stamps and free and reduced lunch programs, or "handouts" as she views them: "You know, you have people who are on [low-income state-provided health insurance], and yet they have the cell phones and the fingernails out to here [*gesturing to suggest long, manicured nails*]. They have the designer whatever. And I know that maybe that's part of black culture or because they don't have so much they might want to spoil themselves a little bit—I totally understand that, but at the same time, when you, you know, and I go back to the same thing." Victoria puts her coffee cup down on the table and looks directly at me before she continues.

> If you can't buy a box of cereal and a gallon of milk, that's less than $5, you know? To feed your child—*you* had this child! So that's part of being a parent, a mother, showing love. And yet now we spend millions of dollars as a nation feeding these children who are going to grow up thinking, I mean, how are they going to think? I don't know how long this program has been going on—free and reduced lunch—but it'd be interesting to track the kids who have been given free lunches, you know? What happens when they grow up? And sometimes, that's their only food, so I'm okay with that. . . . But at the same time, the flip side, why can't a mother afford a gallon of milk, even when they are given food stamps?! Can't you feed your child? That's where I get all caught up with my own, "Why am I thinking like this?" At the same time, responsibility, accountability, you know. . . . If the government has to take care of your child, then you shouldn't have any more. Because then the government is going to have to take care of that child. And then, on and on, you know?

Despite her earlier comments that race is not part of her experience and that everyone is "pretty much equal nowadays," Victoria believes that black moms who receive government assistance in the form of food stamps or free and reduced lunch for their children are bad mothers who waste resources on frivolities. She also makes clear her opinions on the politics of social welfare and her belief in the American Dream: if people work hard and spend their money wisely, they will not need food stamps. I ask Victoria if she thinks kids should go hungry if their parents cannot feed them. She responds, "If you can't feed your kids, Maggie, someone else should have them. It's so basic to me, you know? I mean, it's already my tax money that's already going to support all these kids. Maybe people like me should just, like, adopt these kids or something instead of giving their parents handouts! [*Laughing loudly*] I wonder what my husband would think about that! [*Laughing*]." Victoria and I have this discussion in front of Meredith.

Meredith's mother understands race in the United States today in a way that maps onto dominant "color-blind racial ideology." Researchers have used different language to describe this set of racial understandings and attitudes articulated here by Victoria.[25] The theory overall includes the following:

1. The claim that most people do not "see" or notice race anymore ("I am color blind"; "race doesn't matter to me"; "red, pink, yellow, blue—it's all the same").
2. The claim that racial parity has, for the most part, been achieved ("We are postrace"; "Anyone who is willing to work hard can make it today").
3. The assertion that any persisting patterns of racial inequality are the result of individual- or group-level shortcomings—shortcomings that are typically assumed to be cultural in nature ("If some people aren't successful these days, it is because they aren't motivated"; "Some groups struggle because they don't have the right family values").
4. The claim that because race does not matter anymore, there is no need for institutional remedies (such as affirmative action) to redress racial inequalities and that any attempts to raise questions about race are problematic ("They are playing the race card"; "The real problem today is reverse racism").[26]

This way of thinking about race in the United States is meaningful not only in that it reflects how individuals such as Victoria and Holly understand racial matters but also as "an important ideological pillar in the maintenance of white supremacy because it protects a deeply unequal racial status quo by stigmatizing both personal claims of injustice and systematic attempts to mitigate inequality."[27] In simple terms, the tenets of color-blind ideology "justify" existing racial inequality.

Color-blind ideology is pervasive in Sheridan, but how are kids growing up here making sense of it? Though Victoria draws on color-blind logic and claims that race no longer matters in the United States, Meredith is exposed to both subtle race talk and overt discussion of race and politics by her parents—and often these discussions are rooted in the geography of suburb versus city. Her parents both hold strong conservative views and feel that Petersfield is generally a city filled with "naïve liberals," another reason the Chablis family is grateful that they ended up in a neighborhood with like-minded people. For instance, Victoria describes her perceptions of crime in Petersfield:

> I will say one thing about Petersfield I find kind of humorous sometimes. . . . I couldn't believe how naïve some of the people in Petersfield [are] [*laughing*]. . . . I feel like they are so liberal there, they invite [crime] in, but then they get mad like, "Now there are all these murders!" and I'm like, "You've made it *really* easy for these people to come from the projects of whatever city, and you can't have it both ways!" You know, you can't give them everything they want and then turn around and get mad that crime is going up or whatever! [*Laughing*].

This perception that Petersfield has "made it really easy for these people to come from the projects" connects to very particular locally shared white common sense. Because Petersfield is seen as a socially progressive city and is perceived to offer relatively comprehensive social services, the white logic is that families living in poverty are attracted to this place and bring their "social ills" with them. People both in Sheridan and in parts of Petersfield articulate this same perception—all these social problems are attributable to this negative "changing demographic," by which they invariably mean "black people." I found this to be true not only for white parents in Sheridan but across groups with whom I interacted as part of this ethnography. This includes white adults in the city who work with black children every single day, which painfully and jarringly reveals the harmful mind-set of those adults responsible for teaching, coaching, mentoring, and disciplining black children in this metropolitan community. Ironically, though parents are moving to Sheridan for better public schools, they are quick to criticize the supposed black families (who they believe are) moving to Petersfield "by the droves" for better public services and schools, calling these imagined parents "irresponsible." Even more ironic is that Sheridan parents claim to be "color blind" and yet simultaneously discuss openly the problems with the newcomers, deploying phrases that are sometimes racially coded and sometimes racially explicit but in either case implying something negative about black people. Despite the actual demographics, what matters most with regard to decision making are people's perceptions of these changes—decisions and perceptions that shape children's racial contexts and subsequently shape how they make sense of race.

In addition to understandings of "changing demographics," the Chablises' political beliefs and ideas about race are fundamental to why they construct the racial context of childhood that they do. Ryan and Victoria refuse to live in Petersfield not only because of the perceived low-quality schools and the perceived large influx of poor blacks but because they perceive it be a place filled with white people who are dissimilar from them *politically*. Ryan and Victoria are deeply troubled by what they perceive to be the political perspectives of the other affluent, white people who live in the city—not just because of the "ridiculous" ideas they hold but because those ideas matter in applied, real ways in relation to local public policy decisions. As a result, families such as the Chablis purposefully choose to segregate themselves into an affluent, white, but also politically conservative community, raising their kids here in this racial context deliberately.

The Racial Context of Wheaton Hills

Located in the city of Petersfield is the large neighborhood of Wheaton Hills. The streets that form the boundaries of this neighborhood are popular areas in the city for shopping and eating. Expensive restaurants, fashion boutiques, salons, upscale coffee and wine bars, and expensive grocery stores are located along one of the main streets here. A small lake with a large public park is also located near Wheaton Hills, which is where many children socialize, play soccer, use the jungle gym, learn how to sail, and have school picnics. Groggy teenagers slowly walk with giant backpacks from their houses to the nearby high school in the early morning while middle-aged women run with baby jogger strollers and big dogs down the sidewalks. There is a lot of traffic here, but it is mostly kids getting dropped off at piano lessons or at friends' houses, moms talking on the sidewalk after picking their kids up at the bus stop, or groups of teenagers playing an intense game of basketball in someone's driveway. Everyone seems to know each other here. And almost everyone is white.

While the neighborhood is certainly affluent, it is by no means ostentatious. The homes in Wheaton Hills vary quite significantly in size and style. Some homes are old historic brick Colonials, while others are small ranches or Capes that have had numerous additions built onto them over the years. The average home price in this neighborhood is approximately $400,000. Most of the homes in this neighborhood show clear evidence of children living within them. Basketball hoops exist on almost every driveway, chalk drawings paint the sidewalks, and toys and bicycles and sports equipment litter the lawns and backyards of the families who live here. Groups of neighborhood children can often be seen after school playing street hockey, soccer, or hide-and-seek.

People whom I interviewed who live in Wheaton Hills describe this neighborhood as "the perfect place to live," "a great place to raise a family," and "the most ideal neighborhood politically and geographically to live in." People who live across town in Evergreen tend to associate this neighborhood with "more middle-of-the-road Democrats" and "the medical and hard sciences professors and their families" and "a little too uptight" and even "hypocritical liberals." Sheridan families in this study consider all Petersfield families, regardless of where they live in the city, to be "union thugs" or "naïve academics" or "bleeding-heart liberals." Clearly, political identity matters a great deal in Wheaton Hills, as it does in all three of the neighborhoods in this study, and members of this community think of themselves as being liberal but not as liberal or "idealistic to a fault" as the people in Evergreen.

Wheaton Hills' families are also commonly known for being—and think of themselves as being—extremely focused on academic achievement. Wheaton Hills is zoned in the school district with the perceived "best" public high school in town. The neighborhood is also within close proximity to the multitude of private schooling options in Petersfield. As a result, many families with children live here, particularly parents with professional careers who want school options that work for their schedules and an educational environment that corresponds with their own values. As a result of this common priority of academic excellence and achievement among the affluent, white Wheaton Hills families here, many families opt in and out of the public schools at different moments. These public-school-versus-private-school dynamics make understanding this context particularly complex.

One of the more complicated and contentious issues here is that the boundaries between elementary schools cut in multiple directions through Wheaton Hills. One half of Wheaton Hills is assigned to attend one elementary school (A1), which is paired with another elementary school (A2), while the other half is assigned to attend another elementary school (B1), which is paired with yet another elementary school (B2). Thus, two elementary school "pairings" exist. The parents here understand this to be because, at some point in time, a superintendent was, as one mom puts it, "striving for race diversity in the classroom." In practical terms, this means that a kid may live next door to another kid who attends a different public elementary school. And, perhaps unsurprisingly, there are racial meanings mapped onto these particular schools—meanings that shed light on the local racial politics at play in this community and how these racial politics inform parents' decisions, which in turn shape how the kids growing up here think about race.

The first pairing, Pairing A, is perceived to combine children who live in an international-graduate-student housing area with children from some of the more affluent, white blocks in Wheaton Hills. Many of the students of color in Pairing A are thus understood to be children of graduate students, most of whom, the parents here tell me, are from China and Korea. Pairing B, on the other hand, connects children through a busing system from the "other side of town," many of whom are living in poverty and are black, with another part of the Wheaton Hills neighborhood, which includes both very affluent, white families and solidly middle-class white families. Pairing B is assumed to have a very small Asian population. Across both schools, there is little discussion of the Latinx population, with the exception of an emerging dual-language-immersion program. These kids, no matter which elementary and middle school they attend, go to the same desirable high school in town. The middle and elementary years, however, are distinct from each other in ways that are highly racialized with regard to how people think about these schools. While some existing research examines private school choices,[28] there is something unique about this pattern of affluent, white parents opting *out* of public schools when children are younger but then opting *in* to the public high school.

The local racial commonsense knowledge that leads to the emergence of a range of private elementary school choices in this neighborhood is based on inaccurate racialized assumptions. The actual demographics for each are shown in table 2.1. The data show that the largest difference in racial composition is actually the percentage of Latinx students enrolled in Pairing B as well as the number of white students in Pairing A. Further, a much-larger population that identifies as Asian or Asian American exists at Pairing B than in Pairing A. Despite this demographic reality, the perception on the behalf of the parents is that Pairing B has a particularly large black population. For reasons tied to local, word-of-mouth, parent-to-parent, colleague-to-colleague, realtor-to-home-buyer understandings about race and purported demographic shifts, cloaked in racially coded language, the many white, affluent parents here assume that the minority population in these schools is largely black. This trend reflects a deep disconnect for many parents between what they think and what is actually true at their own local schools and reflects their negative perception of black children and parents.

TABLE 2.1. Racial Composition of Elementary School Pairings, by Percentage

	A1 (grades 1–3)	A2 (grades 4–6)	B1 (grades 1–3)	B2 (grades 4–6)
White	69	68	30	31
Black	5	8	13	16
Latinx	9	9	39	35
Asian	9	8	13	14
Multiracial	8	6	5	4

The Norbrook Family

The Norbrook family lives in a large blue Cape with flower-filled window boxes and yellow shutters. Their home is located on one of the busy streets that runs through Wheaton Hills. But their backyard leads into a neighborhood park where all of the children on the street gather in the winter for massive snowball fights and play games together, such as soccer and capture the flag, in the summer months. Many of the families who live near this park have young children. They live within close walking distance of Wheaton Hills High School, an elementary school, one of many nearby private schools, a library, and an ice-cream shop, which is a favorite hangout spot for middle-school kids after school.

Ralph Norbrook is a professor at the local university, while Gina Norbrook works as a researcher for a nonprofit organization. Both parents describe their midwestern childhoods as being racially "homogeneous," explain how this homogeneity was problematic for them in their own racial meaning-making processes when they were younger, and tell me how they want something different for their own kids. This view is shared by many parents living in Wheaton Hills and reflects a dominant theme: these parents want their kids to grow up in a "diverse" environment.

Given the Norbrooks' parenting priority, unlike many of their neighbors who have opted out of the Pairing B elementary school, they have kept their children in public school. Monica (8) attends Wheaton Hills Pairing B elementary school—the school other parents view as undesirable—while Robert (12), who finished at Pairing B last year, is in his first year at Wheaton Hills Middle School. Gina describes their process of school choice:

> We are big public school advocates. We've always kind of had that view. . . . But when we moved in this house and started going to the park and stuff, . . . we met other parents and were like, "Oh what school do your kids go to?" and everyone was like, "Catholic school." And we were sort of like, "Huh, okay." It makes sense. There is a Catholic school near us. People would move here that would want to go there. But, um, then it just became a little bit weird where, you know, we started to sense that there was this thing in the neighborhood against the school, which is [Pairing B].

I ask Gina what she means by people being "a little bit weird" and how she made sense of that as a new mom to the neighborhood. She explains:

> People were like, "Oh, I just don't want my kid to be bused across town," you know, they'd say that. And we were sort of like, "Okaaaay???" . . . But, um, then we found a couple families that did go to [Pairing B], and they were like, "We love it!" so we kind of did some background—I don't remember how we looked it up—but we kind of saw that there was this controversy with the schools in the '90s and, you know, the schools had been paired together in, I think, 1980, for racial—it had to do with racial desegregation.

Gina is very animated and speaking with a great deal of passion, putting down her coffee mug and gesturing with her hands as she speaks. She speaks critically of the other affluent whites in her community for their choices to send their children to private schools when the public schools are so strong. She believes that this is because these other parents do not want their children to be in "diverse" spaces:

> One thing about living in this neighborhood and going to Pairing B is the school, because of its diversity, it selects out extremely liberal parents who care about diversity. Anyone who is more conservative or middle of the road, whatever you want to call it, they might go to parochial for the test scores and all that. They are the ones who say diversity isn't important. And so in this neighborhood, that's one of the things about living here is we've got kids right here [on our street] who go to . . . five different schools! But it's the parents who care about diversity who stay in the public schools.

Gina brings political affiliation into this conversation about school choice, suggesting that in Petersfield, one's politics shape the decisions one makes about school choice. She goes on:

> I *wanted* my kids to not go to a homogeneous school. . . . And when we moved to Petersfield, we actually thought that Petersfield wasn't going to be very diverse. We kind of had our own assumptions about Petersfield, which were actually wrong. So we didn't even think about diversity when

we bought a house because we didn't even think it was possible. But I remember Robert started kindergarten at Pairing B, . . . and, um, his kindergarten class was 15 kids, so very small, and there was literally—it was the most diverse group I have ever been involved with, was his kindergarten classroom. I mean, there was like three white children, three or four black children, you know, a couple of Latinos, a Native American boy. . . . It was just, like, very diverse, and we were like, "Wow! This is amazing." We had a really great experience with the school. The diversity was celebrated rather than ignored, you know?

"Diversity" in this case is tied to different languages, foods, customs, and celebrating cultural differences. Gina wants to provide her children with an experience of racial socialization that challenges the status quo, and she distinguishes this goal from those of her neighbors whom she believes are "hypocrites" because of their private school choices. Certainly she stands apart from them. Yet, at times, the multiculturalism she embraces is one that celebrates "ethnic" food but fails to acknowledge how power and inequality are also part of understanding the United States as multicultural. Although she offers tremendous praise for the classroom demographics and the community atmosphere of celebrating cultural diversity, Gina never mentions oppression, racism, or racial inequality.[29] The problem with this sort of uncritical "diversity discourse" or "shallow multiculturalism" is that participation in it has the potential to reify, or construct as real, who is "ethnic," who has "culture," and who is "normal" while ignoring how racial hierarchies and power actually work.[30] However well meaning parents such as Gina may be, when they fail to acknowledge inequality and racism, in a way, they are unintentionally complicit in the reproduction of it.[31]

When Gina does talk about racism, these conversations are focused on the past. For instance, Gina talks about residential segregation with her son and me:

This neighborhood did not allow black people to live in it when it was built in the 1930s. It had a restrictive covenant against, um, African Americans. . . . So when we bought our house, I remember, you get, like, these documents, like historical kind of deed thing, and I remember—I'm the kind of person who likes to look at that kind of thing, and I was, like, reading through it, and I was like, "*Oh my Godddd!*" . . . I think a lot of the neighborhoods in the early 20th century had these covenants. Like, you couldn't sell your house to a black person, and it may have had other ones too, religious ones or—I can't remember the details. It was institutionalized. It is horrifying.

Robert asks a few follow-up questions, which Gina answers. But this conversation is largely about residential segregation of the past rather than the present.

Unlike the Sheridan parents, Gina does not think inequality persists today because some people are lazy or lack an appreciation for education. But she also does not think inequality persists because of racism. Instead, Gina's understanding of inequality is connected to class: "Race isn't the real issue here. It's class." It is a sentiment shared by many of her peers in Wheaton Hills—that the problem facing the Petersfield community is rooted in economic inequality, not racial inequality. For instance, many of the parents, including Gina, tell me how they wish there were more black or Latinx professionals in Petersfield—that they would have more friends of color if more people of color shared their class position. Gina reminisces fondly about her days living in a northern suburb of Chicago. She tells me how she lived next door to a black doctor and across the street from a black lawyer. This neighborhood was "ideal" in her mind.

Another common discussion in Wheaton Hills is why parents of black children are not involved in the parent-teacher organization (PTO). Gina explains:

If you went to programs at night, like, um, different PTO things or whatever, it would be mostly the white families, some Latino families. Sometimes there would be an interpreter to understand the program. And there would be almost no African American families. And, um, it was kind of, over time though, it—because, you know, it bothered you. The African American families would come out for musical shows, so anytime the kids performed, like, concerts, they would come out in full force. So it's like, what's going on? I guess, you know, I always wonder, do they not feel comfortable? Do they have no experience about what a PTO was? You know, maybe they hadn't gone to schools where there even was one.

I just don't even know. So there was, like, these weird little things that manifested over time.

While Gina sounds like she is making an argument about race here, instead she tells me over and over again that this is not a "race issue." Instead, she insists to me, as many other parents do, that it is a "class issue"—she would be friends with other parents, but due to class divides, they just "live different lives." She tells me that she connects more with families whose lives "in many ways resemble" her family's, such as the black doctor she lived next door to in the Chicago suburb. Almost all of the other Wheaton Hills parents echo her comments, the logic being that while yes, there are many black and Latinx people in Petersfield who are also poor, if the poverty problem could be fixed, then all of the other social problems within the community would be resolved. Reducing complex forms of race and class inequality to a simplistic class-based explanation is similar to "diversity discourse" used by many parents—in both cases, structural racism is ignored.

Monica and Robert, then, are growing up surrounded by white, affluent children who attend a variety of schools and who have parents with a variety of views about race, public education, and inequality. These are the kids with whom they have water-balloon fights and go trick-or-treating. In addition, at school, Monica and Robert interact with kids who live in different parts of the city and who are of a different race and class background than they are. The school celebrates diversity and multiculturalism, but by and large, a critical lens on how this diversity is connected to inequality is missing.

Getting the best education is a theme for many Wheaton Hills parents, though the Norbrooks and other families are also concerned about "diversity" in their children's life. As such, when it comes to schools, families here make a range of different choices about schools, oftentimes opting into private school during the elementary and middle-school years, and as a result, the kids here often have friendship groups that are shaped by these choices. Parents here identify as liberals, though some are far more moderate than others. Growing up in Wheaton Hills in this sense is contextually different from growing up in exclusively white and affluent, politically conservative Sheridan or growing up in the eclectic, politically progressive neighborhood of Evergreen—even if some parallels can be drawn.

The Racial Context of Evergreen

Across the city from Wheaton Hills is the eclectic neighborhood of Evergreen. Most affluent, white Evergreen families live in expensive Victorian homes of all colors built very close to one another, some perched alongside the nearby lake. There are choices about what kind of house to live in, unlike the sprawling "cookie-cutter" housing developments of nearby suburbs. The average house value here depends on how the boundaries of this diverse neighborhood are drawn. Some blocks are composed of homes with an average value of $700,000, while others are valued closer to $200,000. Some houses in Evergreen have been divided up into apartments, serving as housing for graduate students at the local university or families renting apartments. Some are big, some are small. And some have been remodeled into modern, stylish, and eco-friendly homes that could be featured in a magazine; these homes are valued at well over $1 million. As such, Evergreen is far more diverse than Sheridan and Wheaton Hills are, particularly with respect to class. Instead of well-manicured lawns, there are popular public parks every few blocks, and many of the yards here are filled with wildflowers and overgrown bushes.

Family-run restaurants line the main street along with an assortment of bars, including a host of dive bars, an LGBTQ nightclub, and upscale creative cocktail establishments. All of these amenities are within walking distance of neighborhood homes, as are multiple large and small businesses such as hole-in-the-wall yoga studios, art studios, a small theater, bike repair shops, a busy cooperative supermarket complete with an electric-car-charging station in the parking lot, and a local pharmacy. Many social service / outreach offices and social justice organizations are headquartered along this main street, and almost everyone who is not riding a bike or taking public transportation seems to drive either an expensive hybrid car or a very well-used vehicle.

Perhaps the most noticeable characteristic of this neighborhood is the unequivocal and unapologetic progressive political identity of families who live here. Political signs, both professionally made and homemade, litter the lawns of this community, particularly during the election season. Neighborhood cars are riddled with bumper stickers that mock conservative politicians, promote liberal ideals (e.g., "COEXIST"), or play on old advertising campaigns in curiously antiracist ways: "Got white privilege?"

As one respondent told me, "Evergreen is earthy-crunchy"; as another put it, Evergreen is "filled with a bunch of old hippies." Whether or not the people of Evergreen consider themselves to be "old hippies," certainly they choose to live in this community in large part because of their politics.

The Lacey Family

The Laceys' home is located one block from the edge of a large lake. (The lake helps sustain the Evergreen neighborhood's high property values, especially for those homes located immediately on the waterfront.) Two political signs are displayed in the front yard supporting the local unions and the Democratic Party, though it is hard to know if the signs belong to the Laceys or the next-door neighbors. The Laceys' next-door neighbors have a pride flag flying on their porch, and other neighbors down the street have a homemade wooden sign attached to their house that reads in painted letters, "END THE WAR." An Obama sticker is on the bumper of an old junky car parked in the driveway across the street, along with long stickers displaying names of prestigious liberal arts colleges stuck to the back windshield.

Although the immediate neighborhood of Evergreen is predominantly white, it is heterogeneous in other ways: in addition to families such as the Laceys, same-sex-parent families, graduate students, housing co-op members, interracial families, adoptive families, and halfway house residents live in this community. Some families of color also live in Evergreen, many of whom rent apartments along the main street. Evergreen is also located within somewhat close proximity to a predominantly black neighborhood. Interaction between these two places does not occur frequently in the neighborhood, but the children who live in these two places attend the same public schools. As such, the school that Charlotte (13) attends is racially diverse, and there is a wide range of children from different class backgrounds who attend. This is a fact that Janet Lacey, Charlotte's mom, who works as an environmentalist, explicitly states she wants for her child:

> I like that my daughter sees black people in our house and on our street. We have friends who are black, and we have friends who have adopted from Ethiopia and another neighbor from Guatemala. And you know, in

this area, there's a fair number of gay and lesbian couples, so she's used to seeing that. It's just integrated into her life. Like in kindergarten, she was a flower girl in a lesbian wedding. And I remember being at the bus stop afterwards, and one girl was saying something to another girl about how "girls can't get married." And Charlotte's like, "Oh yeah they can! Girls can marry girls, and boys can marry boys. I was there and I saw it, and two girls got married!" She also sees a lot of people with piercings, covered with tattoos, so she's just, like, used to all these different kinds of people.

Janet tells me that she likes living in this neighborhood for the fact that her daughter will be exposed to people who are different from her. Her remarks about how diversity is "integrated into her life" suggests that it is part of her everyday reality.

Tom, a social scientist, shares a similar view to his wife and tells me that he likes this neighborhood—and the public schools that come with living here—because of the racial and class diversity as well as shared political beliefs of those who live here:

> I think the diversity was one of the things we liked the most—we liked the idea of [Charlotte] going to a school that wasn't like the school I grew up in. . . . I think we were nervous about sending her to a school where it was just a bunch of upper-middle-class white kids. . . . We like the politics of the people here. . . . People are outside all the time, so you're seeing people out and talking and interacting. So that is what drove us there. But we did like that the school was mixed. . . . I don't know that I want her to have that super white-bread, sit around with a bunch of, you know, overachieving, you know, wealthy, white Americans, having them as her entire base of everyone she knows. That made me nervous. So coming to a school that had more racial and economic mixes was appealing.

Tom tells me that for him growing up, he "liked being on the edges of lots of different groups of people." He thinks that having a diverse set of friends made him a "better-rounded sort of person" and "more empathetic to people." He continues:

> I think you grow as a person by getting to know different people. . . . It should help you be a kinder human being and to be more thoughtful

about different kinds of people, and that means not just the color of their skin or their family background but sort of what generation they are or income in the United States, in terms of their finances, you know. . . . I have some hostility towards people of great wealth who—who think that they somehow deserve it. . . . But that's why I want Charlotte to have that [exposure to diversity].

Tom expresses his desire for his daughter to be able to cross social boundaries or "divides" that separate people from communicating and interacting with one another. He connects this to the polarized nature of current US politics, offering self-reflective and even self-critical comments about his own approach to engaging (or not) with others. In his case, he tells me that he avoids the very affluent who refuse to acknowledge their unearned privileges and spends the majority of his social time in an entirely liberal community. Notably, Tom, while perhaps not quite as wealthy as the Chablis family living in Sheridan, is affluent himself and certainly in a position of class privilege and race privilege himself, which he acknowledges at various moments during the interview. But he wants his daughter to think about these privileges, as he believes to ignore them is to fail to be a good person.

Janet also believes that good things come from spending time in diverse spaces. She reflects on how other parents she knows in Petersfield refuse to send their children to Evergreen High School—the school Holly Schultz found so repugnant. Janet rejects this view. "Being exposed to things will give you skills and experiences. Exposure brings more understanding and growth than sheltering does, and so, you know, I think kids should be more exposed than sheltered," she tells me. When I ask Janet what kinds of things she thinks Charlotte is being exposed to that she would not be elsewhere, she explains that Charlotte has exposure to both racial difference and class difference, specifically poverty, which introduces some unique challenges. Given the social geography of Evergreen, when Charlotte goes to school, most of the children living in wealthy households are white, while most of the children living in impoverished or working-class households are black or Latinx. Janet tells me that she wishes Charlotte could be in an environment where this pattern did not hold true. Janet is especially worried that Charlotte's intergroup contact at school will reinforce rather than rework dominant

racial stereotypes that she and her husband are seeking to resist reproducing in their daughter. Indeed, Janet speaks openly with her daughter
about contemporary racial injustice in the United States. Despite these
concerns about messages Charlotte may pick up at school as a result of
broader inequalities, however, Janet is committed to "staying" in public
schools: "If we are not going to keep our kid in, who is going to keep their
kid in? Seriously. You know, if this is stuff that we think is important, if
we don't do it, who is going to do it?" Like Tom, Janet believes that the
good outweighs the bad at the Evergreen public schools and that one
way to improve public schools is to invest resources in them, including the resources of affluent families that would otherwise benefit private schools. In addition, regardless of what goes on at school, Tom and
Janet Lacey want their daughter to grow up in a politically progressive
community, as they view these types of communities as more inclusive
and representative of their own values and beliefs. These choices about
designing a particular kind of racial context for Charlotte were made
with very concrete parenting priorities and goals in mind—priorities
informed largely by these parents' racial politics.

Unlike the color-blind ideology that informs much of what transpires
in Sheridan, parents opting to live in Evergreen deploy color-conscious
narratives about race. Their decision making about where to live and
what schools to send their children to map onto these narratives and
are informed by a commitment to what they often refer to as "social
justice." While "social justice" encompasses a range of topics, parents
in Evergreen are particularly focused on issues of injustice surrounding
sexuality, gender, and race. When it comes to racial injustice specifically,
Evergreen parents deliberately seek to cultivate what Pamela Perry and
Alexis Shotwell define as "anti-racist praxis" in their children, or "constant thought and action to dismantle racism and end racial inequities
in the United States."[32] This is an important priority to all of the parents
interviewed in Evergreen.

Even with these priorities of working to confront inequality, Tom and
Janet Lacey at times unintentionally reproduce the very inequality they
seek to disrupt. For instance, they supplement their daughter's education by providing Charlotte with a number of additional extracurricular
learning opportunities such as tutoring, private music lessons, summer
programs, and elaborate trips and vacations, among others. They pro-

vide Charlotte with private opportunities not available to other students, a reality that at times contradicts their stated intention of supporting equal public educational opportunities for all. Tom and Janet, along with other affluent, white parents in this study who identify as progressive, are often faced with what I refer to as a *conundrum of privilege*: how much work is enough? How does one raise children in ways that truly cultivate antiracist praxis while still receiving unearned white advantage and the benefits of class privilege? Is it possible to raise privileged children at the individual level in a way that maps onto ideals of equality at the structural level? And to what extent do these parents exert their privileges even within this context of race and class diversity and even given their good intentions to get what they want for their children?

The education policy scholar Linn Posey-Maddox documented in her ethnographic research how middle-class and upper-middle-class white parents dominate parent-teacher associations.[33] Studies have also shown how white parents "undermin[e] attempts to rethink the current tracking structure" and "campaig[n] against such change" because tracking benefits their own children.[34] Further research has shown how middle-class parents advocate for their children and teach their children to advocate for themselves in ways that fit with the expectations of school officials,[35] which also leads these same kids to engage in more help-seeking behavior.[36] In short, parents of privileged children work to maintain that privilege, even when they do not intend to do so.

Even though Janet and Tom want to match their values with their actions, they harness their race and class privileges in ways that construct the particular childhood context they see as ideal for their own child. They work hard to promote a social justice upbringing for their daughter, yet they are raising her in a society structured by race and class, which is not entirely possible for them to change. As such, their individual-level behaviors do not address, and likely cannot address, these broader structural inequalities. While certainly Janet and Tom are doing the best they can to make choices they view as ethical and just—and choices they believe will help their child cultivate antiracist praxis and empathy and an awareness of their unearned privileges—the simple fact that Janet and Tom live in a stratified society and subsequently have choices to make in the first place speaks to their power as affluent, white parents. And yet there is something important about parents like Tom and Janet who are committed to trying to raise a child conscious and aware of race and racial injustice, perhaps even a moment of possibility.

The Norton-Smith Family

Moving to the big, purple Victorian house with the white trim in Evergreen was an "intentional" decision, according to Greg and Jennifer, not only for them but for most of their neighbors. Greg, an attorney, describes the neighborhood as well as how the family ended up here:

> I would say Evergreen is an intentional community. I mean, we moved here on purpose. . . . Initially, we rented a house in Wheaton Hills, and we had friends here—lots of people from Boston live here, and we would visit them and think, "[Evergreen] is not exactly who we are, but it's who we want to be." The people who live here live here because of what it is. They don't just sorta end up here and stay here. 'Cause, you know [*laughing*], a lot of people would *not* like living here. It's crazy, and sometimes, when a lot of different people live together, you have all sorts of reactions to things, and there's some goofy stuff that goes down. But that's why the people who live here live here. . . . It's funny because it feels like we are the "righties" of the neighborhood because no one else wears a suit to work every day.

Underlying Greg's final comment about viewing himself as a "righty" is the understanding that Evergreen is where politically progressive people live: "It was a progressive place that would be cozy enough to raise your family but yet the right kind of place—not too closed-minded. We liked the idea of what the neighborhood was and the people who lived here. . . . There are a lot of people here who live what they believe. It's totally impressive. They live it in the community, they live it in their own families, they live it individually. . . . That's what this neighborhood means." While there were other considerations that brought this family to Petersfield in the first place, the politics of Evergreen are what attracted this family to this neighborhood.

Jennifer also describes how "fortunate" she feels that Evergreen is located in close proximity to a predominantly black neighborhood, as this leads to racially and economically integrated public schools—"a rare

occurrence in America," she tells me. Greg too comments on a different occasion that while there is "more diversity and sexual-preference
diversity," he "wishes the diversity was a bit better." I ask him what he
means by this, as does Conor, who is participating in our conversation
and interjects at the same time as me, "I thought there was diversity
here!" The word "diversity" gets repeated over and over. Greg explains to
us both that he worries about the way in which race and class are interrelated in Petersfield:

> I think, Conor, that sometimes the kids at school with behavioral issues, or
> the kids with the extra issues, are usually ones that come from a different
> background than you. I guess I am speaking a little bit in code here. What
> I mean is [*turning to me and away from his son*], it worries me that Conor
> goes to a school where all the black and Latino kids are also the poor kids
> and kids with extra struggles. I wonder how that affects him. I think about
> if we lived in a bigger place where that wasn't always true, like Atlanta—
> Atlanta always comes to mind. Maybe it would be better to live in a place
> that really has a middle class of people who are not majority culture. I
> guess I am talking in code again.

Catching himself and calling himself out for speaking in racially coded
language, Greg expresses his concerns to his son as well as to me about
why in some ways Evergreen is not ideal. Much like other parents in
Evergreen, Greg is concerned that because there are only a handful of
affluent or middle-class students of color at Conor's school, perhaps
this will lead Conor to make associations between people of color and
poverty—the same concern shared by Charlotte's mother, as well as
all of the other Evergreen parents I interviewed. Greg is worried that
Conor will form negative views of his black and Latinx peers and that
he will associate all children of color with poverty. Aware that he keeps
reverting to coded language rather than saying "black" or "Latino," Greg
suggests that Petersfield would be a "better" place to live and attend
school if more of the families of color in town were affluent or at least
middle class and if there was more social equality between the families
who live here.

Both Greg and Jennifer also express to me that they take issue with
the small number of black teachers, coaches, administrators, and politi-

cians in the community because of what this pattern teaches kids such as Conor. These parents do not talk about how this pattern potentially harms black children. The Norton-Smiths are also concerned that practices at the school such as tracking or unfair discipline policies may send Conor messages about race that they are working hard to combat. For instance, Jennifer comments on Evergreen High School and the recent discovery she made about security guards and metal detectors:

> I found out there are security guards at Evergreen High School and metal detectors—I was horrified! It's completely insane. And it's amazing to me what people moralize. When I found this out, . . . I talked to a lot of people, and they were like, "Sure! You know, it's a lot of different kids." And I said, "There are no security guards at the public library. There's no security guards or metal detectors at the grocery store!" I mean, I can think of a lot of places that have that many people in them without armed people walking around, right? It's just crazy to me! But what actually makes me nervous about Evergreen High is that I have heard it is broken down racially and economically, which is what I grew up with and it's awful. Having said all that, I think, what I know about the people like us who choose to send their kids to Evergreen, they are people who think a lot about it and wanting to fix it. There's a program there . . . that helps minority, lower-income kids get access to college, so I do think there's opportunity there. But I'm not going to lie: I worry about going in and our kids getting syphoned off into AP classes and being in all-white classrooms, and no! I want them to be in diverse spaces. That's part of why we are sending them there!

Jennifer talks about "the people who choose to send their kids to Evergreen" as "people who think a lot about it and wanting to fix it," "it" presumably referring to the racial inequity at the school and "people" presumably referring to people such as herself. Yet Jennifer is also concerned about matters far beyond the presumed criminality and misbehavior of the children who attend the school, articulated by parents in Sheridan such as Holly. She is most concerned about how patterns of tracking in which all of the white, affluent kids are in AP classes, a sort of school-within-a-school scenario, is harmful for the school community at large. Jennifer views her child's taking an AP class as less important than her child's being in a diverse class. And the fact that she views tracking as a racialized problem that negatively impacts her own child is what motivates her to work for change. Ironically, it seems that parents of black kids in this school who likely have little choice in where their child attends school given this context may be overlooked by parents such as Jennifer.

Jennifer struggles to balance her concerns about the diversity in her own children's lives with the lack of real educational opportunities for kids of color that result from racialized tracking and school discipline practices. While the Norton-Smiths suggest that these goals are interrelated and ought to be considered together, school-based research finds that many white parents who are committed to integrated, urban public schools tend to "rule the school," pushing their own agendas while ignoring the voices of minority parents.[37] Further research demonstrates how private businesses and policy makers seek to retain middle-class families in urban schools, valuing them more highly than their working-class or poor peers.[38] Questions emerge in Evergreen about how to be a responsible white member of a racially diverse parent population within a community in which structural inequality and privilege persist and define much of people's everyday experiences, opportunities, and outcomes.

Jennifer also tells me how she "mourns" public education and how she mourns the fact that she has to "supplement" her own children's education, similar to the Lacey parents, through enrichment activities and extra education outside of school to make up for what her children are missing out on by not attending other schools in town:

> I think public access to a good education is just core to a democratic model, and I think, you know, . . . more lobbyists for charter schools— they put in more money for charter school lobbyists in this state than in, like, all other lobbyists combined, and that is because they have a *shit-ton* of money. I mean, they are privatizing education, and I mourn that. Because, I mean, my kids are going to be fine. But it's the low-income black kids of the world that aren't going to be fine. They already aren't fine. And we are in a safe-enough place where we're not going to make a guinea pig out of our kids, but what about elsewhere? I mean, we can supplement our kids' education, and we will. We are going to have to navigate some

issues. And we're going to have to have a lot of conversations about race and inequality.

This example further illuminates the complexity of the conundrum of privilege. Even when parents want to teach their kids to recognize and fight against injustice, how much commitment is enough, especially when this commitment implicates their own children's futures or includes elements perceived to be beyond their control? How does one advocate for one's own child as well as "other people's children," all at the same time?[39] What are the politics of advocating for other people's children from a position of privilege?

In the specific case of the Norton-Smiths, on the one hand, Jennifer passionately and genuinely wants to support the principle of equal educational opportunity through public schooling, expressing anger at the fact that her children will "be fine" while children of color may not be. Yet, on the other hand, she does not want to make her child a "guinea pig," and therefore she makes trade-offs, such as providing her son with tutoring, a choice that she tells me she knows contradicts the notion of an equal education for all children. Part of the challenge for parents such as Jennifer and Greg or Janet and Tom is that they attempt to solve a structural problem on the individual level and feel regularly conflicted about their choices. And this challenge is tied to a broader dilemma: what does it mean to be white and progressive and well resourced in a world rife with structural inequality? And what does this mean for raising kids?

This conundrum of privilege is not limited to schools. Greg also discusses his concerns about Evergreen itself, in terms of both the racial diversity but also what appears to be ongoing gentrification practices and increasing property values that he worries will drive out poorer families, renters, and graduate students and attract more white, affluent families, leading to the community becoming the homogeneous place that people such as he are trying to escape. Greg has faith that the current residents of Evergreen "won't let this happen," suggesting that people such as he can control what happens to the future of his neighborhood, again a reminder of his privilege. However, he admits, "if people like us keep moving in, soon it is going to just be a place full of a bunch of people who look like us!"

Most important to the central question of this book is the fact that Greg discusses all of these conflicting thoughts and concerns in front of his son, evidence that Conor is exposed to these kinds of complex, political, sociological conversations. Greg does not hold back discussing any of these topics in front of his child. For instance, following our discussion of his concerns about Evergreen, he talks about what he perceives as the biggest problem white people have. "So many white people get defensive and stop listening about so many things and don't want to admit their own biases. I do plenty of things wrong, but I am a pretty confident person; and so I feel that I am better equipped to handle criticism and being called out, which is what people in the majority all need." Greg continues, describing himself as full of unintentional racial bias, something that he admits openly to me and in front of his son:

> I am a racist, for sure. If I can identify it, all the better because maybe I can deal with it. I mean, it happens all the time. We have innate issues of racist thinking, you know, in the law, the issue of cross-racial identification: so if you have a lineup of people, you have a much harder time identifying someone of another race. So, you know, if you're walking down the street and there are people different than me and it's late at night, I'm more likely to be tensed up about it. And, you know, I believe the less you are around people who are different, the more you will have that and act on it because you just haven't had the experience to say, "Ugh, that is so dumb."

Given these concerns about implicit racial bias, Greg works explicitly and aggressively to encourage critical thinking about race in his children. Greg tells me (and Conor) that he always thinks it is better to provide kids with more information than they perhaps even ask for or want and to recognize that kids pay attention to "the things that we do" as parents. "We tell them why something is important, you know, like politics or whatever is happening, and we talk about it. We just want them to be informed because it is so easy not to be." Unlike many of the families in this study overall, and unlike many popular assumptions about how white children learn about race in the family context, Greg acknowledges in this moment the ways in which his son likely learns a great deal about race in the United States through "the things that we do." In addition to recognizing how conversations may shape his children's ideas, Greg believes that it is the choices he and Jennifer make as parents that truly inform how their child will come to develop his ideas about the social world around him.

Overall, Evergreen parents construct a color-conscious racial context of childhood for their kids. This is true across all 10 of the families in this study. These parents also seek to cultivate an antiracist praxis in their children and therefore behave in ways that promote both antiracist consciousness and practice, even if they are not always successful or consistent. And the foundational aspect of this process rests with the choice to live in this particular neighborhood, despite other and perhaps less complicated alternatives, so that children can attend public schools with brown and black peers and so that they can grow up in an environment structured by politically progressive values and beliefs. Much like in Sheridan and Wheaton Hills, Evergreen parents choose to live here because of the public schools, the people who live here, and the political perspective that dominates this community. And much like in Sheridan and Wheaton Hills, all of these aspects of Evergreen define the racial context of this place, shaping how the young people growing up here make sense of their social worlds and how they make sense of the racial politics around them.

Three Racial Contexts of Childhood

Parents choose to live in Sheridan for the predominantly white neighborhoods and what they perceive to be better public schools. They tend to identify as conservative and want to live apart from the liberal white community of Petersfield and the social problems that are caused by a perceived influx of poor people of color. These parents do not want their children to talk about race, and color-blind ideology shapes much of what goes on in this community. In Wheaton Hills, more complexity is found, largely because of the many private schooling options that are available here and racialized dynamics at the public elementary schools. However, for parents who choose to send their kids to public school here, they identify as liberal and are focused on celebrating diversity and multiculturalism but are less interested in doing antiracist work that addresses persistent inequality. Instead, these parents understand many of the problems around them as tied to class inequality. In Evergreen, parents reject outright private schooling as an option and instead choose to live in a somewhat more diverse neighborhood filled with people who strongly identify as politically progressive. Parents here want their children not only to recognize racism but to resist and fight against it.

Overall, white comprehensive racial learning starts with the choices parents make about where to live. Sheridan, Wheaton Hills, and Evergreen are three affluent, white neighborhoods that represent distinct white racial contexts of childhood. The choice to raise children within each of these neighborhoods is shaped in part by these parents' commonsense racial knowledge, and growing up within these neighborhoods plays a crucial role in shaping kids' racial views.

3

"We're Not a Racial School"

Being a Private School Kid

It is a midfall afternoon, brisk enough for sweatshirts but not cold enough for gloves. I am driving Chris (11) home from Saint Anne's elementary and middle school and his little brother, Oliver (5), home from Montessori school. We stop at a red light about a mile from the boys' house. As we wait for the long light to change, I try to think of a way to distract the restless boys from horsing around, poking and kicking each other in the backseat. I look to my right, and on the sidewalk I see a group of high-school-aged girls, running in a big cluster, a few girls chugging along from behind, losing ground from the rest of the group as they struggle to keep up. Two tall, white, blond girls lead the pack, laughing and jogging, their cheeks pink in the brisk air. As a distraction technique, I randomly say to the boys, "Hey look! It is the Wheaton Hills cross-country team!" The boys stop jabbing each other for a moment and look where I am pointing.

Chris takes one look and then says, "That doesn't look like the Wheaton Hills team to me!"

Genuinely confused, I ask him, "What do you mean?"

"Maggie, they are all white!" he says. "Those girls probably go to Shelbourne."

I look closer at their T-shirts and notice that indeed one of the girls is wearing a T-shirt with "Shelbourne Academy" printed in block letters across the front. "You're right!" I tell him. "Look at that girl's shirt!"

Chris looks and says with disdain in his voice, "Those girls are all so rich and snobby and think they are better than everyone else. I can't wait to go to Wheaton Hills for high school and get away from private school kids."

Oliver slides down in his booster seat, stretches his leg across the backseat, and kicks Chris in the shin.

* * *

Country Day. Gifted and Talented. Parochial. Waldorf. Montessori. Progressive. The Petersfield metropolitan area is filled with private school options for families with the resources to access them. Chris is a "private school kid." Like many of his peers in Wheaton Hills, he knows that his parents intend to send him to public school when he reaches the ninth grade. Unlike many of his peers, though, Chris is critical of his own status as a "private school kid." He tells me on numerous occasions how disgusted he is by his classmates' performances of affluence and their sense of superiority. Despite growing up in a family with upper-middle-class wealth himself, Chris rejects the sense of entitlement and privilege that he says he notices in the other kids at his school or that he believes the cross-country girls represent.[1] In Chris's words, "Those kids and their parents are just so out of touch with reality. It is pathetic. Like, 'Oh, look at me and my Hummer.' Who drives a Hummer? That is so environmentally irresponsible! I mean, you do *not* need a Hummer." Chris is frustrated by how the kids at his school "think they are sooo much better than other people" because they attend a school that Chris would, quite frankly, like to escape. And Chris, like all of the kids in this study, understands that to be "a private school kid" also means to be affluent and white.

Scholars have examined extensively the processes through which parents make school choice decisions, the motivations that undergird their choices, and how these choices lead to increasing levels of racial segregation. Less is understood about how these choices "influence children's perceptions of opportunities and of their places in the world."[2] As the sociologists Kimberly Goyette and Annette Lareau write, it "may be hard to measure in empirical research" the effects of neighborhoods and schools on kids' perceptions of their place in the world, but these effects are "no less important than the measurable effects of test scores, or of college attendance or selectivity."[3] How does "being a private school kid" shape kids' ideas about race and privilege? In this chapter, I explore how white kids receive, interpret, and produce ideas about race as a result of the private school they attend—ideas about race that inform kids' views of who belongs and who does not, who is smart and who is not, and who is special and who is not. I also document how parents' racial common sense, or racial ideological positions, shape these private school choices in the first place.

"My School Is Not for Everyone:" Being a Gifted and Talented Kid

Unlike Chris, Aaron Hayes loves his private gifted school. He shares his teacher with only 10 other students. He has good relationships with his classmates, he feels "at home" when he walks into the building, and his sixth-grade classes are challenging and exciting. He boasts about how much homework he has and talks in detail about his current global politics unit in social studies. His face lights up as he speaks, and he passionately shares his perspectives on current events and reveres his teachers. He is proud of how hard he and his peers work at his school, and he is proud that everyone at his school is designated as "gifted."

Aaron feels very fortunate to be able to attend his private school. "There's a lot more opportunity for people to do what they love at my school," he tells me. "The public schools are a lot more loose: less rules and just, you know, everyone kind of plays along." He tells me how when the teacher does not know the answer to a student's question, the kids gather around her desk, researching the topic on her computer as a group. From Aaron's perspective, the public schools in Petersfield do not help students think as critically or as creatively as his school does. He mentions how he has heard they have "a lot of tests" at the public schools and how he prefers to "really study stuff to learn it" rather than "fill in bubble sheets" about it. He also says that the kids who go to public school "misbehave a lot" and "do not care about school" the way he does, but he qualifies his comments by admitting that he has "never been inside a public school"—this is just what he has "heard from friends." When I ask him about the racial composition of his private school, he says, "It is diverse. There's not really a black or African American population, but there are quite a few Indian people. And mainly white people." For Aaron and many of his peers, the presence of any person of color in a classroom or on a sports team or in an extracurricular activity makes it a "diverse" space.[4] And like many of his peers, Aaron tells me that while white kids attend "a mix" of schools, black kids almost never attend private school. Elite private schools are understood to be places where white kids such as they go to school, and their perceptions map closely onto reality.[5]

Really Smart or Really Privileged?

"I didn't honestly ever physically go to visit Pairing B," Aaron's mom tells me. "I just sort of had the sense that my kids would be bored there. . . . It was the right decision. We made a decision for Aaron's education based on . . . his ability and what he needed to be getting from his school." She goes on to tell me that "the community of students" at the public schools "was going to be such that [teachers] wouldn't have the time or the resources to really give [Aaron] what he needed, because they were spending time on, you know, just getting everybody the basics for the other kids." As an afterthought, she also adds, "And I mean, all the, you know, everything you sort of pick up from other people over time, that was not going to get [my kids] what they want in life."

The Hayeses always knew that their children would go to private school. They firmly believe that Aaron is too smart to attend public school, but they also do not want him to be around what his father refers to as "the less opportunity kids" or the kids who will not help his son "get what he wants in life," which represents a clear inconsistency in their argument of why they opted out of public school. Is it that Aaron is too smart for public school, or is it that he is too privileged to go to school with "less opportunity kids"? The Hayeses waver back and forth between these two positions in their comments. Mr. Hayes explains, "In elementary school, Aaron was at a place intelligence-wise where I think going to Pairing B, just because of the opportunities he had and most importantly just because of who he is on top of that, . . . he was going into a system that because of the lower-income, less opportunity kids, there would be a lot of remedial ABC kind of stuff, and . . . we figured he'd be completely bored out of his mind." The "less opportunity kids" in this context is a racially coded way of saying "black and Latino kids from poor neighborhoods." Opting out of public school allowed the Hayeses to avoid needy, low-income, remedial students—"less opportunity" students of color—who, they felt, would take resources away from their child. But they were able to explain their choice in terms that appear fair and reasonable: their child is really smart. In this way, the Hayeses attempt to justify their avoidance of the public schools by claiming that they are simply doing what is best for their child, as any "good" parent would and should do.

I clearly strike a nerve when I start asking these parents about school choice. The defensiveness of many parents is perhaps understandable given the local context in which these parents are raising their private school kids. Many members of the affluent community in Petersfield at large, and particularly those who live across the city in Evergreen, have absolutely no patience for parents who opt in to private schooling. They look down at those who choose private school and believe that the institution as a whole reproduces inequities that parents ought to reject rather than accept. For example, as Conor (11, Evergreen) puts it, "My parents thought that private schools were just wrong. I had the chance to go to a private school, but I—they didn't want me to. They'd rather have me go to public school. . . . I don't think that people with more money should get a better education. . . . People that don't have money should get that opportunity [too]. It's not fair." Parents such as those of Conor and other children believe that they must act in ways that correspond with their political views and perspectives on the importance of maintaining and supporting public education.[6]

The Hayeses though, like many parents in Wheaton Hills, believe that giving their child the best education is more important than any social justice ideals, no matter how "liberal" or "progressive" they might understand themselves to be. "My kid is not a guinea pig" is a very common phrase among private school parents in Wheaton Hills—and one that I hear used in the same conversation in which a parent explains to me how progressive he is, how much he loves Michelle Alexander's *The New Jim Crow*, and how we, as a society, need to fix institutional racism. As Mrs. Hayes puts it to me, "I know someone . . . [who once] said to me, 'You're just the kind of parent we need in public schools.' And my reaction was, 'Yeah, but I'm not doing this for the public schools. That may be true, but I'm doing this for my kids, and I've got to do what I think is best for my kids and where they'll get the best education for what they need. And given everything I see about my kids, they need more than what the public schools are going to give.'" The goals that the Hayeses have for their children include a prestigious college experience, a stimulating career, and the capacity to pursue a good life—goals that are likely shared by many parents, regardless of race or class. Yet, unlike the majority of parents raising children in a stratified society such as the United States, the Hayeses have the resources to provide a top-notch academic experience for their children starting even before first grade. They believe that their child needs and deserves more than other children "because of who he is." This is the message that Aaron hears and interprets on a regular basis.

"The expectation is that I will attend college," Aaron tells me—hopefully an Ivy League school, he adds—but before that, he has to face the reality that he will go to public high school in ninth grade. He is concerned about this transition, even though it is still a few years down the road. I ask him why, and he says, "I think that if I did stay in a private school, I think that I would probably be more prepared for college." Aaron is not fearful of public school kids or worried about gangs or drugs, topics that other private school kids associate with black and Latinx public school kids. In fact, Aaron tells me that he is looking forward to going to school with kids who are different from him. But, nevertheless, he is not sure if the classes will be hard enough or if he will be competitive enough when it comes to college admissions in comparison to kids at private high schools across the country.[7]

Securing Advantages under the Veneer of Fairness

The Hayeses' decision about Aaron transitioning to public school in the ninth grade is not one made at the last minute. They mapped out his education plan and secured that plan when he was only in elementary school and attending the private gifted school. These efforts included joining with other similarly minded parents to advocate for more Advanced Placement courses at the public high school—courses for which many universities will award students college credit hours. This group of parents worked to protect resources for their children long before they would even be able to access them. A powerful and well-funded legal challenge was presented as the school district considered "allocating more resources to the students at the bottom rather than students at the top," as one parent described to me, or "breaking the laws about special ed and not supporting gifted programing," as another parent put it.

Wheaton Hills High School has what scholars refer to as a large racial achievement gap—during the time of this research, almost 95% of white students graduated in four years at this school, compared to not even

60% of black students. In the context of this disparity, a fight emerged over limited resources. As many people on the periphery told me, this fight pitted affluent, white, gifted parents against parents and advocates of children of color in "really unfortunate ways." While the gifted parents had long since won the legal case by the time of my data collection, the memory of this case was fresh in the minds of the parents I interviewed. Mr. Hayes shares his perspective: "A lot of the opposition to [supporting gifted students] is because of this whole achievement gap thing [*rolling his eyes*], and people think that tracking is going to abandon people on the lower end, basically, minorities, which I think is appalling, because it implies that there's no such thing as a gifted minority student, and that's not true." There are certainly gifted minority students, but most of the students who are tracked into AP classes in Wheaton Hills are white. The parents of these white gifted students, however, as well as others in the study, do not see their actions or these programs as racially inflected because they perceive these resources to be "for everyone," including gifted minority students. They do not see how their own actions regarding private school choice have the effect of perpetuating racial segregation, and they explain away their effort to maintain their child's advantage by justifying their decisions as being "best" for their child. Justifying avoidance of these public elementary and middle schools under a guise of fairness, these parents make decisions that maintain advantage for their own kids that simultaneously have the effect of perpetuating racial inequality.

Ironically, many of these parents told me, "We want diversity in the gifted classroom!" but did not see themselves as responsible for turning that statement into reality. In essence, these parents want diversity at the same time that they choose to opt out of diverse spaces. They are not alone. According to the education scholars Allison Roda and Amy Stuart Wells, other similarly positioned advantaged white parents claim to want diverse classrooms for their children but still deliberately choose racially homogeneous gifted and talented spaces.[8] Certainly, parents such as the Hayeses make these choices in what Roda describes as "a constrained and stratified school choice environment" as well as within a particular political economy that encourages these kinds of behaviors.[9] But the consequences of these choices ultimately secure educational advantages for kids such as Aaron now and into the future.

The debate around gifted programing has close ties to similar debates around the process of "tracking" and within-school segregation in high schools across the country. As the education scholar Jeannie Oakes explains, "tracking" has roots in early 20th-century social Darwinism, which justified differentiated education on the assumption that different kinds of people (i.e., African Americans, new immigrants, the impoverished) were biologically, morally, and intellectually inferior to white, Anglo-Saxon Protestants.[10] Tracking is the process "whereby students are divided into categories so that they can be assigned in groups to various kinds of classes. . . . However it's done, tracking, in essence, is sorting—a sorting of students that has certain predictable outcomes."[11] Despite popular assumptions that tracking is the best model of education, research shows how tracking reinforces privileges and disadvantages and has tenuous educational benefits.[12] Both gifted and talented debates and tracking debates share underlying assumptions about who deserves what: should students who have been socially constructed as "advanced," often through subjective processes that have been cited as highly susceptible to racial bias, receive more school resources than those who are not constructed as "advanced"?

Overall, Mr. Hayes does not see himself as advocating for white advantages. Instead, he views this entire process as race neutral, and if any racial patterns do emerge, they are unintentional. Mr. Hayes tells me that he thinks teachers in elementary schools need to do a better job determining who is gifted and that if the teachers were better, there would be more black students in the gifted classes—a potential scenario that he embraces but does not see himself or his children as playing a role in achieving. Indeed, studies have been conducted on precisely this topic of teachers' perceptions of who is gifted. Research finds that white kids with glasses are more likely to be presumed to be gifted than black kids are,[13] while other research shows that "high-achieving English students [are] more likely to be nominated by teachers for advanced work in the subject if they had high intrinsic motivation to read, if they were female, and if they were not black."[14] Similarly, the sociologists Amanda Lewis and Michelle Manno discuss the ways in which determinations of students' behavioral problems, or "soft" special education designations, are often shaped by race, decisions that not only put minority students in lower tracks or label them as having behavioral problems but also put white students in higher tracks or label them as gifted and talented.[15] Mr. Hayes's views that these patterns are largely due to teachers' inability to designate children properly are part of how he justifies avoidance of public schools for his own children, as well as how he justifies advocating for the advantages that he does for his own kid. To him, it is not about giving the white kids educational advantages; rather, it is about giving his kid what his kid deserves.

For Mrs. Hayes, the question of "diversity" in gifted environments is not her problem. "*I advocate for my child* because that is the job of a mother. . . . Why don't other mothers do that too?" she poses to me. Rather than questioning the role that teachers or administrators play in these patterns or the role that privileged parents such as she play, Mrs. Hayes instead questions the mothering of "others," suggesting that they are not doing their job in advocating for their child. In doing so, she draws on the readily available racist mythology of the "dysfunctional" or "pathological" black family that is pervasive in American culture.[16] As the legal scholar Dorothy Roberts writes, "Images of black maternal unfitness have been around so long that many Americans don't even notice them. They are reincarnated so persistently and disseminated so thoroughly that they become part of the unconscious psyche, part of the assumed meaning of blackness."[17] This seems to be reflected in Mrs. Hayes's remarks about black mothers supposedly failing their children.

Chris's mom, Gail, helps to articulate this aspect of education in Wheaton Hills in a different way:

> I feel like for families that have embraced public high school here, one way that's happened is, they've created these gifted programs, and it becomes a way to segregate within an otherwise-integrated school. Because if you look at the numbers, it's mostly white kids, and, you know, there's an affluence. Because these are the parents who are going to go and say, "My kid is really bright. Test them. And if they don't qualify, test them again until they do." Meanwhile, we have an enormous racial achievement gap that none of these parents want to address. Because they feel like it isn't their problem. This really frustrates me.

As a person in a position of privilege herself, Gail is frustrated by the choices of her fellow privileged parents, such as the Hayeses, as well as the tactics they use to place their children in these coveted programs. She understands this behavior as a strategy fellow parents use to demonstrate support for racially integrated public education while simultaneously demanding segregated, elite spaces for their own children within the walls of the high school. This is similar to what Roda found in her study of New York City parents as they use their privilege to maintain educational advantages within the public schools through "the social construction of giftedness." Roda discusses how going through the process of having one's child tested in and of itself is indicative of being a good parent because "being a good parent" to many affluent people means to "give your child every advantage."[18] "That's what you do," Roda's participants tell her.[19] And "what you do" in Wheaton Hills inherently contradicts the abstract values that many of the parents here simultaneously hold.

As the sociologists Tyrone Forman and Amanda Lewis write, "It is a mistake to view . . . expressions of lack of care for or disinterest in the social circumstances of ethnoracial minorities as benign, because prejudice is increasingly 'expressed in a failure to help rather than in a conscious desire to hurt.' "[20] And this seems to be the case for parents such as the Hayeses. They are faced with a conflict between their *abstract values* of fairness and their own personal *interests* of securing for their own child the best education possible. This contradiction is resolved through this process of justifying avoidance and drawing on a veneer of fairness: advantages and opportunities are secured and hoarded for affluent, white kids, while these actions are portrayed as being about what is fair and "what my child deserves."[21]

Being a Gifted Kid

"It makes me realize how special I am to have these opportunities," Aaron tells me, reflecting on all that his parents have done for him. "My school puts quite a challenge on the kids. Like they really pile them [with work], so I think, definitely I'm getting more in a shorter amount of time than if I went to a public school." It is for this reason that he tells me he wishes he could stay in private school instead of attending Wheaton Hills High. "It's just a better education," he tells me. On the one hand, Aaron's comment, "It makes me realize how special I am to have these opportunities," reflects some degree of his understanding about social stratification. Aaron knows that his race and class privileges help him succeed in ways that are inherently unfair. Aaron tells me that it is not fair that different kids get different educations, drawing on both race and class in his response: "Well, a lot of the time, it seems to me like money is a big factor. . . . Like blacks, just, you know, they don't have as high income for some reason, so they don't have as much money to send their kids to better schools. So they just send them to, sometimes, the bare minimum, so it's not really fair. Because everyone should kind of get the same education, but sometimes it's just not possible for that to happen." Aaron is critical in the abstract: the world ought to be fair. But Aaron simultaneously embraces his privileges and hopes that his parents will miraculously change their minds about leaving private school. As a special student, Aaron believes that he should attend a "better" school than almost all other kids. Underlying this contradiction between abstract values and personal interest is of course the race and class composition of these schools. As everyone in the community knows, the public schools are "more diverse." While Aaron does not outright tell me that he does not want to go to school with black and brown kids, he does tell me that going to school with "other kids" will present undesirable challenges to his educational achievement and threaten his future potential at success. "My school is not for everyone," he tells me. He is right, of course. His school is not for everyone, and the parents at this school want to keep it that way, as this is precisely why they pay lots of money to send their child to this school. For instance, some call for more rigid admission standards: "They've decided that kids can be gifted in one of like five different areas or something. . . . It wasn't just academic. It was like the arts and leadership and things like that, which is not really what gifted is supposed to be about. It is supposed to be about intelligence." Aaron's mom is frustrated because she thinks that the public school is attempting to expand the gifted program for the sake of inclusion alone, meaning getting more kids of color into these classes in an effort to reduce the racial achievement gap, at a cost to her own child.

The Hayes parents have constructed this component of Aaron's racial context of childhood through strategies of what I call *justified avoidance*, or strategies of vehemently claiming not to be racist while simultaneously acting in ways that secure advantages for their own child. Having a gifted child makes avoidance of public schools about the specialness of kids rather than their whiteness. And, as the sociologist Karolyn Tyson finds in her research, these kinds of racialized tracking processes "influence students' perceptions of the link between race and achievement, their self-perceptions of ability, how they view one another, and where they think they and others belong."[22] In this case, the whiteness of gifted programs, such as the school Aaron attends, reinforces racial stereotypes about achievement for the students themselves.

Aaron is growing up in the particular racial context designed for him by his parents, and he and his private school peers form answers to questions about race that emerge over time as they interpret their social world. Together, they think about where they fit in that world and where others fit. Of course, their private school status is not the only factor shaping their racial views, but certainly it plays a major role in this local context. It is this status, for instance, that informs their view that they are special and more deserving of resources than other kids around them are.

Beyond Academic Excellence

Not all parents make their decision as the Hayeses did. Some parents, if even only once, give the public schools a try. Mrs. Anderson, for instance, explains to me the range of school options she and her husband explored for their three children, Emily (13), Rachel (12), and Simon (11), over the years, starting in pre-K: "I took my eldest daughter to pre-K. It was the pre-K meeting actually, and it was, like, crazy. It was loud. Kids were climbing the walls. All the little siblings were there. It was mostly nonwhite. And she wouldn't go off with the reading lady." Mrs. Anderson does not shy away from making racially explicit observations about the public school environment, and she does not shy away from her own decision to avoid the schools filled with "loud" kids. She justifies her decision by drawing on the emotional well-being of her kids. Deciding that the public pre-K option was not going to work on the basis of this initial meeting, she moved her daughter, and later her other two children, to a progressive, private school in town. For a while, she and her family loved this school and were highly involved. "We gave a lot of money," she adds. But, over time, she decided the progressive school also was not right for her children. "There were some very good years, very nurturing years there, but it was mixed with some classrooms being out of control. My kids started getting migraines because it was a stressful environment. . . . Like, so anyways, so [my kids] ended up at the gifted school." While Mrs. Anderson has left the public system, unlike the Hayeses, she is critical of her decision to opt in to the gifted school. She shares some sentiments with parents such as Gail, and she is less convinced that all the children who attend this school, including her own, are actually "off the charts" in their "gifted" capabilities.

> I had been opposed to it. There's a lot of elitism about the gifted thing, and I had, from a values perspective, you know, I had been opposed to it. But here we were, you know, desperate, so the kids went over there. . . . I think you have to watch out for how a school bills itself. Because I think the progressive school billed itself as a place that was really sensitive to kids' feelings, and it ended up being really harmful to our kids' feelings. And I think that the gifted school bills itself as a place for gifted kids. But I think, really, there are a lot of kids there. There's a range. And there are kids who are super gifted, and then there are kids who are just a little above average. And so really, there's room for everyone. . . . I guess I would even say that a couple of our kids are gifted, but not all of them. But they are all happy and thriving at the gifted school so we are happy.

Rather than academic rigor serving as the basis of whether the school is good or not, Mrs. Anderson instead looks to her own children's sense of happiness and the extent to which they are thriving. While she knows that it is due to her privilege that she and her husband can offer this educational experience to her kids, she also seems to recognize that not all children can have this kind of childhood. She thinks carefully about the elitist implications of sending her children to the gifted school, but at the end of the day, like many parents, Mrs. Anderson makes a choice that she perceives is best for her children. And as she adds, "Truth be told, I think that if we had been in a neighborhood with a different public school where our kids could have had peers who would have been—who they would have had more in common with, I think that it would have been a better experience than what they ended up with." When I ask Emily (13) about her school, like Aaron, she tells me that she perceives the school to be diverse: "You know, I have, I mean, my friends—I have, like, three of my best friends are, like, Caucasian, and then I've got one Chinese friend. And, you know, one of my other best friends is from India. So it's like, it's kind of, you know—everybody is mixed together. And I think they do that on purpose. They say in the handbook, like, we try to like—it's not discriminate. Like, it's not like racially—like, we have no preference, but we try to achieve a balance. And I think they do that pretty well." Emily says she likes her school, and like Aaron, and she draws a clear distinction between the kids with whom she goes to school and who live near her and kids from other parts of the city. "Most of the people we do know are pretty, like, white. But there's, like, neighborhoods with, like, a ton of African Americans and, you know, high crime rate and stuff like that." I ask her if she knows any of those kids, and she tells me she does not. "If I went to public school, maybe I would," she explains.

Her younger brother, Simon (11), also explains to me that he does not know very many black people but that he does have friends who are from China and India at his school. Simon tells me he is "really happy" at his school and that the progressive school he attended was "a joke" where "they didn't teach you anything": "You sit around and play on your iPod or just talk or like, I don't know. I could finish all the work super, super easily." He also complains to me that the school did not give grades: "Grades are something that I really, really like, because it gives you feedback." He also references things his parents have said about the school: "My mom told me that it was completely dysfunctional." I ask him what he thinks the public schools are like. He tells me that he has heard from friends two things: first, there are lots of "white, country-type boys, and they're all like—they're all, like, super, super racist"; and second, the black kids cause a lot of problems at the public schools, especially when it comes to violence and fighting. He tells me a story about a big fight he heard about that happened at the public middle school among a large group of black boys. "That would never happen at my school," he tells me, referring to both the racist, country white boys and the black boys fighting.

Simon's comments reflect his understandings of whiteness with respect to class—in this context, "country" boys refer to kids from the local, relatively rural, working-class communities. But his comments also reflect his understanding that black boys fighting also never happens at his school—because kids at his school do not fight but also because there are no large groups of black boys at his school. "I think there are two black kids at my school, and they are siblings adopted by white parents," he tells me, confirming that while he and his sister might both identify their schools as "diverse," they do not go to school with the kind of black kids who go to public school—or, similarly, the kind of white kids.

The children who attend the private gifted school in Petersfield learn how to justify privilege through interactions they have with their families, peer, and teachers. While many of these same kids who attend this school can talk extensively about inequality in abstract terms, in making sense of their own lives and understanding who they are and where they fit into the world and what is in their best interest, these children embrace their privileges far less critically. These kids articulate racialized notions of who cares about school (us: private school white kids) and who does not (them: public school kids of color or white country boys), who is special and important and smart and sensitive (us) and who is not (them), who needs to be protected and nurtured (us) and who is behaving in violent ways (them). Additionally, when it comes to white public school kids, the private school kids in this study interpret ideas about who is not racist (us) and who is (them), who actually knows about the world (us) and who thinks they do but really does not (them), and who is going to be the one to get into a position of power as an adult to solve social problems (us) and who will just get in the way (them).

Private schools not only benefit children materially but also have a significant ideological impact. Like neighborhoods and public schools, private schools are also part of a white, affluent child's racial context of childhood—another realm, constructed by parents for reasons that are racialized themselves, in which kids receive, interpret, and produce their own understandings about race and privilege in the United States.

"My Old School Was Racist:" Being a Former Public School Kid

"Second grade was horrible," Lindsay Kerner (11) tells me. "My teacher was, like, racist and mean, and she kept, like, making fun of this one kid who was my friend. . . . He's my buddy. He's African American. And I would go home crying a lot, and I wasn't really learning anything." I ask her what the teacher did to her friend. "He didn't really do well in school, so like, she would, like, hold up his work and then make fun of it in front of the whole class. And she would yell at him for no apparent reason a lot. . . . She only did that kind of thing to *that* race." Like her buddy, most of the kids who got in trouble were black. I ask her why she thinks this was the case.

> Well, a lot of the kids, like [my friend], he's really, really poor. . . . I remember one time, he was late to school, and it was in the middle of winter, and so him and his brother were getting yelled at. And so I was—I overheard, like, I was listening in, but whatever, on their conversation— and so, like, I heard them say that the bus never came, so they had to walk to school. And then they didn't have any boots, so their shoes were all wet, and they didn't really have coats. It was really sad.

Lindsay draws a link between race and class and describes a moment at her public school when she witnessed what she identifies as racism happening right in front of her. She is agitated and emotional while recounting this story to me, her voice shaking as she speaks.

Mr. Kerner, Lindsay's father, also brings up this same episode at the public school to me separately, in an interview when his daughter is not around:

> Though [Lindsay's] needs are academic, her stronger needs are justice. Her talented and gifted coordinator for the first two or three years, kept trying to find a social justice mentor, not a math mentor but a social justice mentor. . . . She was coming home with these stories every night, until she was in tears and so depressed that she couldn't take it anymore. That is why we had to move schools. So we moved away from an integrated public school into a small, private, progressive school because of racism. . . . And she has blossomed since then in a progressive school that promotes social justice, social concerns. . . . Putting Lindsay into a private environment allowed her to be in an environment where she could see justice as opposed to prejudice.

Before all of this happened, the Kerners were opposed to private schooling for their children. Though Mr. Kerner denies that politics shaped the choice he and his wife made about where to buy a home, he tells me, "We wanted the best house in the nicest neighborhood that we could afford in a neighborhood that had a really good public school, and it would be really nice if that school was integrated along a number of different dimensions." He goes on to tell me that as a parent, one of his goals is to place his children in situations in which there are all kinds of diversity. "We want to make sure we are not living in a pocket community where they will only see people of the same stratification that we are, economic, racially, developmentally, etcetera." For these reasons, the Kerners bought the home they did, in a different part of Wheaton Hills than the Hayeses that feeds into a school that is not part of the Pairing A or B scenario but that similarly serves two very different demographics of kids: white, affluent children such as the Kerners living on the edge of Wheaton Hills and kids living in Hampton Court, a low-income, predominantly black neighborhood. "In a city of any size, you're always going to have people who are struggling due to health, addiction, poverty, etcetera, and there will always be areas. . . . It represents a troubled area and is therefore more subject than any other area of high poverty—increased crime, decreased home values, unemployment, drugs," Mr. Kerner explains to me. Unlike many of their peers who opt immediately for private school, the Kerner family gave the public schools a try. And yet, in the end, academic reasons did not pull Lindsay from this school. In fact, Mr. Kerner tells me that both of his children are gifted, like the Hayeses, but that he was able to get the public school to accommodate his kids appropriately. He never had a problem with what the kids were learning in math or science class. His eldest daughter stayed in public school.

Lindsay was pulled from this particular public school because of the traumatic experiences of witnessing mistreatment by white teachers of the economically marginalized kids of color, such as Lindsay's buddy, from Hampton Court. There are very few teachers of color at most of the schools in Petersfield. What was especially difficult for Lindsay, according to both her and her father, was that the teachers were so nice and accommodating to her:

> There was another teacher—an old-guard, white woman, by all counts a
> talented teacher, particularly good with gifted and talented—and we were

excited, especially for Lindsay for the academic match. Turns out this woman was, in my opinion—and I do not use these terms lightly—overtly racist. And one of the troubled African American boys was in this classroom and was consistently wrongly accused of things he didn't do! So the other little second graders knew, "Hey, I can do something wrong and just point my finger at him, and I'm off scot-free." And Lindsay would come home so upset about this. And there were rules such as nobody could go to the bathroom unless they all went as a group. And so for my anxious little Lindsay, that meant she was holding it all day long—not good for a second grader! And so I went and talked to the teacher about this, and I'll never forget what she said. Remember she had the English as a Learned Language block. I said, "Lindsay is traumatized and interprets that rule to mean she can't go," and she's like, "Oh. Reassure her. This rule isn't for her. It's for the slippery kids. The ones we can't trust in the hallway." Granted, I'm an old-fashioned liberal, but if you have an English as a Learned Language block, I think the word "slippery" should be excised from your vocabulary for fear that it would ever be misinterpreted, let alone used in that context.

Mr. Kerner's disgust with the actions of the teacher, particularly with respect to what she told him behind closed doors, including a reference to a racial slur, led to the family's collective decision to pull Lindsay from the integrated public school and send her to a more racially homogeneous private school with a progressive curriculum in place.

"Real-World Stuff" in Private School

"I love my school now!" Lindsay tells me, referring to the private progressive school she now attends: "The people there are nice, and I'm learning, and it's good there. . . . We, like, talk about social issues and stuff, so I don't know, race comes up all the time, and people will talk about it. We just pretty much say whatever is on our mind. . . . We talk about gender and stereotypes a lot . . . Our teachers are really weird [*laughing*]. [My one teacher] will just randomly break out into song throughout the day. It's really funny." She goes on to tell me that she does not necessarily think she is getting a better education at her school than she would at the public school but that she does think she is learning more about "real-world stuff" than she would otherwise:

It's just different. Like when my public school friends, people, talk, most of the things they're saying are "I'm bored" or "Science sucks." But they're learning, like, facts about certain things, and we're learning more facts and *skills*. . . . One time they dumped us in the middle of downtown and gave us a paper and a bus schedule. And so on the paper, it had different locations where we had to go, and so we had to, like, take buses around and figure out what to do and then how to get back. One team got really lost. I mean, we all had chaperones because, duh, but it was really funny.

Lindsay believes that she is more prepared for the real world than her public school friends are. Rather than an academic elitism like some of her peers at the gifted school, Lindsay instead views being a private school kid in terms of knowing more about reality. She describes how her public school friends are different from her in this regard:

So one of my favorite examples is Chelsea, who is one of my closest friends who is really smart, told me that I was going to fail in high school, because I went to [the progressive school]. She thinks that because it's so different. And [public school kids] are so ignorant that they just don't get it. They're not really willing to talk about it. Apparently my school isn't the real world, which, I mean, I kind of get where they're coming from, but I think I deal with more problems than they ever have going to a public school.

Mentioning a friend in crisis at her school as well as some of the other challenges that kids at her school face, such as learning disabilities, in addition to the real-life skills she learns at her school, Lindsay interprets public school kids as being snobby with respect to how "real world" they think they are.

Sometimes I get frustrated with the [public school] kids, because they think that just because they have more racial separation and problems at their school that they're more in the real world, and they understand more things, and how life is hard. But the way I see it is they're exposed to the racism, but are they talking about it with their teachers? And, obviously, they're seeing stuff—like there's this one girl who got raped, and she's pregnant at their school—and so they see that and they think, "Oh, this is the real world." And they think that since no one is pregnant at my school, then they must live in the real world and I don't. And so I think they're just—they just don't understand, so, I mean, I cut them some slack.

Rather than drawing primarily on racialized distinctions between the kids at public school as black and Latinx and private school kids as white and Asian, as many of her private school peers do, Lindsay instead compares herself to other white kids at public schools. Lindsay views public schools as racist spaces that hurt all kids—both the black kids with no boots in the winter and the white kids who are put in positions of privilege in ways that they do not know how to navigate. Lindsay views herself in a more positive light than she does her public school peers of all races, and she tells me that because her school will talk openly about these social problems, such as rape and racism, she actually knows more about these topics and is more prepared for a future in the real world than her public school peers are. She tells me that she also talks a lot at her school about the privilege of going to private school: "I think that it's frustrating that some kids get, like, all the resources they need, and some kids don't get any at all. But I don't know how much that's able to change, because that's just, like, circumstance and what's what and stuff and luck sometimes. Like in class, . . . we hear a lot of weird stories about everyone's old schools and why they're at [the progressive school] and what they think about it and how fortunate we are and everything."

One does need to be "fortunate" to attend Lindsay's school, as the tuition and fees add up to roughly $14,000 per year. Lindsay does not mention this, but her father puts the tuition bill in the context of his daughter's well-being and mental health. He is willing to send his daughter to this school, even if it is in some ways less academically rigorous in his opinion, if it makes her happier and more successful at doing the work he believes she is cut out to do. "You know, pedagogically, progressive education is about social justice, is about contributing back to the environment; it is about a social democracy. . . . It's easy to supplement her math and science, her two strongest academic areas. It is not easy to supplement social justice when you are in an unhealthy environment." When it comes to justifying privilege, Mr. Kerner's motivation for avoiding public schools is very different from that of parents such as the Hayeses or Andersons. And he is not the only parent to express these views. Other parents of children who attend the progressive private school share similar stories with me, discussing in detail the ways that the public schools are too racist for their kids and send their children messages they as parents believe are harmful emotionally and threaten the antiracist ideals they hope their own kids will develop. While some parents avoid the public schools because they worry about their own children "wearing their pants at their knees" or "listening to misogynistic rap music," parents such as the Kerners want their child to grow up in an environment free from overt forms of racism, to the extent that that is possible. And paradoxically that means avoiding the schools where there are kids of color. Though justifying avoidance of people of color in this example is motivated from a different place than for the Hayeses, the same pattern emerges: white, affluent kids attending private schools who perceive themselves to be receiving a better educational experience than their public school peers are.

Not only does privilege allow parents to pick and choose where their child will be educated, but it also allows parents to change their mind, removing their kid from a school environment when they deem it necessary. Many of the affluent parents in this study reevaluate their school choices as their kids progress through the schools. When a school is no longer working for a child, a new school is selected, and the child is moved. Or, when a new sibling enters a school that does not work for her or him, perhaps the parents send different children to different private schools. Because of the availability of choice in Petersfield, many of the families in this study utilize different schools, both public and private, at different points in time. Lindsay, as compassionate as she is, learns that her own happiness is the most important thing in her life. As she puts it, "We walked away. . . . Sometimes you have to walk away." This practice of disengaging when things get too contentious or too difficult or too racist sends messages to kids about the limits of what one must do to fight for the things they believe to be true, even when they mean well.

"We're Not a Racial School": Being a Catholic School Kid

Rosie Stewart (10) is also a private school kid with parents who have perhaps the most wealth of any of the families in this study. Her father is a very high-profile, world-renowned medical professional. Her mother is a lawyer. Though living in the most exclusive part of Evergreen alongside local celebrities and politicians, Rosie plays competitive basketball, so her peer group is larger and includes more black girls than that of most other private school kids. As such, she can draw comparisons in ways that other children cannot: "Everyone at my school seems so, like, friendly, and the teachers don't really care if you do anything wrong. Like, they care if you do something wrong, but they give you second chances and stuff, and if you screw up, they end up forgiving you. That's not what happens at public schools. Like, they—I think [my] teachers have really good methods. And I just really like it there! It's a lot of fun!" Rosie feels safe and comfortable at her school, appreciating the fact that if she gets in trouble or does something wrong, she will have a second chance. She knows from talking to her basketball friends that this is not the case at the public school—that kids even get arrested at public schools for doing things kids at her school do all the time, such as talking back to the teacher. "At my school, we are all white. In our grade, we might get a new kid who is black, but we are all white. Yeah, so, there [are] no racial differences." I ask her why she thinks this is true: "Maybe it's because more black people are going to public schools because they think they will be with other black people? But I think, I'm pretty sure, most of the people who have signed up at Saint Anne's, they've been welcomed in. It's not like—we're not a racial school. We don't turn people away." Unlike the children who attend the gifted school who believe any person of color makes a school diverse, Rosie speaks openly about the lack of diversity at her school. But kids such as Rosie do not think that the school is predominantly white because their school is preventing students of color from enrolling. Color-blind rhetoric of the naturalization of racial patterns (i.e., "black people want to be with other black people") blends fluidly with Rosie's genuine belief that the school is not "racial" or that the school administrators do not see race when they decide whom to admit.

The Obesity Epidemic, "Crazy Kids," and Religion

Jessica (11) also attends Saint Anne's. With the exception of a few boys in her class, everyone who goes to her school is "nice," she likes her teachers, and she has a large group of friends. Students who attend Saint Anne's are predominantly white: "Our school isn't fully di*verse*. . . . Different hair colors, of course, but they'll be the one or two families that have, like, the dark skin and, um, a couple who are Indian. It's not totally white, and, um, all of our teachers are mainly white women. We have a black computer teacher, um, but other than that, we have a few lunch ladies who are black and a cafeteria guy who is black—he's actually really nice!" Unlike her peers at the gifted school, Jessica does not believe that a few students of color constitute true diversity—and her notion of diversity includes more than race. She expresses some surprise that the black cafeteria employee is "nice," and she goes on to tell me how the Indian kids at her school have parents with "big Indian PhDs." She is also quick to point out to me that aside from recent immigrants from Nigeria, very few black students attend her school. "African Americans go to the worse schools more. I don't really know why, but that's just what comes into my head," she explains. "They are also more poor than European Americans," she states.

Unlike Aaron, Jessica does not believe that she is smarter than the kids who attend public school, but she does say that she is scared of the kids who attend public school. "I would be a little bit more scared of going to [a public] school because of the fear of the bad facilities and crazy students stopping me from learning and the teachers always having to control them," she tells me. Jessica tells me that being a private school kid means getting to go to a good school where people care about learning, where the facilities are new and clean, where there are no "crazy" students, and where she does not have to worry about her teachers focusing on the bad kids rather than the ones that "want" an education, such as her. And the kids who go to these schools, though she cannot explain why, are African American mostly. The comment that this idea just "came into her head" speaks to the implicit messages about race that Jessica has most likely received over time. These messages are conveyed at a level so subtle, messages so taken for granted in her community, that she cannot even identify why she holds this particular belief.

Despite moving to Wheaton Hills "because of the good schools," Mr. and Mrs. Boone have opted out of the public elementary and middle schools and, like the Hayeses and Andersons, plan to transition their children to public school in ninth grade. Their son, Josh, is currently a freshman at Wheaton Hills High School, and Jessica attends Saint Anne's. I ask Mrs. Boone about their elementary and middle school choices, particularly in light of a previous conversation she and I had in which she expressed her view that private schools, such as the gifted school in particular, give some kids an unfair advantage:

> MRS. BOONE: We made the decision, um, based on a religion compo-
> nent primarily. Second component is, it's two blocks from my house.
> And I fully believe the importance of grade school should be part
> of the community. You should be able to walk there. Kids shouldn't
> have to be transported, and, um, the way *this* neighborhood is, you
> would have to be bused to the other side of town. Kindergarten, one,
> two, and three is three blocks from here, and then you get bused to
> the other side of town: *20* minutes on the [highway] for four, five, six.
> MAGGIE: So what is the goal of the busing?
> MRS. BOONE: Well, it was to integrate the, um, the—the blacks and
> the whites in other parts of town, but people just fled this neighbor-
> hood and moved to suburbs like Sheridan. So, there was, um, quite a
> community drain of kids in this area because they didn't want to be
> bused, you know, 20 minutes away.

The Boones live in the Pairing B part of Wheaton Hills. Mrs. Boone describes to me how white, affluent parents associate Pairing A with hardworking, international students who are typically Asian and equate Pairing B with black and Latinx Americans who are "impoverished," "needy," and "troublemakers"—very similar comments to those of the Hayes parents and others. She tells me that this is a problem and that she wishes more white, affluent parents would be more open to Pairing B—she, however, cannot be one of these parents. Despite all her stated values of fairness and her frustration that kids who attend the gifted school are better prepared for high school, her children are also the recipients of a private school education. Rather than seeing herself as someone who wants to avoid the school pairings, however, Mrs. Boone tells me that she wants her children to receive a Catholic education and that this is the reason why she and her husband opted to send the children to private school. Almost in the same breath, though, she presents a secondary reason for choosing Saint Anne's that has nothing to do with religion: she does not want her children bused across town, which is the same logic she assigns to parents in the past who engaged in white flight to the suburbs during school desegregation efforts. Mrs. Boone simultaneously disavows parents who engage in this logic both in the past and in the present (i.e., parents who choose the gifted school), while she herself embraces it (by choosing the parochial school). One way Mrs. Boone reconciles these ideas is in reference to the obesity epidemic: "There's a lot of people in Petersfield who are concerned about childhood obesity. Well, you're on a bus, you're standing at a bus stop as opposed to walking three or four blocks? Just the play[ing outside], looking at water trickle down, birds, things like that. I think that's a component of childhood that we have compromised by making them sit in the car. And now there is an obesity epidemic!" Mrs. Boone draws on what she perceives to be socially acceptable explanations for opting out of the public schools—and specifically opting out of Pairing B, since initially the Boones moved to this neighborhood because of the public schools, not the close proximity to a Catholic school—and justifies her avoidance of Pairing B schools. This allows her to maintain consistency in her values and actions: she is not opting out of the public schools because she is racist like those parents who choose the gifted school; she is opting out because she wants her children to have a religious upbringing and in an effort to fight the obesity epidemic by having her children walk to school. She believes this is a very different motivation from all the other whites around her who choose, for instance, the gifted and talented school, because her choice, she believes, is not motivated by race. She can justify her avoidance of these schools—and the kids who attend them—in nonracial terms.

The most explicit example of this process of justifying avoidance occurs when I ask Mrs. Boone about the population of students of color at Saint Anne's:

> It just so happens that in Jessica's class, she has the Nigerian and the Indian and a half Native American, and then you've got all your Swedes and your Germans, and they're all in there [*laughing*]. Jessica is best friends with the Nigerian, and what we're seeing is a *ton* of parental involvement from this child's parents! You know, this kid is *bah-laack* [*pointing to her skin on her arm, implying that the child's skin is a very dark color*]. She's an

African American, but her parents are first generation—well, they aren't even a generation; they are right from Nigeria, and they know the importance of staying together and of education and their faith, and they're conveying that to their kids. And they live somewhat close to Hampton Court.... And honestly, I don't think [this family] even associate[s] with American blacks. Um, because the ideology is so different. There is more of an educational component. This child could blow the doors off of great grades and attention and preparedness. She's very bright! And her parents are great. It's very interesting.

Mrs. Boone is excited about her daughter's friendship as she values having international diversity in Jessica's life. And certainly Mrs. Boone does not see herself as someone who avoids Pairing B because of the perceived racial composition of the school. Yet Mrs. Boone acts in ways that do not seem to align with what she says. When asked, Mrs. Boone shares further thoughts about the differences between blacks living in poverty and what she considers to be "educated blacks":

> I see the distinction more of as, um, education. Because [President Obama] is a black educated man and talks eloquently, and nobody would think twice. If someone is speaking with a very thick—what is that? you-bonics?—or other ethnic, black language, I think that colors a [white] person's perspective and then just the education level and how they carry themselves. But if you have someone who is white and carrying themselves not eloquently, that would also categorize them, and they would be comparable. So I think it's more now toward your education and how you carry yourself as opposed to what color your skin is.

Mrs. Boone engages in explicit color-blind logic in which she minimizes the significance of race in the United States and makes a class-based argument for why she approves of the Nigerian friend and not of the other black kids living in Hampton Court. Mrs. Boone also tells me how enriching it is for her children to experience the culture, language, and food of people around the world, both in Petersfield through acquaintances and also through travel. Most importantly, she states that "the Nigerian" will provide Jessica with exposure to a positive culture instead of the negative culture of "American black" kids.

Rejecting Catholic School

Chris, the child depicted at the start of this chapter, is also a student at Saint Anne's. As mentioned, he finds the school elitist and the other kids "snobby" and "ridiculous," and he cannot wait for the ninth grade. His mom, Gail, and I discuss his views: "I'm really proud of how he's sort of stepping up and was willing to say, 'These are my politics, and I think this is wrong.' Even when he was kind of surrounded by people who thought the [newly passed conservative legislative] agenda was terrific, and you know, that shows a character that I'm really glad is there. . . . Now, he has a little bit of an explosive temper that we have to work on a bit [*laughing*]." Chris has a very deep sense of fairness and justice, refusing to eat animals because of their treatment by factory farms and purposely wearing political buttons and shirts to school that he knows will antagonize his politically conservative peers. Chris is appalled by the reactions of his peers when Osama bin Laden is assassinated. I pick him up from school that day, and he looks at me after slamming the car door behind him with anger in his voice and says, "Maggie, I cannot believe everyone is celebrating this. That is just sick. And you should have heard all the racist things people were saying today about Muslims."

Over the course of my research, Chris convinces his parents (who also have their doubts about the school) to take him out of private school and send him instead to public school. I speak to his mom about all of this, and she provides her own interpretations of some of the dynamics that are at play within the Wheaton Hills community as well as within Saint Anne's and what troubles her about it. She tells me that she believes some of the parents truly want a Catholic education "partly because they have a perception that the public schools lack values, and they tend to be socially conservative, and so, they don't want their kids learning about same-sex marriage, and they don't want their kids learning sex ed in fourth grade." But she also has some more serious critiques about the authenticity of such claims: "But then again, the flipside of it is, when recently, Chris announced he was going to [public school], the little community, meaning Chris's community, his peers, the perception is, why would you want to go there? It's scary. There are bullies. You know, people are drinking, and people are doing drugs, and people are having sex. And, like, there's this perception that there is this, like, wild, deviant behavior going on in the public schools that doesn't happen in Catholic schools, which, of course, is ridiculous." Similar to what some of the private school kids told me, so too did Chris hear these things from his peers and later discuss them with his mother.

Gail continues and speaks explicitly and straightforwardly about how race matters in this context. "More than wanting even religious values, there's a sense of protecting kids from negative social influence that people want when they go there. And I probably wanted that too. I think I did." I ask Gail what she means by this, and she speaks to me in perhaps the most blunt terms of any participant at any time during this study:

> Everyone wants what's best for his or her kids, and they want their kids to have advantages. And if you're not really confident you're going to get the best, it's hard to really be on board with it, especially when you feel like the stakes are so high. Honestly, I think—and this is going to sound unbelievably racist because it is—I don't see this educated side of the Petersfield community seeing the underprivileged black community as having a lot to offer. I hear people say, "Well, what do we get out of it, you know? We potentially compromise our kids' education, there are maybe some risks, and there might be some danger? Why would we want that?" . . . People really believe without any hesitation that the people coming into the school environment are transient, and maybe they're not up to speed academically, or maybe they have some social behavioral issues or whatever, and that they're distracting time and attention from teachers. And the perception is that kids aren't getting as good an education. And nobody is going to say, "These are the black kids in the classroom," but, you know, there's this sort of euphemism.
>
> I think people here, they don't want to give up what they've got. Like, what they've got for their kids is good; they don't want to mess with it. And I think there's this fear that with limited resources, if we focus our resources on closing the race achievement gap, the fear is that they're going to do it by closing it from the top down and that then, the opportunities for their bright, well-prepared, educated, affluent kids are going to be less. And no one is willing to compromise when it comes to their children.

Gail's words tear down the veneer of fairness and the justifications of privilege that her fellow parents work hard to construct about what is going on in Petersfield. She speaks openly about what she believes is the actual underlying motive behind all the private school choices in Wheaton Hills: affluent, white parents' fears that black kids will lessen the educational success of their own kids. This racial logic is nothing new, with direct links to the push for legal school segregation in the United States' not-so-distant past.

Gail continues:

> We are all parents who can provide a lot of support, but at the same time, we're also parents who tend to really value academic achievement and want our kids to be poised to do well, successfully, and are afraid of anything that might undermine that. So that's why there is so much private schooling in my opinion [around here]. Parents are scared that their white kid won't get the best schooling because of the black kids in the public school classroom. It's a huge problem. And it makes me feel really uncomfortable about keeping the kids in private school.

Though few parents are willing to *say* these sorts of things so bluntly, Gail's analysis fits with much of what her fellow parents are willing to *do* in their everyday lives. As the examples in this chapter have illustrated, there is fear on the behalf of parents—fears about what their children will not learn at school but also fears about what they will learn. And, across the board, limited attention appears to be paid by parents to the messages that one's own child is interpreting growing up in this environment.

As the next school year unfolds and Gail moves Chris to public school, he meets new friends, has new teachers, is exposed to many more students of color along with a different set of issues at school. He tells me one night over a year later, when I am having pizza with the family, that there are still "jerks" and "annoying people" at school but that he likes being a public school kid "way better" than being a private school kid.

Lessons of Being a Private School Kid

Part of how Chris, Aaron, Emily, Simon, Lindsay, Jessica, and Rosie and other private school kids form ideas about race and privilege is connected to the fact that they attend private school. The specifics of these white children's views vary, but with the exception of Chris, the children maintain an understanding of themselves as special. They believe that their school is "not for everyone" and that public school kids are "ignorant" or "misbehaved" or "loose" or "loud" or have "bad" parents and racist teachers. When these interpretations of public school kids operate alongside the popularly shared assumption that to be a private school kid also means to be white, being a private school kid shapes how these young people talk about race and privilege. And, except for Chris, they have learned strategies of how to go about justifying privilege, even when they hold contradictory ideas at the same time, such as abstract ideas about fairness but also desires to do whatever it takes to go to Harvard.

Researchers have examined the ways that white parents have consistently hoarded educational resources over time, evinced in persistent separate school systems for children of color in the United States[23] or in the logic derived from scientific racism of long-supported practices such as tracking[24] or in the actions of parents who "work cumulatively to protect the advantages their kids receive from the way the schooling is currently organized."[25] However, little attention has been paid to the consequences of this process for the white kids who attend these private schools or who are in "high tracks." Certainly, the material consequences are clear. But on the basis of this research, other consequences emerge as well.

As sociologists have documented extensively, "many families go to great lengths to place their children in the schools they believe are best, to the extent their resources will allow."[26] These "great lengths" include not only putting children into the "best" schools but also securing the "best" education once children are there. For instance, the parents in this study support lawsuits on kids' behalf, advocate for more AP courses, spend thousands of dollars a year on kids' education,[27] tell other adults in front of children about just how unique their child is, respond immediately when kids report negative experiences at school by going in to yell at the teacher or even to remove the child from a particular school, make subtle suggestions that the black kids who just joined the school are problematic, and so forth, with a veneer of fairness covering it all. Even if parents also accompany these actions with telling their kids that they are "fortunate" and need to appreciate their unearned privileges and even if they express progressive political views in their homes or reject meritocratic ideology in theory, in practice, these parents' actions, especially those informed by justified avoidance, speak louder than their words. These actions, like choosing a school, play a powerful role in shaping their children's understandings of who they are—as well as who they are not. The majority of the private school kids in this study interpret their status to mean that they are unique, special, deserving, extraordinarily talented, more hardworking, more sensitive to the problems of the world, more in need of protection from gangs and drugs and loud black kids, more knowledgeable about real-life skills or current events, or really, as the one private school child critic, Chris, puts it, just "better than everyone else." At times, these interpretations mirror meritocratic ideology; other times, they embrace the color-blind frame of cultural racism; and other times, they suggest the emergence of what Tyrone Forman calls "racial apathy," or little concern for ongoing racial injustices and a lack of action to try to fix them.[28]

In addition, these kids *are*, in many ways, attending better schools. This is hard to deny when kids' friends at public school tell them they are bored in science class but the private school kids cannot wait for their science class because of the "cool lab equipment" and hands-on experiments they know they will be doing. This is hard to deny when a kid's school has only 10 students in a classroom as opposed to 30 or when a kid feels that his voice is heard when he gets to talk critically about the world and practice real-life skills rather than completing bubble sheets or when a child knows that she will enter high school ahead of everyone else or when kids are given second chances. This is hard to deny when one's highly qualified teacher is willing to admit that she does not know the answer to one's question, and instead student and teacher look it up together and learn side-by-side, and when kids are well nourished emotionally inside the classroom and when going to school makes one feel happy and safe and excited and confident. Unsurprisingly, given the structural advantages that these white, affluent kids have, most of these children are already thriving. Their successes in their private schools, however, serve to reinforce their parents' justifications that they are deserving of special opportunities in the first place. They are good students, so they deserve good schools, so they are good students. Like what Gail articulates, what parent would not want these kinds of opportunities for their own child in a society that is so unequal?

And yet these opportunities also come at a cost: a material cost, in tuition dollars spent by parents, but also an ideological cost to these kids. The understandings that these children interpret and produce and retell to and among themselves, the frameworks for understanding patterns in the world around them, and their road map for making sense of inequality in the United States are all produced through a lens of privilege, even when counterevidence is provided through rich history lessons that decenter whiteness or invigorating political debates that focus on concepts such as structural racism. As evidenced by the kids' voices themselves, while they are aware of racial inequality in the United States in abstract terms—in some cases being able to speak more fluently about it and in more sophisticated terms than almost any other kids in the entire project—they are also interpreting the "specialness of white kids" and their own vested personal interest in maintaining privilege.[29] These Wheaton Hills kids tell me they care about fairness and justness and equality. They want everyone to have an equal chance. They want to live in a society where there are no poor people and everyone has enough food to eat. They think rich people should give away some of their money to help poor people. And yet, despite wanting to idealistically change the world, they also want to have power and influence within it.[30] As such, evidence of the ideological costs of private schooling comes from the voices of these kids themselves—kids who can speak fluently and critically about race and racial inequality in the United States but who simultaneously believe they are better and more deserving than everyone else.

4

"That's So Racist!"

Interacting with Peers and Siblings

Me and my friend Liam were at the beach, and these two cars pulled up, and there were a bunch of teenagers who looked like they were Hispanic or something. They were wearing gangster-kind-of-looking clothes. They were drinking a lot of alcohol or something. So Liam was going, "Andrew, we have to leave *now*." And so we biked for a while. They followed us, and eventually we were able to get away. But like afterwards, we were saying, "Oh my God, that was the scariest thing ever." And we were going into all these different things about why they were doing that—maybe they were trying to actually attack us or something, maybe they were just trying to scare us. And then Liam was like, "Maybe they're just trying to see how racist we are." And I was like, "Really?" And he said, "Well, if you think about it, you're not going to be as threatened by people who are white wearing gangster outfits, drinking alcohol and in two cars." And I thought about that for a while, and I guess it kind of made sense. But it just didn't really feel right to think that that made sense because it doesn't. But at the same time it does.
—Andrew (12, Wheaton Hills)

Kids spend a lot of time with other kids. They play capture the flag together in their neighborhoods, they sit together in classrooms and school cafeterias, and they ride their bikes to the beach with their best friends. They wait at the bus stop together and ride together in carpool minivans. They have sleepovers and birthday parties, they play video games, and they participate in a range of kid-centered activities, such as Boy Scouts or baseball or soccer or swimming or science club or ballet. These everyday spaces are where kids interpret the world around them and produce their own ideas about race. These spaces are also where kids say and do kind and hurtful things to one another, ask one another questions, and contest one another's ideas.

Andrew and Liam in the example in the epigraph work together to try to make sense of what happened at the beach. They critically analyze their own behavior and call into question the assumptions they both made upon encountering the teenagers. Andrew and Liam conclude sheepishly to each other that yes, race did inform their decision to run away from the Latino boys, even if their recognition of this fact makes them feel badly about themselves. They admit to each other that if the teenagers had been white, Andrew and Liam would have carried on without panicking or fleeing to the woods on their bikes and without thinking the encounter was "the scariest thing ever." These two boys decide that next time something similar happens, they will try to behave differently. This entire episode, from the first moment on the beach to the kids' talk later, happens entirely without the presence of any adults.

Andrew and Liam are not the only children in this study who talk with white friends about race when grown-ups are not around. Natalie (11, Sheridan) tells me about a recent sleepover she had with her friends: "I've been to a big slumber party, and everyone was like gossiping. . . . They were talking about other people and like how they're not as good as us . . . and like how [the two black girls in the entire school] were not as smart and everything and how, like, they don't have any friends and, like, how they don't really feel too bad for them . . . and how, like, sometimes they would even say how [the black girls'] clothes are so ugly and all." I ask her if her friends were talking about the race of the two black girls specifically. Natalie replies, "I think they were. I mean, I think they were just judging people like . . . a book on the cover. Like, a lot of [these girls at the party] wouldn't, if they're a different race, they wouldn't include them . . . in their group. . . . Sometimes it felt like [the black girls didn't] . . . have any friends. Because no one would really want to hang out with them." I ask Natalie how she felt when her friends were gossiping. Her response is matter-of-fact: "That's just what we do. We gossip," she explains. Gossiping about other kids at school in private places such as someone's basement during a sleepover party, a form of "backstage racetalk," appears to be a common practice among middle-school-aged children.[1] I hear kids constantly talking about other kids when they are not around over the course of this research. However, in this case, the gossip is very narrowly focused on the two black students at the almost entirely white Sheridan Middle School—girls who were not invited to the sleepover party. Natalie does not seem emotionally impacted by her friends' behavior, and she describes their comments as typical and as just part of their everyday life. "That's just what we do."

Peers and siblings play a powerful role in shaping white comprehensive racial learning processes and outcomes. Kids learn about race, racism, privilege, and inequality in part through their interactions and conversations with other kids—both peers of color and peers who are white. These interactions and conversations happen on bike rides and at sleepovers but also at soccer practice, at the ice-cream shop, in the hallway at school, at the country club, in the living room, and so forth. Often, these conversations take place when adults are either not present or seemingly not paying attention to the children. In fact, many of the moments depicted in this chapter are incidents that children told me happened in exclusively child spaces with no adults present or are based on observations I made of kids when they were not paying much attention to my adult presence. Despite what is commonly assumed, both by parents I spoke to and by many sociologists writing theoretically about how racial ideologies are socially reproduced by whites, children *do not* simply take on the views of their parents or their environment. White kids do not uncritically adopt the dominant narratives about race in a way that is "uninterrupted" or in a prescriptive way that "creates . . . their view on racial matters."[2] Rather, all young people, regardless of their race, actively *participate* in the production of their own ideas. Rather than children simply mirroring the views of their parents, much of what they believe to be true is produced through interactions with peers as ideas are shared and challenged. The kids in this study specifically develop ideas within a particular peer culture; these ideas reproduce, rework, and sometimes even reject components of the dominant racial ideologies present in their particular context of childhood, such as color-blind ideology or different forms of antiracist ideology.[3]

Although parents have very little control over what children say to one another in adult-free spaces or the ideas kids collectively produce as they interpret the world around them, parents do play an important role in establishing these spaces in the first place—establishing, that is, another aspect of a child's racial context. For instance, parents shape their kids' friendship options when they decide where to live, indirectly determining with whom their child will play capture the flag, for instance. Parents also play significant roles in making decisions about their child's participation in extracurricular and social activities, spaces outside of school in which children play and have fun with each other.[4] When parents advocate for their kid to be on a particular soccer team or when they enroll their children in a high-level summer basketball program, parents are making choices about the possible interactions available to their kids. Of course, these spaces not only are where kids produce meanings about race but also are racialized to begin with, such as soccer teams with predominantly affluent, white or predominantly Latinx players or summer basketball camps with predominantly black kids. Similarly, when it comes to socializing or planning a sleepover or a laser-tag birthday party, parents often play a role in decisions about who gets invited, who gets left out, which child "lives too far away" to come, or which child "must be invited" even at the dismay of the birthday girl or boy.

Finally, parents also shape their own children's perceptions of other children through their own behavior. For instance, I frequently observed parents talking about other kids at school or on the sports team in front of their own child, sending their kids subtle or overt messages about which kids are "good" and which are "bad," which kids should be invited to the next party and which kids should be kept at a distance. Parents also talk openly about other parents sometimes in critical ways, drawing comparisons between parenting decisions, such as, "Yes, Sarah's mother lets Sarah go to the mall on Fridays after school. But I'm not Sarah's mother, and you are not Sarah. You're not going to the mall." These kinds of statements send children messages about both who has responsible parents and who has parents who are fun or cool.

In this chapter, I explore the ways that extracurricular activities are places where comprehensive racial learning processes occur. In these spaces, kids interact with siblings and peers, receiving, interpreting, and producing ideas about race. And although parents set up these kid spaces, kids do not simply adopt their parents' views as they interact within them.

"You Don't Know Anything!": The Role of Siblings

All of the middle-school-aged kids in this study, with the exception of two, have siblings. Siblings shape how they make sense of race. In particular, older siblings often share information with younger siblings, telling them "how it really is." Take for instance, Chris (11, Wheaton Hills) telling me that the girls running past the car are snobby (see chapter 3). He does this in front of Oliver (6), his younger brother, who may or may not be paying attention but who nonetheless is exposed to those ideas. In other moments, though, Chris interacts instead with his older brother, George (15), who is in high school. For instance, one late summer afternoon right before the start of the new school year, I observe Chris and George. Chris is very worried about how to use a combination lock—his old school had only lock-free cubbies. Chris twists the combination lock around and around and gets more frustrated every time his efforts do not lead to the unclicking of the lock. George looks on, giving Chris step-by-step instructions. After a few minutes of impatient struggling, George says, "Honestly Chris, this is going to sound racist, but just find a locker buddy who isn't black, and he can help you if you need help. Plus, you won't have to worry about him putting drugs in the locker." Chris looks at his older brother with more fear in his eyes than at the beginning of the conversation. "What do you mean?" he asks timidly. George seems to suddenly feel a little bad for making things worse for Chris by introducing a new potential problem: black kids with drugs. Trying to lighten the mood, George says, "You know, if you learn how to open the lock with just one hand, you can totally impress the girls!" Chris looks skeptical. He thinks for a moment, and then his face lights up. He replies with a grin, "I know! What if I learned how to do it with one foot!" Chris waits expectantly for his brother to laugh, but George just looks at him and flatly states, "No. That won't impress girls. But it might impress a bunch of guys. Or it might just be weird." Chris frowns and looks down at the lock and starts twisting it again, muttering "22-15-3" under his breath.

George is (most of the time) the "cool" older brother who knows a lot about everything. While he is willing to help his younger brother, he is also not afraid to prod Chris's anxieties and, on occasion, make Chris feel badly about himself. In this interaction, Chris takes George's comments for granted; he accepts that what George is saying is accurate and does not question him. If anyone knows anything about lockers and black kids and drugs, it must be George. It is also important to note that this interaction is all happening in front of Oliver, who is playing Doodle Jump on my iPhone and humming to himself, seemingly ignoring everyone around him. Nonetheless, like the episode in the car with the cross-country team, Oliver is exposed to his two older brothers discussing topics that he might otherwise never hear about until years down the road.

Older siblings play a role in transmitting racial lessons and "common sense," but their younger siblings are not always as receptive as Chris is to George in this particular interaction. I also observe children who push back at their siblings and kids who reject or at least challenge the racial logic their sibling insists is accurate. For example, one afternoon I am with the Avery children, and Alicia (14) is texting with her friend who goes to school in Petersfield. "Oh my God, Caitlyn is telling me that she is soooo mad because she couldn't get to her locker today because the police were searching the locker next to hers," Alicia announces to Lauren (12) and Edward (12). She goes on to tell us that Caitlyn's locker is located next to a black student who "*always* has pot in there." Lauren asks, "Has Caitlyn, like, actually *seen* it, though?" Alicia, glancing up and giving her sister a dismissive look, replies, "Oh my God, Lauren, you are so naïve. All of the black kids have pot on them at her school. You don't know anything." Lauren, immediately grumpy, shouts, "Well, how am I supposed to know that? God, you are so mean, Alicia!!" Lauren mutters something rude under her breath in the direction of both of her siblings about how they think they know everything when they do not. In this scenario, Alicia passes information to her younger siblings, explaining to them what "everyone" knows to be true. The content of this information is clearly part of "commonsense knowledge" passed around between many white kids in Petersfield, as this information is almost identical to what George conveys to Chris—that all black kids at public schools have drugs on them. While this may be a popular view of white kids in this community, Lauren is unwilling just to accept this as fact. Her legitimate question about whether Caitlyn has any actual evidence that the police search is warranted is met with a corrective "you are so naïve" from her older sister. The Avery children are secluded in predominantly white Sheridan. And yet, via text message and friendships with white kids in Petersfield, racial ideas are transmitted and discussed, and a particular racial logic is produced as a result. While Lauren's challenge to this "commonsense" racial logic is brief, this moment is important in that it shows how siblings contest understandings about race, and many other topics, through their interactions, in this case, having a conversation that quickly turns into an argument with kids shouting at each other.

In addition to siblings talking to each other without the input of adults, I also record moments when parents' interactions with older siblings are quietly observed by younger siblings. For example, when Jessica (11, Wheaton Hills) bursts in the door after school one fall afternoon, she yells in a singsongy voice, "Maaaa-maaaa! I'm hooooome!" throwing her backpack on the ground near the front door and tossing her shoes and light jacket aside, running in her socks to greet her mother and cuddle with her for a moment before taking off to the kitchen to grab a snack. Meanwhile, her high-school-aged brother, Josh, is telling me about how recently he got into a scuffle in the hallway with a peer. Josh reluctantly explains that someone came up to him in the hallway and attempted to rob him.

His mother interjects, "Describe this kid to Maggie."

Josh mumbles, "What do you mean?"

"What race was he?" his mom prompts.

"Latino," Josh states without making eye contact with me.

Immediately his mother looks at me and says definitively, "See. I think this boy is in a gang."

Josh says in an embarrassed tone that he does not know, mutters something incomprehensible under his breath, and then leaves to go do his homework. Jessica, at this point, has returned to the living room and is settled nearby in an armchair with a bowl of grapes and her homework. I see her listening to the exchange among her older brother and her mother and me, taking it all in as she gets a folder out of her backpack. She observes her brother awkwardly tell me about getting beaten up at school. Even though Josh is reluctant to give his mother what she wants—a confirmation to me that the boy who stopped him in the hallway is a member of a Latino gang—his little sister sits by, observing the conversation.

The practice of older siblings "schooling" younger siblings on race-related matters either in explicit or implicit ways is a pattern across the families in this study. For instance, in another moment, one sister tells the other, "You should not call people 'African Americans' because some black people are not from Africa." The younger sister follows her older sister's lead and, during her interview, confesses to me about how confused she is and how she does not know what to call "people with dark skin." In another example, an older sibling mocks a younger sibling for admitting that she cannot distinguish between Chinese and Japanese people. In another instance, an older brother tells his younger sister that she should be a distance runner and not a sprinter on the track team because "sprinters are black and distance runners are white." An older sibling tells his younger brother that he will never get into the competitive summer program at the local university because the program is more likely to accept "black and Mexican kids than white kids." How kids talk to each other about race matters because it is through these conversations that kids such as Chris and Lauren interpret, produce, and sometimes even challenge ideas about race.

"I Talk to My Friends about Important Stuff": The Role of Friends

Friends also play a significant role in how white kids learn about race. As Conor (11, Evergreen) explains to me, "I talk to my friends about important stuff," including immigration policy, welfare, unequal schools, unfair teachers, and racism. Unlike Natalie and her friends at the sleepover party who talk at the micro level, talking about the clothes that the black girls at school wear, Conor and his friends talk in more macro terms. These boys share their ideas about politics and race and discuss their opinions on broad issues. Although these topics are brought to these children's attention by the media, parents, and teachers, it is with friends that Conor really hashes out his opinions on the matter, away from his parents with their strongly held views or his teacher who often "tries to control" the class discussion.

Similarly, Danny (12, Evergreen) tells me about conversations he has with his white friends in which they criticize how their teachers negotiate conversations about social injustice in his classroom. "They try to hide reality from us," he tells me, "but my friends, we like talk about how you can hide stuff from students, but eventually they are going to figure it out." I ask him what he means exactly. Though he does not use this term, he spends time describing to me how he and his friends cannot stand how color blind their teacher is: "By ignoring race, some people are still going to be in that stuck position where you think, 'We don't need to talk about it because we shouldn't let that divide people. But when I talk about it, I always mess up and sound really racist, so we shouldn't talk about it!' And one person gets that idea, and then everyone gets that idea. And that's the place we are at right now. The teachers do not want to talk about it. But we do." Here, Danny and his friends, who are both white and black, have conversations that his teacher is unwilling to have—thus, it is not that these kids do not talk about race at school but that they just do so with each other when the adults are not paying attention. Danny explains that he and his friends have decided that their teachers not only avoid talking about race with students but also lie to them all the time about "real-world stuff." Danny says that when his teachers are not listening, he and his friends make fun of them for their unrealistic portrayals of society:

> Teachers say, "Oh, your dreams can come true! You can do anything you want!" But that doesn't mean anything to me! Come on! Like, you can say that, but I mean it's—it will only go so far. Because depending on where you are born and your race and how much money your family makes, you might not be able to go to college. . . . But if you're born into a really rich family that pays for college easily and you live off your parents' salary until you find the perfect job, that person is going to be—they will have a chance of finding their dreams a whole lot easier if they don't need to worry about feeding themselves or feeding their kids or anything as long—because they are just living off their parents' salary, and their parents are making so much money, they don't feel a dent. And they just keep giving them money 'cause he's looking for that dream job. . . . But that's not possible for everyone, and it just won't happen.

Danny goes on to give me an example that one of his friends devised about how no matter how hard someone works, he might not be able to achieve his dreams, like inventing an invisibility cloak: "My friend made a good point. He was like, 'Say I want to make an invisible cloak.' . . . I feel like people can come very close to their dreams, but you can't really tell kids they can be or do whatever they want because it's not true. And it's not actually going to happen. There is only so far you can go." Telling a child he can develop a magical cloak if he works hard is foolish in Danny's mind. I ask him what he and his friends propose would be a better way to talk about "real-world stuff" at school or how he would prefer his teachers approach topics such as inequality. He replies,

We *always* talk about how the teachers need to start talking about more things in the real world rather than textbook stuff, 'cause I hate it when teachers use textbooks, and they say, "Okay! Chapter 3 in this textbook" and we are all like "Uggggh, we've learned about this stuff for the past four years. Giving us this worksheet, it will slip right through our minds, and there is nothing for it to stick to." . . . But if you give us something to do, like this is something *you* can do to stop it, let's go out into the world and help stop it! Or, like, these penguins have died because some guy is dumping sewage into the water. Let's all write this guy a letter to tell him not to dump sewage. Just let the students, let them into the real world because not everything is going to be in a textbook and tell them the world is not a nice place and especially for black people, [the world] is not going to like you no matter what you do. So let's go learn about it so all of us can help fix it!

Danny and his friends are outraged that their teachers are willing to present the standard American Dream story and ignore the ways in which race and class shape people's lives and opportunities. Through talking—and complaining—with each other about their teachers and what is taught in their school, this group of kids, composed of both white and black boys, develops its own understandings about race, social stratification, and the difference between talking about problems and doing something to fix them.

Kids also use each other as resources to try to make sense of a topic that for some of the children in this study is frequently taboo. Unlike kids such as Danny and Conor (Evergreen kids), some children in this study are growing up in communities and in families where their parents do not think it is necessary or even appropriate to talk about race (although certainly they do communicate often in subtle, racially coded terms, perhaps without realizing it). These parents do not believe their children even think about race. They are confused when I tell them about my research and cannot understand what their child would possibly have to say about race. "I can try to connect you with my colleague at work who is black. She might be more helpful," one Sheridan parent tells me when I invite her family to participate in this research. These parents have in fact gone to considerable lengths to reinforce color blindness: their children are not even allowed to accuse one another of being racist in school. Perhaps unsurprisingly, however, these children have lots of questions about race—questions that they attempt to sort out for themselves when their parents are not paying close attention.

While eating string cheese one afternoon, Edward (12) and his friend debate whether or not black people have an extra muscle in their leg that allows them to be more successful athletes, jumping higher, running faster, being stronger, and so forth. Edward is skeptical. His friend insists that there are anatomical differences between white and black athletes and points to the predominance of elite black basketball players to prove the point. Edward peels his string cheese, dangles it above his mouth, and chews this over. Without any direction from their parents, these two boys determine that race is biological.[5]

On another afternoon, Carly (12, Wheaton Hills), her younger sister, and a friend discuss the famous musician Rihanna. The girls disagree about what race the celebrity is, one believing that Rihanna is black "or at least a mix" while the other believes that Rihanna is white and is just wearing a lot of bronzer makeup to look tan. The girls spend a long time debating this and eventually discuss plans to rub as much bronzer makeup as they can onto their white skin to see if they can get their skin as dark as Rihanna's. Carly really wants Rihanna to be "white with bronzer" like her, rather than black.

For all the kids in the study, moments of debate between children about race emerge organically in daily life.[6] These debates do not necessarily happen often, but when they do, the kids are very invested in them. When these debates cannot be resolved by the children, the kids sometimes lose patience with each other and ask me what I think the answer to their question is. They ask me, "Do black kids have to wear sunscreen?" and "Are there Mexican gangs in Petersfield or just black gangs?" and "Are Asian kids actually smarter than white kids?" and "Why do all the black kids live over there?" and "How come so many homeless people are black?" Other questions they ask focus on black hair (e.g., "Do black girls wash their braids?" "How do you make dreads?" "How do the boys get it so flat on the top?"), "you-bonics," the meaning behind lyrics in rap songs, how biracial kids understand their identity (and why "biracial girls are always so pretty" and Asian babies are "so cute"), and debates over whether "all Mexicans can speak Spanish" or whether all Latinos are Mexicans, and on and on. My response is often, "What do you think?"

"That's Racist": The Role of Peer Culture

More than anything else, these kids ask me, "Is *this/that/xyz* racist?" These white kids spend a lot of time worrying about, talking about, and joking about whether something or someone is racist. This practice is an aspect of their unique, white, kid peer culture. Some kids think talking about race is racist, some kids think not talking about race is racist, some kids think only people of color are allowed to talk about race, and some kids think white people need to talk about race the most. How children make sense of what "racist" means varies from neighborhood to neighborhood, but—surprisingly—all of these children use or know someone who uses the phrase "that's racist" in moments that have nothing to do with race.[7] For instance, as Meredith (12, Sheridan) explains, if a white kid does not do something for another white kid, such as share a snack, the first kid may call the second kid "racist." In predominantly white spaces, in other words, "That's racist" has become a joke among middle-school-age kids—a joke that insults, polices, and delegitimizes actual claims of racism in their everyday lives.

For children living in Sheridan, any mention of race could be considered racist. But few children here believe that anyone in their community is "actually" racist. Because so many kids accuse one another of being "racist," the Sheridan public middle school has a rule in which kids are not allowed to identify people or things as "racist." According to the children who attend this school, this rule was put into place because kids were using "racist" the same way kids were using the word "fag"—as an insult.

ERICA (13, SHERIDAN): They put signs with things that we shouldn't
say in our school up in every classroom. . . . One of them is like, "You
shouldn't call someone racist . . . or gay." Like, there's always better
words to use. And if you're hearing a conversation like, "Oh, that's so
gay," or "Oh, that's so racist," you know, you can probably use better
words. . . .

MAGGIE: So "racist" was one of the words that people aren't supposed
to say?

ERICA: Yeah, mm-hmm. Like there's "fag," "gay," "racist." So, yeah.

MAGGIE: What if someone is doing something you think is racist?

ERICA: Kids at my school aren't racist, so that wouldn't be a problem.

Kids in Sheridan are taking ideas of color blindness and combining
them with ideas about sexuality in order to produce a new logic of
color blindness.[8] As a result, not only are these children minimizing racism, but they are doing so in a slightly new way. These kids
are rearticulating color-blind ideology, adding their own twist to it.
As Edward (12, Sheridan) explains to me, "Sometimes people just get
mad at [each other] or whatever and, like, call each other racists. It's
just, like, an insult." This aspect of these kids' peer culture can also be
seen as evidence of kids policing and upholding color-blind ideology.
For many of these kids, any suggestion that racism exists threatens
their interpretations of the world around them. Among themselves,
these kids simultaneously reject that anyone is *actually* racist while
using the term "racist" to insult one another. Racism may be a serious
offense in their parents' world, but in the kids' world, it has become
a joke.[9]

For children living in Wheaton Hills, there are no formal rules in
place that prohibit kids from using the phrase "that's racist," but kids
still use it. Similar to what Sheridan kids tell me about how other kids
use this phrase in their community, the use of the phrase "that's racist"
is also frequently used as a joke relating to colors, such as when Matthew
(12, Wheaton Hills) and his friend Alex are doing their social studies
homework and Matthew asks Alex if he wants to use the black marker.
Alex declines, and then Matthew, grinning, states, "You're racist!" I also
observe kids choosing chess pieces. They jokingly accuse one another of
racism when they say they want to be white or black. When I talk to kids

about this behavior, many of them tell me things such as, "It's just a joke" or "It doesn't mean anything—we are just kidding around."

For children living in Evergreen, however, talking about race is a common practice and happens almost every day in their lives. Many report that their peers at Evergreen Middle School use the phrase "that's racist" as a joke, but the kids I interviewed think it is offensive. For instance, Charlotte (12, Evergreen) explains to me her interpretation of why white kids do this:

> Usually when a white person calls the other person racist, they really— they don't mean it seriously at all. They try to make it as a joke. And sometimes people think it's funny, and sometimes people, like me, don't think it's funny at all. So like, . . . we have pinneys for teams: white pinneys and black pinneys. And you will be like, "Oh, I want to be on the black team," and then some white kids will say, "Oh, that's racist," and they are like, "ha ha." I think when people call each other racist, it's kinda like—they kinda want to point [race] out, but then they also want to be making a joke.

I ask Charlotte what she thinks they are trying to point out. "I think that—I think that people have this thing where they know people can be racist and they're not quite sure how to point that out seriously, so they point that out through a joke. . . . It's, like, the same with health class. You know the stuff is happening, like, in sex ed or whatever, and people can't talk about sex or race or any of that stuff seriously, so they kinda have to say it through a joke." Charlotte interprets the behavior of the other white kids at school critically, but she also tries to understand where they are coming from—what motivates them to engage in this behavior that she personally rejects. Conor is also critical of this aspect of his peer culture: "It's kinda the same thing as when kids say, like, 'Oh, you're gay'—it doesn't mean anything. It means they don't know what else to say, but it is wrong. . . . It is just some stupid thing that people come up with because they don't know what else to say. They can't think of anything else to say when they are mad at you." I ask him what he thinks when he hears kids call each other racist in moments that have little to do with racism. "You think, 'Well, he obviously doesn't have any idea what that even means.' Then you get mad at him and think they are stupid because that is stupid, what they just said." Conor tells me that there are real issues of racism to contend with—and there is nothing about racism that is a joke.

"Sometimes My Friends Are a Little Bit Racist": Noticing Racism in Peers

Not all accusations of "that's racist" are jokes, however. In some cases, children tell me about friends they think are *actually* racist or, as Robert (12, Wheaton Hills) puts it, "a little bit racist." When I ask Robert if he has ever witnessed any racism at school, he tells me about the use of racist jokes:

> ROBERT: Sometimes my friends are a little bit racist. . . . Like, this one
> time, one of my friends made this slightly racist joke, but I don't
> think he was *trying* to be racist.
> MAGGIE: Did anyone say anything to him after he did that?
> ROBERT: Well, before he said it, he said it was kind of racist . . . but
> it's still funny. Yeah. That's what he said, I think. . . . It didn't make it
> okay, but it was still better than not acknowledging it.

I ask Robert if he can think of any other examples of racism in his daily life. He replies, "I haven't seen any open—haven't really seen any people be openly racist. Maybe in private they say things, though." I push Robert on his final point of the possibility of people saying things in private that are racist. "I mean, like, everyone has tiny prejudices with people, . . . tiny little things that I might not even know that you have them, like subconsciously thinking. I think that is where people don't realize, like, if they are racist without realizing it." Robert goes on to tell me that "light-skinned people" have "lots of advantages that they don't even realize," in addition to negative stereotypes about "darker-skin colors" about which they are unaware.[10] Robert specifically references his friends when he discusses his observations—not in a way that demonizes his friends but in a way that seeks to understand them and where their "little prejudices" come from. Later, I ask Robert's mom if she remembers ever hearing Robert talk about this, and she is surprised with her son's answer, telling me that she has no idea where he came up with that. She laughs and tells me, "Raising children has made me realize how smart and perceptive kids really are." His mom also tells me that she intends to discuss this idea further with Robert after I leave, evidence of how kids shape the way their parents think about race, or the transactional nature of comprehensive racial learning.[11]

Meredith (12), growing up in Sheridan, also shares with me an example in which she witnessed her friends "being racist":

> Like sometimes when I go downtown [Petersfield] with my mom or my friends, like if we see a group of black people, so, um, we . . . we—and they are all like shouting and loud, I don't freak out about it because it's just a stereotype that they're going to jump you and hurt you. But some of my other friends freak out, and they are like, "Oh my gosh, we need to cross [the street] right now! They're probably going to do something!" And I'm just like, "It's going to be fine. I don't think we need to move. Just be wary of your surroundings. Be aware of your surroundings but don't be a racist!" This is like my *best* friends!

I ask Meredith why she thinks her friends behave this way and if she ever talks to them about this behavior. She replies with frustration in her voice: "It's just because, like, they have these, like, stereotypes, but like, whenever I try to tell them, they just get mad at me. It's, like, we can't even have a *normal* discussion about [race] without them getting mad at me! It's so stupid!" Interacting within a white, segregated context of childhood such as Sheridan, many of the kids have formed ideas about race that reflect hegemonic, color-blind racial ideology. Clearly, in this context, it is not "normal" to talk openly about race or to call each other out on racist actions.

Evidence that confirms Meredith's comments about how unwilling her friends are to "have a normal discussion about race" can be seen in this representative interview interaction between Britney (11) and me. Britney also is growing up in Sheridan and is otherwise chatty and open with me. However, she literally shuts down when I ask her to talk about race:

MAGGIE: Do you ever hear kids at your school—or do you and your friends ever talk about race? Or talk about any of that kind of stuff?

BRITNEY: No [*very quickly*].

MAGGIE: Can you think of any times where you heard other kids like talking about race

BRITNEY: [*shakes head no*]

MAGGIE: Or making comments that you thought are not very nice about people of different races than them?

BRITNEY: No [*avoiding eye contact with me*].

MAGGIE: So you never talk about race at school or with friends?

BRITNEY: No [*shifting in her seat*].

MAGGIE: Why do you think that is?

BRITNEY: It's not right.

MAGGIE: So outside of your school, do you think that racism is a problem in America?

BRITNEY: No. Like I said before, it's *not* a problem! [*Frustrated with me, looking around the room uncomfortably.*]

Not only are race, racism, and privilege rarely discussed in Sheridan, but many children are very uncomfortable when these topics are brought up—not making eye contact, shifting in their seat, and expressing frustration, both with me as an interviewer and also to their friends such as Meredith who have a desire to talk about race. Of course, these are the same kids whom I overhear talking about race all the time with their friends, kids who—outside of the formal interview—ask me all kinds of questions about race.

"I Have a Friend Who Is Not White": The Role of Interracial Friendships

Up until this point, this discussion has focused on the interactions among white children. What about interactions across race among kids of the same age? Does having a friend of color lead to a reduction in prejudice or encourage antiracist behaviors? Take, for instance, Jessica (11, Wheaton Hills). Out of her many friends, Jessica has two friends of color: one friend who is Indian and one friend who is black. All three girls attend private Catholic school, and Jessica's two friends are both recent immigrants to the United States, a fact that is important to Jessica as it signals something special about these two girls. Jessica tells me that she was very worried about her black friend when her teacher made the class talk about race after reading the book *Sounder*, which includes racial epithets: "We had to talk about the racial barriers in the story and the Civil War and all that, and they used the n-word. And, um, so I think [my black friend] just kind of, you know—they didn't feel like total outsider, shut out. I think they just kind of felt a little bit more awkward in that situation, especially my African American friend, um, just because, I mean, she knows that that's out there, but she knows that none of her friends would ever [treat her poorly because of her race]. I *hope* she knows that!" I ask Jessica if she talked to her friend after class about the story or how her friend was feeling. "Not really," she replies slowly with a sad tone. Then, swiftly changing moods, she says in an upbeat, cheerful voice,

> I mean, we talk about how she's sooo lucky because her hair is, like, soooo much more, like—the texture, it just looks so cool and different, you know? And she can do more spikey-type hairstyles, where mine is, like, just kind of there [*laughing*]. But I dunno. We just—we never really talk about *how bad the skin tone is* or anything like that. But, um, head lice was going around, and, um, she can't get head lice because her hair is textured, and they can't stay on. And so I was like, "Ugh, you're soooo lucky," and I'm, like, wearing my hair in a tight pony tail or a bun or something like that to keep it all up. (emphasis added)

Like her mom, Jessica is very excited to tell me that she has friends who are a different race than she. But when racist incidents happen at school, such as boys bullying her black friend on the playground, or when her class reads a story with racial epithets, Jessica does not know how to talk to her friends or be supportive of them. Despite having two friends of color, Jessica does not appear to have developed "affective knowledge" about "race-based suffering" or a "felt recognition of the wrongs of racism" through the intergroup contact that she has with her two friends.[12]

As social psychologists and sociologists have long debated, intergroup contact is one strategy cited as minimizing prejudice.[13] Writing during the Jim Crow period of US history, the psychologist Gordon Allport initially theorized that prejudice can be reduced if meaningful, equal-status contact, under a very specific set of conditions, occurs.

These conditions include equal status given the environment, a shared set of goals, intergroup cooperation, and the support of authority figures within the context. This theory of intergroup contact has provided the foundation for scholarship on the social psychology of race. However, what this example with Jessica illustrates is that interracial contact, or having a black friend or an Indian friend, does not necessarily mean that Jessica is immune from the broader, more deeply entrenched ideas, mythologies, and ideologies that operate around her and have operated in the United States before she was even born. For Jessica, caring about a person of color and developing some level of empathy toward a person of color is not enough to eliminate comments about "how bad the skin tone is" or suggestions that it is appropriate to objectify someone's hair and play with it. Perhaps this is because the conditions of contact are not in place. So what about situations in which white children are some of the only white people in an otherwise black space?

Rosie (10) is a superb basketball player. Her family is wealthy, and she attends an almost exclusively white private school. She has been playing in highly competitive leagues since she was very young, and she hopes to go to college on a basketball scholarship, though of course she will be able to afford college without a scholarship. Rosie is one of the only white kids on her competitive basketball team. Rosie describes the team dynamics to me: "I'd say, a lot of us are friendly, except some people have their moments, like they are bad sports or something. I'd say there's a lot of friendship going on there. . . . We have a black coach, and we have a white assistant coach. It's just basically being around friends. We don't find [race] to be a big deal. . . . I think they all come from good families and stuff like that, so it's not a big deal." Rosie tells me that she never talks about race with her teammates. She also explains that while she spends a great deal of time with her basketball friends on the court, she rarely sees her teammates otherwise. She never goes to their houses or has them over, and she does not know them very well, outside the basketball context. Rosie tells me that she knows she is "a lot more fortunate" than most of the other girls on her team. She tells me about how she has "more opportunities that they don't have" because her parents can afford to send her to exclusive summer camps where she gets to train with collegiate coaches and athletes. Rosie also explains how much travel is involved and how difficult it is for some of the other girls on her team to make it to all the games and practices, which are spread out across the state and sometimes even beyond. Although Rosie is aware of her own advantages, she associates these much more with class than with race and, like Jessica, has not developed the "affective knowledge" about race-based suffering that some people may think she would simply by having friends who are black. While Rosie does not make comments the way Jessica does about her teammates, and while Rosie is familiar with being in spaces that are predominantly black, including spaces with a black authority figure, Rosie distinguishes between her own circumstances and those of her teammates on the basis of class. Due to residential segregation, Rosie does not live near her teammates, she does not have many opportunities for socializing outside of practice and games, and she does not have close bonds with her teammates off the court.

For other children in the study, though, having a friend of color does open their eyes to the realities of racism in the United States. For example, Aaron (11) shares his concerns with me about his close friend: "Well, my best friend, who is Korean, just recently moved. . . . And he—he's moving to a very white town, and he is really worried about it. I would be too if I were him. I haven't heard from him yet whether or not, you know, if they're racists or anything. But from what I've heard in general about the area, they're not very accepting of other races. . . . It actually makes me kind of mad, like, to know that maybe he will have to go through that." Aaron's final statement is one of the few moments when he expresses an affective response to racism. We talk a bit more about what it is like to have a best friend who is Korean and how he wishes he had more friends of color. Aaron tells me, "I feel like I don't have the chance to meet people who are black, but I want to. Maybe when I get to high school, I will." It is very true that Aaron has very few opportunities to meet people who are black given the choices his parents have made for him about his everyday racial context of childhood. I ask him why he wants to meet people who are black, and he responds, "I dunno, just 'cause. I learn a lot about Korea from my friend, so I think I could learn a lot about what it is like to be black if I had a black friend."

Rachel (12, Wheaton Hills) tells me how she is friends with many of the Asian American students at her school, the gifted school, mainly because she goes to school with them and the kids are "forced to interact with each other":

> I think that kids are forced to interact with each other in a way that adults aren't. Like, adults can kind of modulate who they want to like talk to or, like, be with, but, I mean, we're placed in classes. And we are, like, partnered up with, you know, whoever the teachers decide to partner us up with, and we have to, like, work with them and get along with them. . . . I think the way that we are forced to be, like, social and interact with each other, we form, like—we have like these experiences that some adults just don't have. And I think that that's important, in, like, forming opinions about these types of issues. And that's how we do it.

Finally, unlike every other child in this study, Tyler (10) has three close friends who are black. The boys hang out together all the time in Evergreen. They play video games together, ride their bikes together, go to soccer practice together, and so forth. They all hope to be in the same class at school, and they hang out at recess—all activities that signal "best friends" to the kids in Petersfield. Tyler tells me how he met Jerome, Shawn, and Derek: "Jerome and Shawn, we met in kindergarten. And we are still friends. That was a while ago, except I [specifically] remember meeting Jerome. I thought he was pretty funny and nice. He liked to play the games I played, and yeah. And then Derek, I met him in third grade because I saw him at [my elementary school] at first, and yeah, and I think, 'He's pretty funny.' He, um, he really likes to jump off things, high things. He likes to jump off play structures and land. And I like to do that, so we became friends." I ask Tyler if he has met his friends' parents, and he says yes and tells me details about his friends' families— how many siblings they have, the races of their parents ("Derek has a white mom and a black dad"), and so forth, information that clearly demonstrates his closeness to Jerome, Shawn, and Derek. Even though Shawn lives too far away for Tyler to walk to his house, he tells me, sometimes Tyler's mom drives him over there, or Shawn's dad brings Shawn over to Tyler's house. Tyler also tells me that he thinks it is "really easy" to have friends who are a different race. I ask him if a lot of white kids at his school are really good friends with black kids. He says, "Yeah, a lot. Like, I know one guy, Shane, who is friends with Jerome. And my other two white friends sometimes hang out with us as a group." Although Tyler perceives that many of the other white kids have close friends who are black, he can think of only a few examples.

I also ask Tyler if he and his black friends ever talk about race. He replies, "No, not that often." And yet, one day after school, when I am spending time with his family, Tyler tells his mom about how Shawn got in trouble for having the hood on his sweatshirt up at school. (Other kids tell me that this "no hoods up" rule is one that a lot of kids break all the time—"They only enforce it only if the teacher really wants to yell at you," as one child reports to me. Another girl tells me, "I wear my hood up all the time, and I never get in trouble.")[14] Tyler's mom calmly talks with him about it, asking Tyler if the rule is applied to all kids or just Shawn. "Just him," he says, telling his mom that he talked to Shawn afterward, that "he was really mad too," and that they thought he got in trouble because Shawn is black. Tyler, usually an even-keeled kid, is clearly frustrated with the teacher. Before he can say anything else, though, his older sister interrupts and offers her perspective about how the black kids at school "always get in trouble." The conversation shifts to her being the focal point. Tyler, who quickly grows tired of listening to his sister, takes his video-game device and wanders upstairs to his bedroom by himself.

Although this interaction is brief, it demonstrates how Tyler and his friends talk to one another, trying to make sense of their teacher's behavior. In addition, Tyler seems to be upset about this incident at school largely because it is his friend who is getting in trouble. Unlike white children who do not care personally for black kids, Tyler's relationship with his friend informs how Tyler reads the teacher's behavior. While Tyler wonders if race played a role in this encounter, other kids tell me that the teacher yells at whomever she wants about the "no hoods up" rule. It seems, then, that although Tyler does not think much about the fact that he has close friends who are black, there are moments that emerge in his daily life that he interprets differently than he perhaps otherwise would as a result at least in part of having close equal-status bonds with kids such as Shawn.

Finally, as Tyler describes, he met these friends on the playground, approaching Derek because they shared an interest in jumping off the playground structure. Tyler would not have had the opportunity to befriend Derek and share in the jumping if they were not both on the same playground. In this sense, the choice of Tyler's parents to send him to the public schools in Evergreen provided the racial context in which he could establish interracial friendships in the first place. Of course, not all kids who go to his school form these friendships with one another. There is no guarantee that by attending an integrated school, interracial friendships will develop. Even when these friendships develop, there is no guarantee that they will lead to more antiracist actions on the behalf of children. Still the potential for positive intergroup contact is greater in social spaces that are racially diverse than at a school that is predominantly white, like so many of the schools that I found.

"Sometimes My Kid Is Racist": Challenges of Cultivating Antiracist Praxis

The popular myth that parents magically dictate or determine the sociopolitical views of their children is debunked when parents tell me how frustrated they are by some of the ideas their children produce—ideas that, as parents, they want their child to reject rather than to replicate. These are ideas that kids produce on their own, in many cases as a result of the things they learn from spending time with other kids.

For example, Margot shares with me her perspectives on some of the boys in her class at school:

> I'm going to start [by telling you about] Malik. He's black. He's really disrespectful and, like, constantly talking out of turn. And like, he's just, like—he's just mean. Just mean. And he's rude and he's mean. He's, like, rude to every-one. He's rude to me. He's rude to this kid Sarah I know. . . . It's not like he bullies, but, like, it's, like, kind of hard to explain. He singles out Charlie. . . . He teases or, like, [is] more annoying and, like, kind of mean to [Charlie]. And so, like, so sometimes, I, like, intercept and I'm like—like, one time he was pulling this girl's hair, which I think he has a crush on. But it's not very likely [that the girl likes him]. I mean, *no one* else likes him, but except for his friends Kerron and Bryon, who recently jumped like seven stairs.

Here, Margot pauses to take a gulp of water out of a cup before launching back into her story. "And I was at the bottom [of the stairs], and Bryon broke my glasses! He jumped down seven stairs and landed on me. I fell. My glasses fell off of my face. And my friend Rebecca, she was like, 'Oh, your glasses are broke.' I was sooo mad." Margot explains how she first went to the nurse, who called her mom, who brought her an old pair of glasses from home. She continues her story, telling about how she stands up to these boys at school: "One other day, Malik sat next to Bree. And she kept moving away from him, and then he reached over farther. And I'm like, 'If she doesn't want to, she probably doesn't want to [sit next to you].' And he's like, 'Shut up talking to me.' So it's a combination of 'shut up' and 'stop talking to me,' which he says a *lot* to me. I don't think I deserve it, and neither do a lot of people. But, like, I don't really care because he's just annoying and mean and kind of a jerk." Margot goes on to tell me that her parents have taught her not to say "shut up" and that Malik's parents must never have taught him that. "I have a moral code against saying 'shut up,'" she explains to me. (Her younger brother yells from the other room, "You tell me to shut up all the time!" She scowls in his direction.) She tells me that she thinks Malik acts the way that he does "to get attention": "He is rude to the teacher and then he'll laugh about it with his buds," she explains. "Mostly Bryon," she adds and makes a disgusted face, still angry about the incident in the stairwell. She tells me that these particular black boys at her school always hang out together. "Mostly Malik is like the worst of them. And I have to sit next to him in *two* classes!" she tells me. I ask her if she likes the black girls in her class. "Yeah, there are a few girls, and they are not, like, mean. But Jasmine, she's not like mean, but she's, like, ehhhhhh." Margot holds her hand out, palm facing down, shaking it back and forth, as if she is on the fence about how she feels toward Jasmine. She tells me that the black girls all hang out together too and are not very interested in being friends with her, from her perspective.

Another evening, when I am watching television with Margot and her mom, Margot talks about how the black girls at school always "segregate themselves off" at recess and in the lunchroom. Her mom, without missing a beat, without even looking away from the television, and without reacting emotionally, simply states, "You don't think that you and your white friends segregate yourself off from them?" Margot pauses and thinks for a moment. "Well, I guess I never thought about it that way," she replies. I talk to Margot's mom later when Margot is not around about how she handles questions from her kids, such as the evening when the topic of segregation came up:

> I just try to take kinda a mundane approach to racial stuff, where it's, like, not a big deal to talk about it, even though it's important to me that we do. Margot has had a few things where there's people she doesn't like, and then she brings up the fact that they are black or not, um, and I'm like, "Well, that's not really relevant, right?" Like, you know, she is just like, "Jasmine doesn't like me," and often it is in the context of—she feels affronted because they claim some sort of status as being oppressed and having to deal with prejudgments or whatever, and Margot doesn't really believe in that, and then she gets very sort of uptight about it. . . . I heard her telling you the other day how she was telling someone that you can be racist against white people. So I get the impression that she is hearing conversations in her school where the students of color are talking about being students of color and the consequences of it, and it seems like that is an issue for her to wrap her mind around. I usually try to be like, "Well, *think* about it" [*in a stern tone*]. She definitely understands the concept of stereotyping and discrimination, but I think she has a really hard time applying it to individuals she knows. . . . I have often framed things as, "Some people think this, and other people think this. This is what I think and do." This is how we have always talked about God and religion and, like, "A lot of people believe in this. I don't, but you can decide whatever, but here is why I think this way." I think with stuff like race and gender, I'm probably more assertive about it.

I ask Margot's mom if she worries about this knowledge Margot produces through interactions at school with other kids. "She is young and still figuring things out," she tells me. "I think my asking leading questions is better than just me telling her what to think. I mean, there is just a certain amount of pushback where even if I'm like, 'You should do this,' I can't actually make her believe or do the things I believe and do." Margot's mother recognizes her own child's agency and freewill and attempts to balance out her desire to help her child formulate ideas with the reality that her child will come to her own conclusions.

Margot's mom is not the only mother who talks to me about these moments when their children's ideas, produced through interactions with peers, do not align with what the parents want their child to think. As Nicole, the mother of two Evergreen middle school boys tells me, her sons sometimes form ideas that reinforce stereotypes that she wants them to reject: "I'll put [the kids] in contexts where they're around a lot of other different people, but I guess research has shown that then there's just as much prejudices that can come out of that as not. You know what I mean? [*Pause*] You know, I don't know. I don't know if we're doing it right." Nicole tells me that she sometimes overhears her boys talking to each other about how their black classmates do not care about school or act out in ways that disrupt class or are disrespectful to teachers. As a public school teacher herself, she is attuned to what goes on inside schools that reproduces inequality in a way that perhaps other parents are not. She tells me how she worries that her children will observe behaviors of teachers and administrators as they "let white kids off the hook while they suspend black kids for similar behavior" or learn to adopt stereotypes based on what other white kids say about black kids when adults are not around. She tells me that she is often less worried about what her children will think as a result of their black peers themselves but rather the way that other whites interact with these black children. She tells me that she notices this happen at her own school—white kids looking on as other white kids tease black kids, or white teachers scolding black kids unfairly—and wonders if similar interactions are happening in her own children's social life.

Nicole also tells me that she does not know if she and her husband are "doing it right," a concern that nearly half of the parents in this study articulate to me at one point or another. The anxiety these parents have about their children's racial views are most obviously reflected by the fact that after my formal interviews with their children, nearly all the parents ask me, "What did my child say?" Some parents ask me if, in my opinion, they need to "do anything to intervene" or "address anything in particular" with their kids on the basis of what they had said to me. These parents face this conundrum of privilege: What is the best way to raise a white, privileged child such that the child not only thrives but also thinks and behaves in ways that challenge the very privileges from which they benefit? What is the best way to raise a privileged child in a society structured by inequality?

Nicole's boys and Margot are not the only children who attend an integrated public school and produce negative ideas about black peers. Danny (12, Evergreen), for example, explains his observations of what happens when new black kids come to his school. "When they first arrive, they raise their hand in class! Or they try to meet new people! That might be because they are new at school, but they just do things that you wouldn't necessarily see black people typically doing. Like, they seem more active. I mean, I hate to say it, but it's true." Danny tells me that new students who are black behave differently when they first arrive compared to a few months down the road. He tells me that the new kids are always nice and follow rules and try to be friends with white kids. Over time, though, they "close off" and become better friends with the other black kids. I ask Danny why he thinks this happens. " 'Yeah, all groups, they are like, 'I have my friends, and I feel no need to move on, so I'm going to stay closed off,' which doesn't really help." Unlike Margot, who does not easily recognize the role that white kids play in the segregation she observes at school, Danny thinks all the kids do it. He tells me that it is getting worse as everyone gets older. "Let's say fifth and sixth grade, it starts to happen more, and you can see it. But before that, I think it's still happening. It's just less visible," he tells me. Danny perceives that all the kids at his school are participating in a sort of norm within their peer culture to hang out exclusively with kids of their same race. I ask him why he thinks this is, and he tells me he does not know but mentions that some of the "really smart" black kids hang out with the "really smart" white kids—suggesting, perhaps, that the beginning stages of tracking are taking place at his school.

As a result of structural limitations that make positive intergroup engagement difficult to achieve, many of the white Evergreen children reproduce negative views about children of color despite their parents' best efforts otherwise. These findings reflect not only the limitations and nuances of intergroup contact and speak to prior social psychological research on this topic but also demonstrate the complexity of and potential contradictions located within even the most politically "progressive" racial context of childhood. The parents in this study have only so much control over their children's lives and experiences outside the family because kids ultimately produce their own ideas about the social world. In the case of parents such as Margot's mom and Nicole, they attempt to cultivate antiracist praxis, or constant, everyday, proactive, civic engagement aimed at dismantling racism in their kids.[15] However, despite their best intentions, these parents must negotiate a context that is at times hostile to the messages and practices they are trying to instill in their children about racial inequality and racial privilege.

The Power of Peers

From sleepovers to playing video games, from debating Rihanna's skin tone to determining what is racist, the kids in this study form ideas about race in part through their interactions with one another. Much as the research of the sociologists Patricia Adler and Peter Adler illustrates, "Preadolescents do not perceive, interpret, form opinions about, or act on the world as unconnected individuals. Rather, they do all these things in concert with their peers, as they collectively experience the world, encounter problems, share their perceptions, and form joint solutions to those problems."[16] Instead of being told what to think or unquestioningly "adopting" a particular racial logic, children actively produce ideas about race in conjunction with other young people. Part of this interpretive model of socialization involves an "appreciation of the importance of collective, communal activity—how children negotiate, share, and create culture with adults *and each other*."[17] As such, peers and siblings clearly play important roles in the process of white comprehensive racial learning.

5

"Everybody Is White"

Volunteering and Vacationing

In Mozambique, we went and visited these people that lived in
these mud huts, which is cool. . . . We visited the school, and there
were all these little black kids. And they've never seen white people
before, and of course, I've seen black people. But it was kind of
like—like, sometimes when you are black in a whole white school,
you feel like everyone is staring at you, and it was kind of the
opposite—the white person with the black people staring. So it
was kind of strange to have that experience because I never had
before. . . . I mean, it happens to black people in America all the
time, . . . that feeling where everyone is looking at you like, "I've
never seen that kind of person before."
—Charlotte (13, Evergreen)

Volunteering in the context of these families' lives often means interacting in the world with other people, oftentimes people with less
power than they have themselves. These families volunteer at the local
food bank or homeless shelter, participate in mentoring programs in
the community, and are involved in a range of religiously based or
social-justice-oriented organizations. Sometimes this community-
service work is presumed to be race neutral—it is done with a religious
organization or as part of a requirement for Girl Scouts. Other times
parents deliberately sign up their children to participate in volunteer work with the explicit goal of exposing them to people of color.
In either case, and given the relationship between race and class in
Petersfield, children receive, interpret, and produce ideas about race
as a result of serving soup in a room in which they are one of the only
white people among almost exclusively families of color or hanging
out with exclusively black homeless kids at their church on Wednes-

day evenings. Certainly, broader philosophical and ethical questions of power emerge in these moments about the entire endeavor of volunteer and charity work, especially the perception of volunteer work as a way for whites to "save" people of color from their problems. And this dynamic, too, is part of comprehensive racial learning for children with race and class privilege.

Similar dynamics emerge when families travel or go on vacation together, particularly when families visit parts of the world where they are a racial/ethnic minority and their whiteness suddenly becomes more visible to them. As the African American studies scholar and expert on racial learning Erin Winkler finds in her research with black children, kids learn about being black "everywhere they go."[1] As Winkler writes, "Travel influences their developing understandings of place as raced and race as placed, especially in relationship to who belongs in which kinds of spaces."[2] A similar pattern emerges with the white kids in this study. Drawing on the "tourist gaze,"[3] they learn more about their whiteness when they find themselves in new environments and make observations and judgments about people of color they do not know. Again, sometimes parents deliberately construct these experiences with the underlying goal of exposure to human difference, while other parents do not think much about the racial meanings that their children will produce while traveling. These latter parents report being presented with questions from their kids while sitting on the beach in the Caribbean, for example, about why all the brown local kids are swimming on the other side of the rope demarking the resort beach from the public beach, or while maneuvering the holiday shoppers on Michigan Avenue in Chicago about why so many of the homeless people begging for money are black.

Trying to Do Good Work: Volunteering

"You gotta walk the talk!" Greg and Jennifer Norton-Smith, the parents of Conor (11, Evergreen), tell me. Rather than teaching children about race through discussions about the news, these Evergreen parents approach the racial socialization of their children in deliberate, active, explicit, and regular ways, including through volunteer and activist work in the local Petersfield community. Greg and Jennifer tell me that they seek to teach their children that one must put one's ideals into action, and they provide their children with real living examples of such action through their own careers in legal advocacy. They both explain to me that they are very privileged and that "with that privilege comes responsibility," which is why they dedicate so much of their time and energy trying to "make life better for other people" and why they spend so much time thinking and talking about social issues with their children. Greg and Jennifer actively work to teach their children previously agreed-on, explicit messages about issues related to social inequality and particularly racial inequality and racial privilege.

Jennifer and Greg tell me that as parents they have conversations about conversations they will have with their kids—or discussions between the two of them about how to best go about talking to their children about race. In this sense, much of their parenting with respect to teaching lessons about social inequality is premeditated and planned ahead of time. I ask them what lessons are most important for their children to acquire. They tell me, in separate individual interviews, very similar things. Greg states,

> The most important thing that I hope my kids grow up with is what their place in the world is and what other people's place in the world is and, you know, how connected we are to all those other people and that you can't really, you know, be content until other people have the same opportunities you have, and you gotta, you know, you gotta be somebody in that space. You can't just let those things happen. You gotta walk the talk. And that would be great if they found their way in life to make sure that, you know, everybody got the same sort of opportunities.

Greg wants his children not only to acknowledge their privilege but also to do something to work for those who have not received the same unearned advantages. Jennifer says something similar: "I'm not really focused on someone being top of their class or getting into the best college or making the most money or being the most famous, which I feel there is more of that [in Sheridan], and it makes me happy to be here [in Evergreen]. . . . It is more important that my child knows how to interact with all kinds of people around him and be aware of his own position in the world."

Greg and Jennifer both indicate to me that they want their kids to grow up recognizing their unearned privileges and social position, acting on that recognition such that they can work to make sure all people have good lives, rich with opportunity and justice. As Jennifer puts it, "Recognizing people's differences and recognizing people's strengths and weaknesses and backgrounds is important—I mean, just being an empathetic human being as you go through the world. And in order to do that, you have to appreciate what their experiences might be vis-à-vis yours. And so Conor is, like, a white male from a privileged household, and he needs to be very cognizant of that. . . . I want him to be informed and nondiscriminatory and empathetic." Jennifer wants her son to recognize that he is privileged not only with respect to race and class but also with respect to gender. In order to do that, she explains, it is all about "presenting [children] with opportunities to think about and talk about their position in the world." Jennifer goes on to describe how challenging this can be:

What is disturbing to me is that there are very few people of color or minorities in positions of power [in Petersfield]. So what's disturbing to me is that my kids—their teachers are white, their coaches are white, their ballet teachers are white, you know, *everybody* is white. . . . So one of the things we thought about when we moved here was how to develop relationships with people of color, how to find arenas where we were going to be able to interact with diverse people. Because just as a general concept, when you raise kids, you are often guided by what they are ready to talk about, and you can't really just give them more than they can digest. But if you present them with opportunities to think about things, then you can talk about them. So I think it's really important to present opportunities.

Jennifer believes that it is important to think about not only how to cultivate interracial spaces but also how these spaces can provide actors within them with equal status and power. As such, she believes that, as difficult as it is, she has a responsibility to try to find ways for her children to interact with people of color *and* to build loving, meaningful relationships across racial lines.

Two ways that Jennifer and Greg do this work is through community engagement and their own interracial friendships. They participate in rallies and protests, they are connected to black and Latinx leaders in the community through their professional lives, and they bring their children with them to cultural events such as the local Juneteenth celebration and racial justice protests in which they are some of the only white families. Jennifer and Greg are close friends with people of color themselves and model interracial friendships to their kids. For instance, Jennifer shares with me a number of conversations that she has had with black women in her life about topics including raising children, the politics of transracial adoption (at one point, she and Greg considered adopting across racial lines), and what happens in the principal's office when a white child calls a black child a racial epithet ("The entire situation became about the white woman's guilt and shame that her child behaved this way rather than about my friend or her kid!").

Jennifer also tells me that she reads as much as she can on the topic of race, particularly as it relates to child development. She is convinced by her reading as well as observing her own children that kids notice racial differences and disparities at very young ages. Silencing the questions that they have for the sake of appearing "color blind," she knows, does little to help children make sense of social inequality and instead encourages fear and avoidance of the topic of race. Jennifer does not want her children to avoid talking and listening to others about the topic of social inequality, particularly that of race inequality. Thus, it is a priority in her parenting to ensure that her children have contextual experiences that encourage them to ask questions and notice human differences and that she is prepared to answer their questions and have real conversations about social position, privilege, and inequality. Jennifer gives me a list of examples of moments in which her children asked her direct questions about race, many of them connected to sports. For instance, "Why are college football teams predominantly black?" or "Why do Ethiopians always win the Boston Marathon?" Jennifer confides to me that those are really "hard conversations," especially the ones about sports and race, as she does not want to promote biological understandings of race: "I mean, we've embraced [their questions], and we try to explore things with them, but it's not an easy thing to talk about with an eight-year-old about. But they are asking because they notice. So you can't just ignore it. You *have* to address it. . . . We're not as subtle as we used to be. We used to be more subtle. But, I mean, Conor is aware when certain arenas are dominated by certain people. They notice this stuff! So we aren't as subtle now." However hard these conversations might be, Jennifer believes strongly in the importance of having them, especially as the kids get older. While she used more "subtle" strategies when the children were younger, such as offering experiences for her kids to interact with children of different races and modeling particular types of behavior, she now tells me that given the kinds of questions the children ask along with their age, she is overt and direct in her approach. Greg describes this as "beating them over the head with it." Both parents tell me that they feel more comfortable being the person providing them with answers than a peer or another parent or a teacher or a television show doing so.

Another way these parents try to build relationships across the color line is through their participation in a local mentoring program. For years now, the family has been paired up with Michael, a black boy who is the same age as Conor, who spends one day a week with the Norton-Smith family. Jennifer explains that it is difficult to navigate the power differential in this relationship and that this relationship presents both challenges and opportunities for everyone involved to talk about their feelings and perspectives. She explains, however, that since the two families have been connected for so many years at this point, mutual trust has been established, and Michael is "part of their family." Jennifer explains that as Conor and Michael get older, they are both increasingly aware of how differently they each get treated as a result of their race, even just walking side-by-side down the street in Petersfield. She thinks it is good that they have each other to talk to about these experiences. Conor is "super curious" and "precocious," Jennifer tells me. "He really just wants to talk about things, so when you have an open dialogue, it's easier to sorta get at what their preconceived notions might be or whatever. . . . While with my daughter, I don't know what kinds of things are being formulated in her mind." Jennifer is aware that her children may not form the ideas that she hopes they form, but through listening to them, she hopes to identify their ideas and then work to deconstruct or dismantle the ones she feels are inaccurate or inappropriate. Jennifer tells me that she is actually not worried about her own kids. "My kids are going to be fine. It's the Michaels of the world who I worry about. And they are already not fine. I worry about him and kids like him," she tells me, in reference to patterns of racial inequality in the education and criminal justice systems in Petersfield.

On the one hand, Jennifer stands apart from many of the other parents in this study. She thinks long and hard about what her children are learning about race through their everyday lives. She has a close relationship with a child of color in the local community whom she worries about and tries to advocate for however she can. She does her own reading and research on race in the United States and works for social justice through her occupation. She and her husband develop plans for parenting their kids, including explicit plans about teaching the kids about race. On the other hand, though, race and class privilege shape Jennifer's ability to maneuver through Michael's life the way she can, and in some ways, Michael is used as a tool to help her own kids learn about black people, racism, and diversity. When Jennifer talks about Michael being part of her family, she does not talk about Conor being part of Michael's family. Additionally, one reading of the Norton-Smith family is that they are attempting to "save" Michael from his life of poverty, inculcating him with various forms of cultural capital, placing him in spaces to which he otherwise would not have access, and so forth. In the same way that white parent-leaders of extracurricular activities in Petersfield can orchestrate diversity when they wish, so too can Jennifer.

Here again emerges the conundrum of privilege and a set of challenging questions that Jennifer herself acknowledges openly with me. What can parents such as Jennifer do to promote antiracism in their own children through experiential learning that does not objectify and commodify people of color such as Michael? How can the power dynamics due to structural inequality along the lines of both race and class be balanced between these two boys, when the person in charge is the white and affluent mother of one of them? Is the relationship between these two families transactional? Or is inequality and privilege unintentionally reproduced through this relationship as this white, affluent family in some way attempts to assimilate Michael into the white, affluent world? Certainly, Jennifer and Greg have the best of intentions, and it is important to distinguish them, I think, from parents who occasionally "help" black people but then vote against affirmative action or make pejorative statements about black moms behind their backs. Rather, Jennifer and Greg try in whatever way they think they can to "walk the talk," devoting their careers to working for social justice and structural level changes, engaging their kids in activist work, supporting detracking and the demilitarization of public schools, and redistributing resources at the individual level, such as through their relationship with Michael and his family. But the ways that structures shape individuals lives cannot be ignored.

Another example of the conundrum of privilege at play involves volunteer work at homeless shelters and soup kitchens. Patricia (Wheaton Hills) volunteers periodically at a local homeless shelter. Patricia tells me that while she does not often talk to her kids about race explicitly, she hopes they will take away positive messages by volunteering alongside her:

> I volunteer at an organization that works with churches and synagogues and faith communities. It's for homeless people. And it's a program where they bring these homeless families in, and they have to be homeless families with children. And they bring them in, and they basically get them— they take care of the necessities, food, shelter, and then they work on helping this person get into affordable housing. But it's a really great program, because they don't just bring people in and throw them into housing and then expect them to figure out how to make it happen. They stay in a church for a week, and at the end of the week, the volunteers, which is what I do, load up all their stuff, and they move to the next church for a week, or synagogue. So that's their—how their housing is taken care of, their meals are taken care of. And at the same time, the social workers are working with them trying to figure out what their issue is.

Patricia thinks that the homeless people she serves have problems that can be explained at the individual level—that with a little help, they can find permanent housing for themselves and their children. She views herself as having a moral obligation to help the poor and goes on to talk about her actual volunteer work as well as how she involves her children in it:

> I make my kids come. . . . We feed them dinner at night. And then after dinner, we have children's activities. It's a time for the parents to have a little bit of a break, and whatever kids are in the shelter at that time go

play. And I purposely bring my children to come play with these kids, because they're kids. The majority of them are African American, not all, but the majority I would say are. And my kids notice that. And we have been doing this now for four years. It wasn't until this year that my daughter finally asked me. She finally realized, "You mean they don't have homes?" She didn't understand. She just thought she was going over to play with some kids at the church. That's all she really knew. And so now I try to explain to her that, "They don't have a home, and so they're staying in this church. And we're helping provide for them so that they can work on trying to get into a house." It wasn't until just this year that she asked the question, "Well, where do they go when they're not at this church?" Because to her it was just all about on Wednesday night, you know, once every couple of months, we go up to the church, and we play with a bunch of kids up there.

While Patricia does not talk to her kids about the program before bringing them to participate, as time goes on, her kids notice not only that the kids here do not have places to live but also that the majority of these kids are black. While certainly volunteering promotes conversations within this family that would not otherwise happen, so too do Patricia's children observe their surroundings, interpreting information on their own about who is homeless (black kids) and who is not (white kids). Here, white kids such as Patricia's daughter interpret racialized messages about who needs help finding a home and who can do the helping, rather than messages about why some groups are in positions of needing help or of being able to provide it in the first place. Certainly, Jennifer approaches teaching her kids about race from a multitude of ways, including talking about structural change and taking action in order to make these changes, both personally and professionally. But kids such as Patricia's children do not appear to be learning much from their parents explicitly about systems that created these racialized patterns in the first place—rather, they learn that individual affluent whites can be the ones to bring good things to poor blacks such as the kids she plays with at church.[4]

White, affluent families in this study often try to do good work for their community and as a way to teach their children about the world around them. Of course, in any community, it is important to help each other in times of need. However, while volunteering may be altruistic and done with the best of intentions, the messages that privileged kids interpret from interactions in these spaces may reinforce ideas about race that run counter to larger antiracist projects.

Traveling the World as a White Family

All of these families travel throughout the United States: they go to Washington, DC, for President Obama's inauguration, to vacation homes in the mountains of Colorado, and to cabins on the Great Lakes. These families also travel internationally to such places as Mozambique, Peru, Israel, South Africa, Hong Kong, and most commonly, throughout western Europe. These kids also travel to major US cities quite frequently to participate in educational enrichment programs, as well as to perform in elite groups based around the arts, particularly dance and music. According to these families, the purpose of this travel is either to gain an appreciation for global human difference or to learn more about forms of social inequality across the world.

A number of the parents in this study explain to me that it is important to them that they bring their children around the world, introducing them to the cultural diversity that spans the international community. These parents spend months planning family vacations, or they arrange their travels such that the kids tag along on a business trip or sabbatical that one of the parents may be taking. Largely, for these parents, the focus of travel is about exposing children to different foods, cultures, traditions, architecture, artwork, history, and music. As Jessica's mom explains in reference to their recent travels to Asia, "We are also very much interested in international travel and bringing international influences . . . and different flavors into our lives."

The Silber family also embraces international travel—as well as actually living abroad. Danny (12) was born in Japan while the Silbers were living there for purposes tied to their work as historians. The family has since lived in France for six months as well as in Germany for a summer. As Danny's mom, Anna, tells me, "The world is a really big place, and it's really important that [the kids] all get out in it. . . . Life is totally, totally, totally about being open-minded, you know, thoughtful. There's lots of ways to skin a cat, and yours might not be the best or the only way. It's real important that we [travel]." In addition to living abroad and being immersed in a particular community, Danny has traveled independently as part of a sports competition to New Zealand, and the family has been to Alaska, Mexico, Canada, and throughout South America, where Danny's sister lives.

Many of the children in this study have traveled abroad by the time they were in middle school. A handful, like Danny, have even lived outside the United States for periods of time. These children are confident travelers, have passports, know all about going through customs and immigration, and look forward to, as Anna puts it, "getting out in it." Some of the kids in this study show me memorabilia from their trips, going into their bedroom to bring out a piece of pottery to show me or a framed photo with the Eiffel Tower in the background or Russian nesting dolls. In addition to the messages these children perceive while they are out in the world, they also gain the cultural capital associated with international travel. These children know how to navigate new countries, at least to some extent, and they are prepared for a lifetime of moving through different spaces and places with ease, even spaces where they are one of the only white Americans.

Like many of the families in this study, the Lacey parents have much to say about travel and how it serves a very specific purpose in the racial education of their daughter, Charlotte (13, Evergreen). They tell me where they have traveled over the past few years, including cities such as Cincinnati and Washington, DC, and countries such as France and Mozambique. They tell me they hope to use travel as a way to teach Charlotte about racism and inequality, nationally and across the globe. For example, Janet explains why they went to Cincinnati: "We recently went to the Underground Railroad Museum in Cincinnati. . . . I have also been doing a lot of reading on the subject of race. I just keep thinking, 'Wow.' We have just screwed over black people *over* and *over* and *over* and *over* again, whether they are people who live in this country or people who don't live in this country. It's partially race, and it's partially capitalism—which I don't think is the greatest system in the world [*laughing*]. Just call me a socialist, I don't care." Janet goes on to talk about some of the exhibits the family saw at the museum in Cincinnati and how this museum provided them all with a better foundation from which to start conversations about slavery in the United States. She tells me that she herself learned new things at the museum that she previously did not know. Because her career involves international health work, she too bridges what she and the family discussed after visiting the museum with health crises in places such as Haiti, bringing in structures of both race and economics into her reflections.

One of the most important ways the Laceys believe they can offer Charlotte exposure to different cultures is through travel. Janet explains:

> I want to teach Charlotte that you need to respect that your knowledge and your experience is limited, and so it's important to ask questions and not make judgments just on a wee bit of information or one experience. Travel is really important to both of us for this reason—we like to expose her to different things through [travel]. She's been to South Africa and Mozambique and France and all over the US, so, um, not for a long period of time, but you know, she's seen all kinds of stuff in all of those places and all different cultures and you know, it's *really* important for her to be exposed to these things.

As Tom also explains, one of the primary purposes behind these trips is to help Charlotte understand not just cultural diversity but also her own position in the world. He wants his daughter to recognize that she is a person who has been granted a tremendous degree of privilege by simple luck of circumstance:

> Charlotte has a knack of keeping an eye out for people and tak[ing] care of them. . . . She sees that people's lives are harder than hers, and of course, we've traveled and seen that. And I remember, it's like that light goes on in her head, and [she's] like, "Wait a minute! These . . . babies, these children that we are seeing in this tiny little village in this country, they are poor because they plopped out of a mother right here. If they had plopped out of my mother back in Petersfield, they'd be thinking about that trip to Paris they want to take someday."

Tom understands travel as a tool that he can use to help Charlotte develop more thoughtful and empathetic understandings of social problems such as poverty. Tom tells me in a number of different ways that he wants his daughter to challenge explanations of poverty tied to ideologies of meritocracy and instead observe for herself evidence that poverty is a structural problem connected to policies, governments, histories of different places, and power. Rather than simply telling her these things, Tom believes she needs to make her own observations by analyzing the world around her for herself. The racial difference between herself and the majority of the people with whom she interacted while in Mozambique clearly shaped Charlotte's experience in impactful ways, as illustrated in Tom's story. Charlotte remembers details from her trip, such as the "mud huts" that she describes as "cool," in a tone that communicates to me that she does not want me to think she is judging these homes. She also seems to be most impacted by being the only white child around, and she draws connections between how she felt in Mozambique and how black kids must feel at her school. Missing from this, of course, is an acknowledgment of the tremendous power differences between affluent, white tourists from the United States visiting a small village in Mozambique and growing up as a black child in predominantly white spaces in the United States.

This trip is not a "mission trip" or driven by any sort of explicit "white savior" agenda on the behalf of Charlotte's parents, although they do hope that she is motivated by what she sees to do good work in her future for the world in which she lives.[5] In this sense, similar dynamics emerge between this type of travel and volunteer work—exposing one's child to people of color whom they do not personally know and with whom they certainly do not share an equal status due to broader structural inequalities. As I have written elsewhere, "Cultivating an awareness of privilege in one's own child may lead them to work for equality in their future lives. Yet . . . the inconsistency lies in that exposure to 'other people' also reflects power dynamics in which the bodies of the marginalized are sites for the privileged to learn something about themselves."[6] As well meaning as Janet and Tom are, this inconsistency appears to send multiple messages to Charlotte—on the one hand, that she ought to appreciate how it feels to be stared at or be out of place in a sense but, on the other, that her experience in the Mozambique school is the same as that of black kids in her honors class at school back in Petersfield. Due to the power differences tied to race, class, and global inequality between nations, of course, these two experiences can never be the same.

The complexity of international travel of this nature is apparent. Charlotte is far more knowledgeable and aware than most of the other children in this study about rural poverty in one part of sub-Saharan Africa and has a much more global understanding of the world around her. She expresses compassion and respect for the people she met while traveling, and she produces critical understandings about her own position in the world through this travel interaction. And yet these interactions are not based in equal status. She does not build meaningful relationships with the children she observes, as she is only visiting for a short period of time. A number of scholars have examined the concept of "poverty tourism" or "slum tourism," in which "privileged tourists . . . visit places for the purpose of experiencing where poor people live, work, and play."[7] As the human geographer Malte Steinbrink explains, drawing on both the long-standing history of this practice and modern-day versions, poverty tourism is "a medium of self-reflexive Othering" in which the slum serves as a way for privileged tourists to draw distinctions between themselves and others.[8] Of course, this kind of tourism is rife with exploitation and voyeurism, particularly as tourists "den[y] residents the opportunity to consent or object."[9] Another example of the Laceys exposing their daughter to experiential racial learning through travel and exposure to people of color unknown to the family was when they brought their daughter to President Obama's inauguration. Charlotte's parents describe how moving this day was to them but also express concern about how their daughter interpreted it. Specifically, they tell me about how surprised they were that race was not central to Charlotte's interpretation at the inauguration, as it was for them. Janet describes the event:

> There was such a mix of people there and there were a *lot*, a *lot*, a *lot* of very old black people who were there. . . . It was so powerful, so powerful. Just to be in the most integrated event, yeah, probably the most integrated event I have ever been to. . . . It was so amazing to have our daughter there. I don't know that she understood all of the significance of it, but it was powerful. And I know she witnessed this moment, and that is powerful—even if she didn't recognize that at the time.

Tom too reflects on what it was like to bring his daughter to the inauguration and how he was in disbelief when his daughter did not mention race in an essay she wrote afterward, something Tom wrestled to understand: "She never mentioned anything about race in the entire thing. And I remember thinking, and of course, Janet and I have tears streaming down our face—we cannot believe that there are hundreds of thousands of black Americans out here celebrating this day. It was unbelievably moving to see disenfranchised people come out, largely— God knows they must have been excited, and there are tons of them that came out for this thing, and we were thinking, 'What an amazing thing,' and Charlotte didn't even write a word about it!" He tells me that he still wonders why Charlotte did not mention anything about race, questioning himself retrospectively as to whether he should have pushed her to think more about it. Janet believes that this moment was important for Charlotte to witness, if only as something she looks back on with a richer and deeper understanding of the significance of the day.

Charlotte and I discuss her thoughts on the election of the first black president in the United States and her experience of going to his inauguration.

> Yeah, the thing is, when I was that age, I don't think I thought about the African American thing. I think it was just my parents saying, "Oh! This is the guy we want!" And [I think about] me and my friend who lives over there [pointing], in our snow pants in the winter and saying, "Vote for Obama!" and yelling it on the street. So I don't think I was thinking he was black more than just—because that was my first age when I really knew about elections. Before Barack Obama, I never knew, like George Bush. I never really understood politics that well. So that was the first time I actually understood—and I think because everyone was making a big deal about it, I was paying more attention, but I wasn't really sure *why* it was a big deal. So that was the first time I was like paying attention to politics. What year was that, 2009? 2008? So I was like 9? So that is like when you first start paying attention to it.

Charlotte tells me that as she gets older, though, she feels more independent of her parents and forms her own ideas about politics and controversial topics. Evidence of this can be found in the political discussions she has with her parents, sometimes agreeing with them but also sometimes taking her own unique position and challenging them to rethink their own. I ask Charlotte what she remembers from attending the inauguration:

I just remember it was *really cold*. And it took us a minute to get in, but we were actually pretty close [to the front], which was cool. But I remember being really cold, and but, like I said, I don't really think I thought about the race thing. Like, I think when you are that age, your parents—like, my parents aren't racist, so if you don't hear your parents saying anything bad about black people, you don't really think about it. Like, when you're that age, unless your parents have actually raised you that way, you don't even think about the diversity between whites and blacks because you are just used to everyone being people. It seems like as you grow older, you learn more about what other people are talking about, and my parents at least talk to me about it more. But when you are younger, you are only around a certain zone of people and what they think. But then you learn what other people think. And then you understand better. That's what is happening to me. I am learning more as I get older.

Charlotte distinguishes her 9-year-old self from her 12-year-old self, commenting that because she is growing up in a "certain zone of people" that do not make outwardly racist comments, she was unable, at age 9, to understand what "the big deal" was about going to the inauguration of the first black president, aside from the fact that it was an exciting time to be on the Mall in Washington, DC. This "zone" also includes people of color, as Charlotte, especially when she was younger, had good relationships with black classmates and playmates. Looking back on it, she appears to offer a color-blind perspective on race relations—that when she was 9, she "didn't even think about the diversity between whites and blacks because you are just used to everyone being people." But, as she explains, the older she gets, the more she understands the significance of the election of President Obama and the more she realizes that even within her same "zone," people do not always think the same way about race. According to this white child, just like with politics, as she gets older, she understands the complexities of race in the United States more and more.

Overall, travel experiences shape how the children in this study make sense of who they are in comparison to others. Through these experiences, boundaries are established by children: Who is American? Who is African? Who is South American? Who is in need? Who can help? As Steinbrink writes, "tourism lives on what is different."[10] Whether families are traveling to gain exposure to cultural difference or whether they are traveling to gain exposure to the realities of global inequality, the politics of consent and the power differentials between tourists and residents shape the interactions. In this sense, there are ways in which well-intended international travel has the potential to actually justify inequality in the minds of some children. Without a doubt, the kids in this study learn a great deal from both volunteering and vacationing, including many positive lessons about community, ethical responsibility, and the reality of inequality. However, one of the lessons they also learn is that they can navigate the world fluidly and with ease and without ever asking for permission, a hallmark of privilege.

6

"Shaking Those Ghetto Booties"

Family Race Talk

Water ballet consists of mainly girls, separated into different age groups, performing a memorized, choreographed dance that starts on the pool deck, includes an acrobatic group jump into the pool, and then continues with synchronized-swimming-type movements in the water. The girls wear waterproof makeup to do this, along with matching expensive dance-costume-esque bathing suits that are purchased for this one performance only, decorated in sparkly sequins and bows. Each age group has its own specific bathing suit and dance routine. High school girls choreograph the dance and teach the moves to the younger kids. These dances are accompanied by the music of artists such as Lady Gaga and Katy Perry, which blasts from loudspeakers on the pool deck. Every single person at the pool is white. The pool is private: you must be a member or with a member to enter.

Parents sit by the side of the pool, cheering on their daughters, a few parents looking at each other with an eyebrow raised as the middle-school-aged kids perform what some people might identify as sexually suggestive dance moves in their bathing suits. I sit with the parents, a crowd of about 30 people, observing this scene and listening to the conversations around me. One mom, with long red fingernails, white linen pants, and black platform sandals, is very excited about water ballet. She sings along to the music, swaying back and forth and clapping her hands up over her head, occasionally yelling out, "Wooo!" to her 11-year-old daughter as her daughter shakes her hips back and forth to Beyoncé's "Single Ladies." At one point, while snapping a picture on her iPhone, she turns to one of the other moms and says, "Look at them pretending to have ghetto booties!" The other mom laughs and replies, "I know! It's so hilarious!" The girls have all turned their backs to the crowd and are sticking out their "booties." The two women start singing along to the song together, waving their arms in the air as they move to the music.

After the performance, the mothers greet the girls by giving them roses. The girls are very excited and giggly after an exhilarating pool dance. One of the mothers gives her daughter a hug and says, "You girls really looked like Beyoncé out there!" The other mother chimes in and says, "Yeah, girls! You were really shaking those ghetto booties!" The girls look at each other, turn their backs to us, and repeat the same hip-shaking dance move they had performed by the pool. Everyone laughs as the girls turn and run off to retrieve five-dollar smoothies, purchased by one of the parents for all 40 girls in the performance. I see the girls checking each other's waterproof lipstick as they scurry toward the smoothies, everyone around me laughing and enjoying themselves in the summer sun.

* * *

All of the families in this study talk about race. Sometimes these conversations are deliberate; at other times, parents do not even realize they are drawing on their own taken-for-granted assumptions about race when they interact with their kids. I observe parents, in the presence of their own children, mocking the names of black kids at school, calling black parents whose children receive free and reduced lunch "lazy" and making fun of their acrylic fingernails and fashion, talking about jury duty and how "obviously" the black guy is guilty, talking about families like their own as "normal," and so forth. I observe parents talking with their kids about participating in political protests, reprimanding their children for mentioning the color of someone's skin, making excuses for racist Grandpa at a family party ("He's from a different generation"), and talking openly about patterns of racial inequality in the United States. Parents confide in me about the racist things their kids say within the walls of their home, asking me for advice on what to say in response. And kids tell me about the racist things their parents say in the car as they leave a particular liquor store or drive through a particular part of town. In some cases, these family conversations attempt to interrupt racism, while in others, they attempt to reinforce racial stereotypes and myths. Sometimes these discussions are serious, sometimes casual. Sometimes race talk is explicit, and sometimes it is subtle. Sometimes parents initiate these discussions, and sometimes kids do. Whether or not family members identify that these conversations are happening, race talk in white families happens all the time. As such, white kids in this study, regardless of the racial politics of their own parents, are constantly receiving messages about race, interpreting these messages, and then producing their own understandings.

Overall, these families are talking about race and reproducing ideas about race in a variety of different ways—and they are all doing so far more than what is commonly assumed about white families. Even in families where parents claim color blindness, it is clear through interviewing kids growing up in these homes and observing these families in their everyday lives that family race talk occurs on a regular basis. Often, this talk is derived from ongoing current events in both the local and broader community presented to families through the various media they consume. This talk also presents itself in relation to what goes on within extracurricular spaces, or places where parents interact not only with their own children but also with other people's children. Both the consumption of media and popular culture and the participation in extracurricular activities contribute in unique ways to the process of comprehensive racial learning and, as such, are part of a child's racial context.

Media and Popular Culture

One of the ways family conversations explicitly about race emerge is through *media* consumption. Like many children, the kids in this study constantly consume media. Only a few of them use social media at this stage in their lives, but most love sports stars, musicians, and celebrities. Some talk constantly about LeBron James's or Tom Brady's most recent athletic feat. Some kids learn the lyrics to new songs they hear on the radio or on their iPod almost immediately upon release, such as "Hey I just met you / And this is crazy / But here's my number / So call me maybe," or "Baby, baby, baby oh / Like baby, baby, baby no," and then sing these songs relentlessly. Some of the kids discuss celebrities' clothes and hair and athletic shoes, occasionally even trying to imitate these fashions by persuading their parents to take them shopping. Some of the kids read the newspaper every day or listen to NPR in the car on the way to school or consume Fox News or national PBS broadcasts or the local news with their parents in the evenings as dinner is prepared. These kids regularly watch films, television programs, and documentaries. Some of them listen to podcasts with their parents on road trips. And they read books. Through all of these different media outlets that their parents allow them to access, the kids in this study receive and interpret messages about race, and subsequently, media often provide opportunities for conversations about race to emerge among family members in my study. Sometimes these opportunities to use media as an entry point to talk about race are intentional and to some degree premeditated. But often these opportunities emerge organically, as part of everyday life, when no one is really expecting it, such as in response to events in the evening news, for example. The family conversations that emerge from these everyday moments are impromptu and unscripted and take place as the family listens to the radio in the car or sits around the dining-room table or watches television at the end of the day. However these media-related moments emerge, they are often when these white families share openly their ideas about race.

"Where They Get Their Diversity": Films and Television Programs

Parents play an active role in guiding children's access to various forms of media, including films and television programs. For example, Mrs. Avery, a Sheridan mom, explains to me how she used a film to teach her daughter about racism:

> The kids get *very, very* little racial diversity in Sheridan, so we try to take different opportunities to expose them to different things. One of the things I did was have Lauren and I read *The Help*. We read the book and, you know, talked about it together. . . . And you read that book, and you're just horrified. You're like, "Oh my God! Seriously?! That is what [black domestic workers] actually dealt with?!" And then it comes out in movie form, and we all went to see the movie. I took some of her girlfriends along with us, and there are parts of it where your mouth is just hanging open because you just can't quite believe what you are seeing. And so from that instance, [the girls] say, "Oh my gosh, thank God I didn't live then! Thank God we live now where it doesn't really matter what the color of your skin is."

Mrs. Avery purposefully introduces her child to a fictional account of black domestic work as a way to teach her daughter about history, diversity, and race in the United States. "I look for those examples to teach them because they are not living it every single day," as she puts it. While her intentions are good, *The Help* has been widely criticized, particularly by the Association of Black Women Historians. In an open letter to "Fans of The Help," the association outlines the ways the film misrepresents black women, black culture, black speech, and black domestic workers. It suggests that *The Help* is in fact a "coming-of-age story of a white protagonist who uses myths about the lives of black women to make sense of her own."[1] The sociologist Matthew Hughey has argued that *The Help* can be classified as a "white savior film"—a film that "helps repair the myth of white supremacy and paternalism in an unsettled and racially charged time."[2] Due to patterns of residential segregation, these films are popular, he argues, because they present narratives of racial reconciliation and redemption, which, when consumed, make white people feel good about themselves and the state of race relations today. These films subsequently serve to downplay all the ways race still matters in the United States. In this sense, the history lessons that are being taught by this film not only are inaccurate but serve to mask the reality of continued racial injustice in the United States: "Thank God we live now where it doesn't really matter what the color of your skin is." When I talk to Lauren about this issue later, she tells me that she really enjoyed reading the book and going to watch the movie. She tells me, "I learned a lot from my mom and the story" and goes on to tell me that she and her friends discussed it together, talking about how horrible the white people were, how brave the main white character was, and most importantly, how good it is that the United States "is no longer racist." Thus, despite overwhelming evidence of the existence of racism in the United States, this film reinforces the color-blind or postracial logic that racial injustice is a thing of the past and presents this narrative to white kids such as Lauren as fact.

Other parents reject using fictional accounts to tell historical stories and instead present information to their children through documentaries or alternative forms of media. For instance, Janet, the mother of Charlotte (12, Evergreen), tells me about their weekly family tradition of watching films together: "We alternate who gets to pick, and I've got the M.O. for the one who is always picking the documentary [*laughing*]. I'll say, 'Oh! So let's watch this movie about these two 19-year-old girls whose parents are trying to get them to get married because that is what their culture is, but now they live in the United States.' Or, 'Let's watch this movie about these indigenous people in Brazil whose land has been taken or this one about race and the death penalty.'" Janet goes on to tell me how important she thinks it is for her daughter to be exposed to topics covered in well-researched, social-justice-oriented documentaries. She also tells me that Charlotte enjoys watching these movies and that the family often has lively discussions afterward. Charlotte confirms what her mother says, telling me that overall she likes the documentaries her mom picks but that sometimes they are "annoying." Charlotte also tells me that she prefers to listen to podcasts such as *This American Life* with her family on the weekends and that they often discuss these podcasts together as a family—not only immediately following the podcast but also weeks later.

In addition to fictional and documentary films, television programs also present opportunities for families to have conversations about race. In fact, for Sheridan parents who typically embrace color-blind ideology, they tell me that their families most often speak about race in relation to the news or to a television program. As one mother of two girls puts it, "That's really the only time we talk about [race]." For other parents, sexuality rather than race is what is often noticed and discussed among family members: "I would say probably more than race, we talk about, you know, gayness or homosexuality, just because it's on television so much. That we're all, you know—I mean, it's a part of pop culture. My kids are really into pop culture. So we probably talk about that more than race. But if race was on television more, we might talk about it more." While the children consume a wide and varied selection of media, a few shows are popular across many of the families, and many of these programs interrogate issues of sexuality in ways that feel new to these parents and children. The most popular shows mentioned include *Glee* and *Modern Family*. As Mrs. Schultz describes, "The TV shows—*Modern Family*, *Glee*, you know—they are bringing all of that diversity into TV shows, so the kids are being exposed to it there if they aren't being exposed in their own communities. And these guys have been exposed to TV shows from before they were born. So, I mean, that's where they get their diversity." In this sense, these parents explain to me that they feel better about living in a predominantly white suburb and sending children to a predominantly white school because they know their kids will have exposure to people who are different from them via television programing.

I find evidence that these programs do shape kids' racial thinking. For example, a handful of children, all girls, bring up the show *That's So Raven* to me, and all of them remember one particular episode. Kelsey (13, Sheridan) tells me what she remembers about this episode: "A long time ago, there was a show on the Disney Channel called *That's So Raven*, and they did an episode on how [Raven] wanted to get a job at the store, but the manager wouldn't let her because she is black. So I definitely think that [racism] is still an issue; otherwise they wouldn't have made an episode about it. I mean, kids all over the world watch this show. [Racism] is obviously a big deal if it's on [the show]." This particular episode is memorable to Kelsey, and what she remembers is a lesson about racism in the United States today. Watching the protagonist of this program, whom Kelsey likes and with whom she identifies, experience racism appears to legitimize the existence of racism for this child viewer, at least in this one scenario on television.

Of course, the media these children consume contain all kinds of messages about race that are interpreted by kids, even when parents do not see evidence as such. Much of children's television programing contains messages about color blindness. Shows often contain either a token person or two of color amid an otherwise white cast, such as in early seasons of *Modern Family*. The most popular show for these families is *Glee*, a musical drama about a diverse group of high school Glee Club members. The communications scholar Rachel Dubrofsky, an expert in examining messages in television programs, argues that *Glee* "downplays racism, avoids the institutional role and presence of racism, racially aligns Jewishness with whiteness, and whitens blackness."[3] Through presenting a diverse cast, this particular show fits within a "postracial media landscape" that she argues normalizes oppression "with the suggestion that overcoming racialized oppression is akin to overcoming one's awkward teen years and learning to celebrate one's uniqueness."[4] Ironically, this is the show that many of the parents point to as an example of what they use to teach their children about diversity or, more specifically, people of color. This is not a new phenomenon. Research shows that beginning in the late 1960s, as more black actors were represented on television, white parents living in segregated white communities used television to provide information about black people to their children.[5] Child psychologists also argue that television often provides kids with representations of race that they otherwise do not observe due to lack of interracial contact in their everyday lives.[6] It is for this reason that critical media scholars, family studies scholars, and child development scholars have been so interested in examining the messages about race in children's television.[7] This research explores the extent to which characters of color are represented in shows produced for children of all ages, what kind of roles characters of color play in the programs, whether and how racial stereotypes are drawn on, and how television producers are increasingly attempting to diversify and integrate multiculturalism into kids' television.

Sheridan mom Mrs. Church tells me that it is precisely because of diversity in programs such as *Glee* that she does not have to have explicit conversations about race with her kids. She draws on diversity in television as a way to confirm her color-blind beliefs that race is no longer a significant factor in US society, unless people of color "make it so." As she explains to me, "The kids are so exposed to [diversity] on TV, so we, as parents, try not to say much of anything about it. . . . I do think it's neat that to them, it's all really natural. We don't even need to talk about it." Believing that her children live race-neutral lives and never think or talk about race, Mrs. Church also believes that diversity is so normalized for her children through television that it is further proof that the United States is beyond race and that race is unnecessary to discuss. This finding confirms Dubrofsky's critique about the risks of presenting a "postracial media landscape." And yet it is also through these shows that kids push back against their "postracial" or color-blind parents in small ways, arguing that discrimination still exists in the United States—just look at what happened to Raven on *That's So Raven*. In this sense, exposure to different perspectives via television provides children with evidence that they sometimes use to challenge their parents in addition to providing a platform to speak openly about race, even if these conversations are rooted in a broader postracial, color-blind perspective, particularly for Sheridan families.

Outrage and Innocence: The News and Current Events

Current events and news media also fuel explicit race talk in white families. For instance, one afternoon, Gail, the mother of Chris (11, Wheaton Hills), comes home from work, puts her work bag down on the front bench, and says "Hello!" enthusiastically. Noah (5) jumps up and then clutches her leg as she tries to walk across the room. She asks Chris and Noah how their days are going. They both say, "Fiiiiine" in a dull and bored tone. She scoffs at them and then announces enthusiastically, "There is a *revolution* going on, people!" Gail goes on to tell the kids all about what had happened that day in Egypt, answering their questions about whether Mubarak is a pharaoh, speaking in an excited and engaging tone. When I talk to her later about her strategies for engaging her kids about current events, she says she always wants to be "on the side of more information." She explains:

> I want my kids to learn about stuff from me. I mean, I'm sure my kids are the ones telling the other kids on the bus about the birds and the bees, but I always sort of thought, give them the information before they're even old enough to be embarrassed by it. So yeah, I don't try to protect my kids the way I see many other parents doing. I want them to have a good sense of what's going on in the world. And with race, what I try to tell my kids is to recognize that everyone harbors prejudice and that you need to see it in yourself and try to overcome it.

Gail is not the only parent who thinks this way. For instance, another Wheaton Hills mother tells me, "We mainly talk about race whenever it comes up in the news or on TV. . . . I'm open about what I have to share. I guess I'd rather have them hear it from me, hear everything from me, than just trying to figure it out on their own or hearing it from friends or from people who don't know the facts." Over the course of my time with Gail's family, I witness her speak openly with her children about the daily reports about the Occupy Movement, the Norway massacre, the Penn State sexual abuse scandal, the complexities of the Arab Spring, the debt-ceiling battle in Congress, the devastating tsunami in Japan, and contentious state politics. Gail is passionate about the importance of understanding both or multiple sides of any argument and talks openly about the different positions with her boys. Gail enjoys debate, and so do her children. The kids engage in these conversations with her, and sometimes the family gets into heated discussions or loud arguments about politics or controversial topics. Most of the media consumed by this family comes in the form of NPR, the *Wall Street Journal*, online news sources, and PBS, a more politically diverse representation of the news than many of the other families in the study who consume either entirely right-leaning news or left-leaning news. Gail also uses print media to convey ideas to her kids. For example, after George Zimmerman was found not guilty of murdering Trayvon Martin, she emails me about her conversation with Chris:

> Chris is outraged. Outraged. I tried to explain the distinction between a tragic event that unquestionably reflects deep and inherent race bias and a court system that is designed to identify whether a specific set of facts meets the elements of a particular crime, as charged. The criminal justice system may reflect social problems, but it is not really well designed to fix social problems. . . . In short—be angry. Be angry at Zimmerman, at us, and at our society. Don't be angry with the jurors. When it was clear he was buying none of this, I printed a few good (short) editorials for him that articulated this better than I can. I don't think he read them. He does not need my input or perspective because he is adamantly of the opinion that the verdict is an outrage and travesty of justice. To his mind, it was flat out and clearly motivated by bigotry. Zimmerman deserves to be put away for a long time, and by failing to do that, the jury failed. That is his perspective, which I do not entirely agree with but I respect. He gets very angry with me when I do not agree with him 100%, so we stopped talking about it.

Despite Gail's presentation of an alternative view, Chris interprets the outcome of the trial for himself, developing his own ideas about what happened, regardless of what his mother attempts to share with him. It is clear that Gail engages with her son and that this particular family speaks very openly about racism and the criminal justice system—not just in this moment but throughout my time with this family. It is also clear, time and time again, that Chris comes to his own conclusions about current events and has the confidence to share these views with the people around him.

On the complete opposite end of the spectrum, some parents firmly believe that their children should not be concerned with tragic events in the news. In efforts to protect their children's "innocence," a term that the historian Robin Bernstein demonstrates is imbued with whiteness itself, these parents tell me that it is essential that they "let them be kids."[8] As Tara (Wheaton Hills) explains, "I know my older daughter is very sensitive. And, you know, if I tell her . . . a bunch of people died, she'll cry. I mean, it will really touch her. She's a very tenderhearted person. And so, you know, I—not that I am trying to shelter her, because she needs to know that this is the world we live in. But I'm not going to divulge more than she really, maturity-wise, can handle." Parents across this study are faced with similar decisions: do you tell your fifth-grade child about a mass shooting or racist comments a politician recently made or tragic natural disasters such as tsunamis or earthquakes? And if you do, what is the best way to approach these discussions? While Gail deliberately chooses to talk to Chris about the murder of Trayvon Martin, other parents email me to say that their kids "have been busy with camps and practices" and "we were just on vacation." One parent tells me, "I don't think [my son] knows about it."

The structural privileges of whiteness are what allow white parents to avoid conversations about racial violence perpetrated against youth of color. While white parents can make the choice not to talk about black youth being shot because they appear "dangerous," parents of black children do not have this luxury—the luxury of protecting the innocence of one's own children. In fact, research shows that many parents of black children spoke to their kids about what happened to Trayvon Martin, and many believed it was required of them to help keep their child safe.[9] This is not the case for the white families in this study.

Yet the news media is consistently present in the everyday background of these families' lives. Stories in the news are available for kids' interpretations, whether parents embrace these conversations or try to avoid them. For instance, one afternoon, Janet Lacey (Evergreen) has the radio tuned to NPR, which is broadcasting state news. She is multitasking, rushing around the kitchen managing a baking project alongside washing tomatoes from her garden while also talking to me about raising white kids. She also periodically answers questions from her daughter, who comes in and out of the kitchen, about the plans for the upcoming weekend. I see the daily newspaper is left open on the kitchen table, as if someone is still reading it. This is a very typical scenario for many of the families—the radio or television on in the background of everyday life with magazines and newspaper lying around the house, available to whoever wants to pick them up and look at them. In addition, in some of these households, stacks of magazines and newspaper appear to be a part of routine life. Radio news is also consumed by these kids and their parents, especially in the car driving to activities or listening to the local pop channel with celebrity "news" or *All Things Considered* on the way home from gymnastics or when parents are cooking or washing dishes. The father of Conor (12, Evergreen) listens to Amy Goodman on *Democracy Now* as he tidies up the kitchen after dinner. In other families, the television is tuned to Fox News and is on constantly in the background of home life.

The kids in this study certainly have thoughts about how current events in the news impact their lives. For some children, current events are for adults, and they just want to "be a kid" and "have fun" and let their parents deal with all the controversy and political arguing. As Britney (11, Sheridan) tells me, "I think adults should worry about [current events], and kids shouldn't really worry about it as much until they are older." Other kids, though, have had enough with the political arguing and "want it to stop." Still other kids are really engaged, inspired, and animated by the ongoing political discussion and want to learn as much as they can about current events. For example, Danny (12, Evergreen) tells me,

> I like reading the news so I can have my opinion. . . . Like, especially lately, teachers have been like, "Okay! Any opinion is right!" And I'll say something, and then they'll start to argue against me. And that makes me feel like they aren't letting me say what I want. They *say* they're letting people say what they want, that they want all the opinions out there, but they really aren't letting people think what they want to think. And I think that's a big problem in the public school just because people don't really realize like how much the teachers control the kids.

In order to prepare himself to stand up to his teacher, Danny skims through the newspaper at the breakfast table every morning before school. In some ways, he is actually motivated to know what is going on in the world so that he can argue with and even antagonize his teacher (whom he strongly dislikes) at school. But this means he also has a solid grasp on current events.

Other children also tell me that they also pay attention to the local news and want to know what is happening in Petersfield. I spend time with some of the kids in this study at a large protest happening downtown, listening to the kids as they talk about the controversy of the proposed legislation and noting their homemade signs or which sign they have picked out of a stack of premade signs to wave. These kids want information so that they can participate in their community, whether that be physically at the protests, at school in classroom debates, or in the privacy of their home, where they can try to figure out what is going on around them. In sum, the kids in this study have different reactions to the news, different levels of interest in current events, and parents who approach conversations about race with different political beliefs. Yet, for almost all of the families in this study, the media encourages families to talk openly about race, another aspect of one's racial context of childhood.

Parents on the Sidelines

While media provide opportunities for family race talk, what goes on in extracurricular spaces between adults and children also leads to open conversations about race. Research shows that children growing up with class privilege tend to participate in a number of highly organized activities.[10] Not only are these formal spaces where kids interact with each other, producing racial meanings as they do, but parents play an important role in these spaces as well. Parents select which activities are best for their children, but as the following examples demonstrate, they also play an active role in shaping what goes on within these spaces by inserting their own racial logic from the sidelines of these activities.

Take, for instance, parents' actions from the sidelines of the water-ballet performance, described in the opening to this chapter. Part of the girls' laughter in response to their mothers talking about their "ghetto booties" may be due to ways in which acting like adults in sexually suggestive ways is sometimes funny to children. However, the use of the term "ghetto booty" to describe the way that the girls are dancing, and the laughter that it incites, is racially coded, despite no explicit mention of race. The flippant use of this term, and everyone's understanding of what it means, specifically suggests that these mothers and daughters alike agree that there is a difference between black women's bodies— such as that of the celebrity Beyoncé—and white women's bodies and that there is something funny about this difference, especially when a black woman's body is mocked, imitated, and culturally appropriated by white children. Existing research documents the ways in which white kids and white performers culturally appropriate hip hop, fashion, language, and black culture for their own purposes, while "removing the racially coded meanings embedded in the music and replacing them with color-blind ones."[11] Lots of the children in this study consume music of black artists including Beyoncé, Rihanna, and Kanye West. Two boys are especially enthused about Drake, Kendrick Lamar, and Lupe Fiasco.

The connection between Beyoncé and "ghetto booties" also demonstrates that the term "ghetto" is a commonly agreed-on term that whites in this community use uncritically to refer to black people, black spaces, and black culture. Generally, this racialized term means people, spaces, and culture that whites view as unfavorable and beneath them. For example, in other instances, Sheridan children refer to something as "so ghetto," such as a decrepit basketball court or playground in disrepair. Parents refer to "ghetto talk" when discussing black children's speech, as one mother demonstrates: "What I like about the few black families that do live in [Sheridan] is that they don't fall into that stereotypical, um, you know, place of an African American which is the ghetto talk, the baggy clothes. If you were to put a picture up of a stereotypical kid, you know, what someone might envision, they don't fall into that." In a similar vein, the term "Afro" is commonly used negatively to describe unwanted humidity-induced curly white hair. In one child's words, "Ugh. I need to straighten my hair. This weather is turning it into a giant Afro!" followed by her mother saying, "Well, then, go straighten it and stop complaining!" The use of terms such as "ghetto" or "Afro" may seem harmless to some of these parents, but as used, they contain and transmit commonsense, agreed-on, subtle racial meaning and are employed in ways to denote difference, disgust, dismissal, or apathy toward black people. Much as school and neighborhood choices are part of the racial context

of childhood for Sheridan children, so too are the everyday subtle behaviors and talk that occur between parents and children about topics
connected to race and, of course, the interactions that take place between
children themselves, such as when they laugh together and "shake their
ghetto booties" at the private pool.

Coaching Soccer and Parent Leadership

While sometimes parents stay on the sidelines, other times they play a
more central role in the operations of extracurricular activities. Perhaps
the most popular extracurricular activity in this community, regardless of
gender, age, or skill level, is soccer.[12] It seems as if most kids in this community, at least at some point or another, have played soccer. Similarly,
many of the parents with whom I spoke play, or have played in the past,
an active role in their child's soccer world, whether it be as a coach, an
assistant coach, or a highly involved parent who brings oranges to the
games and orders the trophies at the end of the season. Even parents who
are not directly involved typically agree to transport their child across the
city, or even region, attending practices and games, washing sweaty shin
guards and removing dried pieces of mud dragged in on soccer cleats
from inside their SUVs. Only one parent in the entire study told me that
she outright despises the hectic world of extracurricular activities, complaining in particular about the demands of soccer: "Frankly, I'm not a
fan of extracurriculars. . . . Like, the parents I'm friends with tend to be
more like me, where they are like, 'Uggggggggghhhh, going to *another*
soccer game. *Again.* It's happening *a lot.* Ugggh!' . . . Also, *no.* I am *not*
fund-raising." This mom may have friends who think similarly, but many
parents in the Petersfield area, even if they privately dread the weekend
sacrifice of soccer game after soccer game or the inevitable fund-raising
efforts they are personally asked to supervise, are very much invested in
their child's soccer life.

Soccer fields are where some important racial dynamics play out
in the Petersfield area. As such, what goes on here is often discussed
back at home between children and parents. In addition, parents talk
to each other on the sidelines about the players, the kids interact with
each other, and everyone interacts with new kids and adults from other
places, especially when the team is a "traveling" team, which many

are. Many youth soccer teams are segregated. As one parent explains, "We have an integrated school, but we choose to be on soccer teams that are all white." In fact, many of the parents in Petersfield describe this dynamic, including Raymond, a parent who also volunteers as a soccer coach.[13] Raymond is proud of the fact that his team is one of the more diverse teams in the city: "We had the most racially diverse soccer team. . . . It was actually a very good, positive racially mixed experience. . . . Everyone had a great time. . . . We had two or three Hispanic kids, we had five or six black kids." Yet, although Raymond is proud of the diversity of the kids on the team, he has negative comments about the black kids' behavior that he believes is the result of his perception of a lack of father figures in these children's lives: "Coaching them was hard because it's like you're coaching a bunch of kids whose parents never say no to them. Some of them don't have fathers who care about their kids. And then you're out there saying, 'Look! If you want to play soccer, you've gotta listen to your coach. You've got to stop screwing around.' And you know, you actually try to lay down the law with some of these kids for whom it is never laid down." Despite Raymond's dedication to coaching a diverse team, he draws on cultural racism and stereotypes about absent black fathers who "don't care about their kids" as he makes sense of the behavior of the black boys on the soccer team. In addition, when he tells me that it is "actually a very good, positive racially mixed experience," he conveys his surprise, as if he expected some other result. All of these thoughts are shared with me but also with his son, who sits next to him on the couch.

However, in spite of these negative assumptions and common racist tropes about black families and the behavior of black boys that Raymond easily draws on, when the kids on his team are faced with blatant forms of racism from kids on an opposing team, he takes a different stance. "There were players on the team that wouldn't shake hands with [our black and Latino players]. *And* the coaches didn't do anything about it. If I were the coach, they all would have been *done*. . . . The coach should have been strung up basically [*laughing*]." Not noticing his own use of a lynching metaphor, Raymond tells me how he stood up to the other coach in front of the kids. He reassured his athletes that they were great, and he tells me how he tried to help the kids make sense of what had happened. The kids also talked to each other about it, sharing ideas about why this team was so discriminatory and what they could do to stand up for each other when bad things happened to one of them in the future. On the one hand, Raymond infuses his own racial logic into soccer practice and games, viewing himself as the man who needs to step in and act like a father figure to the black boys on the team. But, on the other hand, he also helps cultivate an extracurricular environment that does not stand for explicit expressions of racism and is willing to challenge other coaches and children who behave in discriminatory ways, modeling a particular form of antiracist behavior to all the kids on their team and other teams.

Parents also serve as Girl Scout troop leaders, hockey coaches, cross-country coaches, and parent volunteers with after-school activities, such as tutoring, selling hot dogs at the concession stand at basketball games, or coordinating the science and technology team. One father, Seth, explains to me that he is working to make the science and technology team at his daughter's school more inclusive, an endeavor that is more complicated work than Seth appears to recognize: "How racially diverse is this? It's not. And that's something that a few of us are spending some of our time working on," he tells me.[14] Because his daughter's team, which he coaches, has achieved such a high level of success in competitions across the region, the team was recently invited to visit a group of low-income kids in a major city to present their work and try to encourage the kids in this program to want to participate in similar science and technology programs.

> Our team was very excited, and it was a *wild* environment because here you are, taking these Petersfield kids—and we have some economic diversity on our team, but for the most part, it is top heavy on the upper classes—and bringing them where they have to go through metal detectors and past armed guards into this environment. And I was *never* more proud of my kids than when I was seeing them do this and just, you know, what they were able to accomplish and how proud they were at what they were doing and how they were doing it and reaching out and being part of trying to bring new people into science and technology. I've been trying to work in the city to try and get more funding and support too, so that we can get the Boys and Girls Clubs more involved. So there are efforts to do this, and the kids see it. . . . The majority of

learning and activity doesn't happen at school. It happens in enrichment programs.

Because of the race and class privilege of parents such as Seth and the power that comes with it, when they desire a more diverse team, in large part for the benefit of their own kids' exposure to kids of color, they believe they can orchestrate it—and they can. Seth can insert his child into almost any environment, including one that is predominantly black, with metal detectors and armed guards in an economically marginalized neighborhood. It is unlikely that this would be as easily accomplished if roles were reversed. Parents of children of color may also want more diverse spaces for their kids or access to better resources such as top-notch science and technology clubs, but they are not always able to cultivate what they want for their child as easily as parents such as Seth due to race and class barriers. Of course, Seth is doing work that is meaningful, not only in the lives of the white, affluent children on his science and technology team but also for the black girls whom he recruits to join them, encouraging them to pursue science and connecting these kids with real resources. As this example shows, privileged white parents face a conundrum: they risk becoming either opportunity hoarders or white saviors. But perhaps there are other options. For instance, none of the white parents in this study even consider bringing parents of kids of color into the fold to join them in coordinating or leading extracurricular activities.

Parents Observing Kids

Finally, parents also observe their own children in action during theater productions, art shows, music concerts, track meets, and even online, and they base future conversations about race with their kids on what they see. Parents tell me that they learn a lot about their own child through watching her or him interact with other kids in both formal and informal extracurricular spaces—and in comparing how their child acts at school events in comparison to play dates. For instance, Tom tells me that as his daughter, Charlotte, gets older, he notices her socializing with kids of color at school events but far less so in informal spaces outside of school:

I feel like when Charlotte was younger, I sort of wonder if there is an age where suddenly . . . there is more of a racial separation that takes place [between the kids]. I wonder if it's just Charlotte, but I talk to other parents and they notice it too. I think, "Who do I know of the people who are her friends that she used to see more of that she doesn't now?" . . . So when she is bored and complaining about being stuck in the house, I'll say, "Call somebody new up!! These three people [that you always hang out with] are the only three people you can play with?!" Her friend Alana she used to go see a lot more, and, um, Khayla, she used to hang out with—they are both black. It's like, you know, what is driving that split?

Tom wants his daughter to have interracial friendships, as he himself credits much of his own understanding of race to his own interracial friendships that he has had throughout his life. He tells me that he pays attention to what he observes at school events or during extracurricular activities and observes the relationships Charlotte appears to have with other kids.

I'm sitting at . . . a big school family fun night, which is a way of torturing parents. . . . They are running around, and I see her being friendly with [black peers]. Or at her . . . chorus performances, just last time she was standing next to an African American girl, and the two of them were giggling, laughing, having a grand old time the whole time. So I certainly wasn't seeing that separation there. . . . I'm watching in those sort of natural settings. I'm seeing her having friends that are black. . . . I look at her Facebook stuff, and she has tons of friends who are black, tons. So I don't know.

Tom thinks that these relationships will help Charlotte think more carefully about race, different people's experiences, and her own privileged upbringing.

Part of the challenge that parents such as Tom face is that there are deep structural inequalities that make equal-status contact challenging and many times counterproductive to their goals, as previously discussed. Given how race and class map onto each other in this community, creating equal-status interactions is difficult when the white children here almost always have more economic resources than the black children here do. But it is through observing children in extracurricular spaces that parents gain insights into some of the racial dynamics of their children's lives, particularly with respect to peers. These observations of one's own child, much like racial dynamics on the soccer field or current events in the media, lead to future everyday discussions in the private realm of the white home about race.

"It Was Racism"

White Kids on Race

One Saturday morning, I sit in a coffee shop with Meredith (12, Sheridan) and her mother, Veronica Chablis. Veronica and I are drinking coffee while Meredith stirs the whipped cream on top of her hot chocolate with her pointer finger, periodically licking her finger and sticking it back in the cup. I ask Meredith if she has ever witnessed an act of racism firsthand. Given the strong, resounding "No" that I typically hear from kids growing up in Sheridan, I am taken aback when she says, "Yes." Meredith goes on to tell me a story:

> I remember one time I was at [a liquor store in Petersfield] with my mom about a year ago, and there was a bunch of black guys in front of us. And only two of them out of the three or four, I think, had an ID, but they were obviously like 45. But the guy wouldn't let them buy the one bottle of liquor. So they were like, "Oh fine, man," and then they left. And then my mom and I were there, and she was getting her bottle of merlot or whatever, and [the cashier] didn't even ask her for an ID. He was just like, "Okay, you're done." And we went outside and I heard [the black men] talking near their car about white trash and saying all this stuff [about the white cashier].

Meredith's mother suddenly interrupts Meredith's story. "Um, but I think when you buy something at the liquor store, all the people that are in your party need to show—" Meredith interrupts her mother in return, angrily. "Those guys were *not* even standing near the register! And I was with you! And I'm not 21!" Her mother rolls her eyes and replies in a condescending tone, "Okay, honey. If you say so." This sets Meredith off emotionally; she grabs her cell phone and stomps off to the bathroom. She is gone for the next 10 minutes. Her mother goes on to tell me that this is just one of her most recent "teenage antics" and says, "God only know what I have in store for the future." With a look in her eye that seems to suggest that she believes we certainly agree on the matter of Meredith's story and trying to smooth things over, Veronica says, "Of course the cashier wasn't being racist! I mean, come on, you know? How ridiculous."

Later, when Veronica is not around, Meredith insists that her version of the story is accurate; something "was not right" in that interaction, she tells me. "It was racism. And sometimes my mom is racist and tries to pretend like she isn't. . . . My mom just hates talking about that stuff," she confides in me with frustration.

* * *

What do affluent, white kids actually think about race, racism, inequality, and privilege? After I spent nearly two years talking with and observing kids in their everyday worlds, similarities in how these kids make sense of race emerged as well as some patterned distinctions between groupings of kids. These patterns are striking and demonstrate that although these kids share understandings of race with each other in some instances, meaningful differences in how kids think about race also exist—differences that correspond with the racial contexts of childhood constructed by these kids' parents. These kids do not simply reproduce the ideas of their parents; rather, they formulate their own ideas, as Meredith does in the preceding example, drawing on interactions in and observations of their racial context of childhood. Taking seriously the voices and perspectives of these kids, this chapter explores the patterns in what these white, affluent kids actually say about race, racism, inequality, and privilege.

Understandings of "Race": Defining the Concept and White Fragility

Kids growing up in Sheridan, Evergreen, and Wheaton Hills explain that race is defined in terms of *physical appearance* and/or *where people come from*. I ask each of them, "If a 5-year-old asked you what 'race' means, what would you say?" William (12, Evergreen) replies, "Skin tone, maybe like facial looks, hair color." Edward (12, Sheridan) says, "Like the type of their skin." Similarly, Kelsey (13, Sheridan) explains, "Just differences in appearance and stuff like that." Moving away from the color of skin, Kacie (13, Wheaton Hills) replies, "Okay, that's a tricky question. I would say, I would say, probably, um, that's hard. Um, probably like they're—I guess I would be, like, their family background and what countries their parents are from, I dunno, kinda like that." And in a similar way, Danny (12, Evergreen) responds, "I would say to the kid, 'A long, long, long time ago, different people came from different areas, and that's what determines race because it's not by personality, it's not by looks. It's by their background from a long time ago basically." Some of the kids connect place of origin with language or accent. For instance, Erica (13, Sheridan) states, "Africans Americans used to like, when they're from Africa, they speak a different language. Like in Africa. And they—and it sounds like Rihanna's got an accent almost." Here Erica explains that language or accent is an indicator of race because it is an indicator of "where someone is from."

Appearance and Origin

As the preceding quotes illustrate, "race" is understood by many kids as linked to one's skin color and/or one's country of origin, however that might be conceptualized. This is the first major theme with regard to shared meanings of race. For some kids, both of these definitions are important. For instance, Tyler (10, Evergreen) blends these two definitions together: "Um, it's when, like, there's a—it's hard to explain for me. Ahh. I think it's when there—well, there's a normal—they are normal kids. But it's just they have a different color skin that's like darker. Or lighter. Because they came from, like, a different country." The pronoun "they" in Tyler's statement is defined in comparison to whites, evinced by his comment about a "different color skin that's like darker," presumably different from pink or white skin color. To Tyler, to be a person of color in the United States means that one is not essentially "from" the United States. Rather, people of color are from other countries, while whites are from the United States. He talks about everyone as being normal, but the way he talks about it suggests that kids of color "are normal but" rather than just "normal." Here, Tyler puts whiteness at the "normative center," a pattern that sociologists studying whiteness have observed.[1]

Interestingly, Tyler quickly adds, "Or lighter," to his comments, almost as if he has caught himself saying something "wrong."

Tyler is not alone. These children all make sense of race in similar ways. For instance, Aaron (11, Wheaton Hills) explains the approach he would take to talking with a 5-year-old:

> I think I would steer away from talking about the color of skin, because . . . you have the white, and then you have, you know, Latino, which is less white, and then you have Indian populations, and, you know, Spanish, and they're less white but still white. And then you have, you know, African Americans, who are even less white. . . . I think when people are talking about, like, the race of African Americans, they're taking into account the color of their skin, even though when you think of an African American, you don't think that they're originally from Africa way back when. You think that their skin is black. So I don't really know. . . . Usually what I go by is their skin color. But since, you know, it's more of a less-white/more-white thing, it's kind of a difficult gauge. But I guess that is how I would explain it.

Like Tyler, the unmarked racial category here, or the "normal" category to which all other categories are compared, is "white." Aaron suggests that he believes racial categories are determined based on one's proximity to whiteness—that there is a "less white, more white" gauge that people use to determine where one fits within the classification system. And while Aaron begins by suggesting he would *not* use skin color as a way to explain race to a 5-year-old, by the end of his response, he is doing exactly that.

Simon (11, Wheaton Hills) also blends together these two definitions of skin color and family origin but makes a nuanced point about why he believes that it is "more racially sensitive" to talk about origin rather than skin color when discussing human difference: "Races typically have some [particular shared] skin colors, so you could say that. Like, people who have dark skin are African Americans. They're—that's their race. . . . But it's—I think it's a little more racially sensitive to say it as where they come from rather than their skin color. Like, you're being—you're not, like, making fun of them in any way. You're not calling them different, currently. They're not currently different. They're—

they originated from a different country, but, like, they're not just—right now they're not different than you in any way." By noticing skin color, a white person acknowledges difference between oneself and the person of color, making the person of color "currently different," which can quickly lead to "making fun of them," according to Simon. In order not to make people feel "currently different" and not to make fun of them, Simon argues that, instead, one should focus on how "right now they're not different than you in any way," even if they were different from you in the past. To Simon, while human difference exists, it does so only in relation to the past; today everyone is the same. To talk about difference today is to "make fun of people." This logic maps onto color-blind ideology and the frame of the "minimization of racism," though with a small twist.[2] Here, Simon reworks color-blind ideology in a way, suggesting that of course race is something he notices in his everyday life but that it is better to attribute differences in skin color to differences in the past rather than in the present.

Defining Race Is a Racist Act

Many of the kids growing up in Sheridan and those who attend parochial school take Simon's point to an extreme. Jessica (11, Wheaton Hills), who attends parochial school and lives in an almost exclusively white world, explains about race: "[It is] where you come from and just, I dunno, just in general, *who you are as a person instead of who you are just by your features*, you know?" (emphasis added). One reading of this statement is that Jessica has some kind of essentialist understanding of race—that to be a particular race means that you are therefore a particular kind of person. But an alternative reading is that Jessica is rigorously engaging color-blind ideology here: she does not want to tell me that race is based on "features" because she thinks it is racist to talk about someone's physical differences. Instead, she wants me to know that what really matters is "who you are as a person." Similarly, Adam (11, Sheridan) tells me, "Sometimes [race] is facial features. Like, people from the East, like China and Japan, their eyes are slightly different, *which I don't judge them for*. It's just something I've noticed" (emphasis added). Here, Adam immediately wants me to know that while he notices these physical differences between himself and people from East Asia, he is not attaching negative meaning to this comment. He is guarding himself in this moment, anticipating that because he is talking openly about physical differences that he notices, he may be accused of being racist.

In Sheridan—and in the parochial schools—kids believe that it is racist to talk about race. Even defining the concept of race is potentially racist. They believe that no one in their community is racist, and the best evidence for this is that nobody talks about race. Natalie (11, Sheridan) explains her logic: "When you notice the color of a person's skin, you're stereotyping. Like, if you put a label on somebody, like their skin color, that's race. And that's bad." Natalie believes that "race" and "racism" are synonymous—that to identify someone as "black" is to be racist, just as identifying someone as "white" is also racist. This is of course the logical outcome of color-blind ideology: kids who have been told that they should not recognize racial difference feel bad that they do. Yet, of course, when adults are not around or when they forget that I am present or even at other moments in the very same interview, they speak openly about race. They gossip at sleepovers, they debate Rihanna's race, and they argue over whether black athletes have extra muscles in their legs. While they know they are not supposed to talk about race because doing so is "racist," they talk about race all the time. Meanwhile, their peers in Evergreen and Wheaton Hills who attend public school, the gifted school, or the social justice school reject this notion that to talk about race is to be racist altogether. "That makes no sense," Conor (11, Evergreen) tells me when I ask him about it.

White Fragility in Youth

Being called a "racist" "for real" instead of "just as a joke" is the worst possible insult a white kid in Petersfield can receive, kids tells me. As Charlotte (13, Evergreen) puts it, "No one wants to be considered racist." These kids demonstrate what the education scholar Robin DiAngelo defines as "white fragility, or "a state in which even a minimum amount of racial stress becomes intolerable" and leads to, among other things, silence.[3] And this is precisely what emerges as a second theme across kids growing up in different contexts: all of the children express some anxiety when talking about race, even when the conversation is about the definition of the concept of race alone, disentangled for a moment from the more controversial topics of how race works in the United States. Simply talking about "race" means creating "racial stress."

When asked what "race" means, the kids across the sample either respond in quick partial sentences or stumble over their words. They often end up with a conclusion that contradicts their initial point, which indicates that they are not particularly confident in their answers. In research with college students and adults, Eduardo Bonilla-Silva has observed similar increases in repetitive phrases such as "um" and roundabout descriptions of topics tied to race that are ultimately incomprehensible. He labels this speech pattern "rhetorical incoherence" and discusses how this rhetorical pattern increases when whites discuss a sensitive topic such as race.[4] My data suggest that this rhetorical incoherence is tied to white fragility and occurs well before white youth enter college. This pattern of speech for the kids in my study is evident in middle school and perhaps even earlier. Even when asked to talk about race in a creative way such as by looking at photographs of celebrities or thinking about how to talk to a young child about this concept, almost all of the kids in this research express some form of anxiety and discomfort in responding. Those who are not uncomfortable talking about race mention that most of their peers are. This theme of white fragility, then, is common across the children regardless of meaningful differences in their experiences based on the context in which they grow up.

Racialized Emotions Underlying Fragility

Variations in the motivations underlying white fragility emerge and are evident when I talk directly with the kids about their feelings. Kids in Sheridan do not want to be seen as racist, which is why they tell me that they do not talk about race or at least reserve that talk for private spaces where they do not think their talk will be noticed or judged, or the "backstage region."[5] For instance, when I ask kids in Sheridan, such as Kelsey (13, Sheridan), to look at photos of celebrities and tell me what race they are, she refuses. Instead, she says, "Um, I kinda feel kind of racist." I ask her why. She replies, "Because I'm just, like, categorizing them by the color of their skin, and I don't think that's right." Some Sheridan kids are willing to participate in the activity but do so halfheartedly and express awkwardness that requires me to change course within the interview. When I ask these kids why they feel so uncomfortable, their response is consistent: they are scared of me thinking they are racist.

A few Sheridan children perk up when I invite them to look at the photographs. Although the mother of Britney (11, Sheridan) tells me how proud she is that her daughter "does not even see [race]," Britney happily goes through the photographs of the celebrities, pointing excitedly to each picture and stating the name and the race of the people. When she gets to the photo of Malia and Sasha Obama, she pauses for moment, pondering over who they are. "Oh! I know who these are!" she finally exclaims. "These are Michael Jackson's sons!" When I tell her who they really are, she looks at me and starts laughing so hard it is difficult for her to compose herself. Here, the façade of color blindness that defines the Sheridan community quickly crumbles as Britney is of course able to racially classify people such as Beyoncé and Taylor Swift.

Kids in Wheaton Hills and Evergreen also express anxiety associated with white fragility. But, unlike the kids in Sheridan, kids in Wheaton Hills and Evergreen are worried about saying something that will hurt the feelings of a person of color. Because these children are growing up in more heterogeneous contexts, they have developed an awareness of the ways that white kids often *do* hurt the feelings of kids of color. They tell me that they are scared they might unintentionally do this and therefore avoid talking about race in particular moments. For instance, Anthony (12, Evergreen) states, "If someone calls me white, I don't mind, but if I call somebody else black, it gives me a very uneasy feeling. And I don't know if black kids get that feeling if they call somebody white, . . . but it just makes me feel kind of embarrassed and weird and just uncomfortable if I use anything like that because I wouldn't want black kids to think I am trying to hurt them. If someone's race comes up, I probably just choose not to talk about it." Similarly, Charlotte tells me that while she is comfortable talking about race because her parents talk about it all the time, she thinks her peers are less comfortable, particularly her white peers at her diverse public middle school. Charlotte and I talk at length about why white kids are so fearful of talking about race. She explains, "Well, I think they don't really want to be perceived as a snobby, white kid, you know what I mean? They just don't want to be perceived as those kind of kids who are rich and can say and do whatever they want. . . . So people just don't talk about it."

Anthony and Charlotte refer to what DiAngelo calls "entitlement to racial comfort." This is the idea that whites are unaccustomed to feeling discomfort in connection to race or racial matters, and when they do, they "insis[t] on racial comfort, [which] ensures that racism will not be faced."[6] Yet patterns suggest that Sheridan kids and Petersfield kids are motivated by different reasons to disengage in uncomfortable scenarios. Kids such as Anthony and Charlotte do not want to talk about race because they do not want to make a peer of color feel bad or "hurt them," which will, in turn, make them feel bad and will establish that they are, in fact, "racist." For kids such as Natalie and Kelsey, though, kids growing up in a very segregated white environment, they do not believe they are racist or ever could be racist, and their primary concern is protecting that sense of moral superiority and defending themselves against any possible accusations of racism. In simple terms, while none of the kids in this study want to be perceived by their peers or the adults in their lives as "racist" for reasons connected to their own self-images, Sheridan kids believe they are immune to racism, while Evergreen and Wheaton Hills kids believe they are susceptible.

Overall, when it comes to interpretations of the concept of "race," the white kids in this study generally (1) agree that race is based on appearance and/or "where you are from" and (2) share some degree of discomfort in talking about the definition of race openly. However, important variations on this theme also emerge, and these variations reflect different racial contexts of childhood that these kids find themselves growing up within.

Understandings of Racism

Despite sharing similar forms of race and class privilege, despite occupying similar positions within a racialized social system, and despite some shared understandings about the definition of "race," important variations in what these affluent, white kids think about *racism* surface. These patterns offer empirical insights into the powerful role that one's unique racial context of childhood, derived from a bundled set of choices made by one's parents, play in shaping—though not determining—how kids makes sense of racism in the United States. While kids in Wheaton Hills and Evergreen on occasion identify racism as existing at the structural level, many of the kids in this study believe that racism operates exclusively at the individual level and in overt ways. To many of these kids, racism is when people, no matter what race they are, act in ways that are "mean," "bad," or "rude" toward people who are a different race. And this is true across racial contexts. For instance, William tells me that racism is when "people mak[e] fun of another race for not really any reason at all, just to kind of be mean." Similarly, Erica explains to me that "racism is when, if you walk down the street and you see people of different colors, maybe you think about how they must be bad. And so you just go, automatically, to things being bad." Logan (13, Wheaton Hills) tells me, "It's when somebody says something like rude or not true about like different-colored people." For these kids, racism is when someone acts in a negative way toward someone else because of the color of the other person's skin.[7]

Although kids in Wheaton Hills and Evergreen understand racism in individualized terms, many of these kids also draw on words they learn at school, such as "stereotype" and "discrimination." Margot (12, Evergreen) explains, "In third grade, we talked about stereotypes, . . . but we don't anymore. But it's like stuck in my brain. When I hear [people say] things [that I think include a stereotype], I'm like, 'That's a stereotype! That's stereotypical!' I know a lot about them. . . . And we learned about discrimination and how people like discriminate once they have the stereotypes in their head." Margot's discussion of stereotypes and discrimination, which other kids also bring up, demonstrates that she understands that racism is not just about one white person randomly being mean to a person of color but that larger ideas and myths about race operate in American society. Because a number of Evergreen children tell me similar things and talk about learning this material at school, it seems that this way of framing racism is likely part of the formal curriculum at Evergreen's elementary schools—that racism is about affect, behavior, and cognition at the individual level rather than the ideological sphere of a racialized social system that serves to justify and maintain the racial status quo.

Drawing on rhetoric similar to that of Dr. Martin Luther King Jr., many of the children also tell me that they have learned about the word "prejudice" in school. Emily (13, Wheaton Hills) explains, "Racism is when people judge you because you're from a certain place." Her little sister, Rachel (12, Wheaton Hills), adds, "Or, like, bias or prejudice, based on, like, your race."

But kids in Sheridan do not have access to the jargon used by their peers in the city. While all of the kids struggle to talk about race, this is especially true for Sheridan kids, as they stumble over words and consistently insert laughter into their statements, such as Rosie (10, Sheridan): "I'd probably say racism is, um, just a bunch of people who kinda don't like—it's kinda hard to explain!! [*Laughing*] Um, it's—I'd probably just explain it, like, racism . . . just a bunch of people who I guess don't really feel comfortable with other races, I guess? I would say. And just don't agree with their [*laughing*] customs or something. I've never really been around people who are racist, so I don't really have an answer to this but I don't—I guess they wouldn't be as outright friendly to them. I don't know." For many of the kids growing up in Sheridan with parents who embrace color-blind narratives, they have limited tools to talk about race and very little practice doing so with adults. Of course, these kids still do talk about race with each other all the time.

Another way that the kids in Evergreen and Wheaton Hills complicate individual-level understandings of racism is to offer scenarios in which they think racism likely occurs—scenarios that suggest societal patterns. For instance, Ashley (10, Evergreen) talks about potential racism at restaurants: "If you were, like, maybe, like, at a restaurant or something, um, like, maybe the way a customer would treat a waiter if he was black, 'cause if they were racist like that. Like, they would be disrespectful and just expect them to, like, do everything for you." Ashley tells me that she has observed white people mistreat servers of color at restaurants before, though she does not go into any detail about who she has seen behave in this way. Charlotte similarly presents a scenario of potential racism when shopping or at school:

Sometimes teachers or when you are out places like shopping, people think, sometimes how you dress, like if you wear really skimpy clothes *and* you're black or Hispanic, *then* they may treat you differently. But if a black person is wearing a suit and tie and walks in there, I don't think they will treat them any differently. But I think if they look trashy, even if they're not, *and* if they are black or Hispanic and wearing trashy clothes, then people are going to treat them differently. 'Cause I don't think it *just* has to do with race. It's a combination. I think it also has to do with people's judgmental perception of them right away. . . . I mean, white people could wear whatever they want [and not be treated differently].

Charlotte believes that race works in combination with things such as social class or the kinds of clothes people wear that reflect class. When I ask her if she has observed this kind of thing happen before, she says she has.

William also talks about how he thinks race works in combination with how someone talks: "Sometimes people, like, sorta think of the other race, if they have an accent or if they spoke a different language before and are trying to get into the new language, are *dumb* and, like, they, like—even though the person can, like, understand everything and speaks pretty well and can do everything, like, sometimes [the white person will], like, speak really loudly and clearly and that kind of thing, which can discourage them." William tells me that he has observed this happen before, usually between adults.

These examples illustrate that kids pick up on racial dynamics in their local community when they are out to dinner or at the mall or watching adults interact with one another. These kids believe these moments are indicative of the prevalence of racism in their everyday lives. This lies in stark contrast with children in Sheridan, most of whom tell me that racism does not exist and that they cannot think of any examples of racism in their own lives.

Another variation on understandings of explicit forms of racism includes discussions of formal hate groups, particularly the Ku Klux Klan, which most children think exist primarily in the South. As Aaron poses to me rhetorically, "Isn't the KKK still around? If the KKK is still around, obviously we still have racism." Similarly, Danny says, "As you go farther south, [racism] is going to be more present just because of what happened in the past. Um, like, racism was more present there than it was in the northern states, so it's still going to leave its effects and it's still going to be present." Many other kids articulate something similar—they assume that most racist individuals and organizations are in the South, rather than in the Midwest, where they live. Robert (12, Wheaton Hills) talks in more concrete terms about recent hate crimes: "I heard about this guy somewhere in the South who was burning one of the Muslim holy books because there's, like, people who don't like Muslims because of the terrorist attacks, and, like, they think everyone who is Muslim is a terrorist so . . . I also heard about people, like white supremacist groups or something, who don't like dark-skinned people." Drawing on individual- and group-level examples, Robert describes what he perceives to be evidence of racism in the United States. Unlike many of the other kids who reference hate groups abstractly, Robert speaks in concrete terms about one particular act of white supremacy and Islamophobia, which indicates his awareness of ongoing racial hate in the United States today.

Emily and her sister, Rachel, also talk with me about the prevalence of racism today:

> EMILY: I think [racism] still happens, like the Ku Klux Klan and stuff, but—
> RACHEL: I think it's definitely a problem. I think it's—
> EMILY: Yeah, it's better though.
> RACHEL: Well . . .
> EMILY: Like it used to be . . .
> RACHEL: Yeah.
> EMILY: . . . well, like slavery—
> RACHEL: I mean, it's better then since then, definitely. But, I mean, there have been—I've heard about, like, surveys and stuff about, where, like, people, like, will see, like, a black person walking down the street, and they'll, like—are automatically, like, assume, like, stuff.

While Emily identifies the KKK as a site of racism, Rachel pushes back against her sister slightly, bringing up a discussion of surveys that measure racial bias as evidence that racism is found not only in the formalized white-supremacist organization of the KKK but also in "normal" white society. (I find out later that Rachel's school, the gifted school where kids gather around the teacher to look up interesting facts on the Internet, has been doing a unit on implicit attitudes, and the kids have learned about implicit-attitude tests that measure subjective forms of racial bias.)

> RACHEL: And, I mean, there are, like—kids today seem to think it's, like, kind of funny to say and do racist things. Like, I know people

who, like, pretend to be black and stuff, because they think it's, like, funny or something.

MAGGIE: How do they pretend to "be black"? Like, what do they do?

RACHEL: They just, like, talk, like, gangster or whatever [*rolling her eyes*].

EMILY: Or if, like, if they're, like, sagging [their pants] way below their butt. I might judge black kids for that, but I would do that if they were white too, like, pretending to be black.

Rachel carries on, without acknowledging her sister.

RACHEL: So, I mean, I think, in the, like, exact environment that we've been in, it's, like, really, like, not seen so much as a problem because, like, I find our school to be, like, a really, like, open and accepting kind of place. But I feel like it still is a big problem in other environments, like, more so. Even other environments here in Petersfield.

EMILY: Um, well, I *personally* feel like, today, there are a lot of people who *aren't* racist and who, when they see, like, someone walking down the street who has a different skin color, they *don't* automatically think, "Oh, he's trouble."

RACHEL: [*Sighing*] No, Emily. I think it's—like, I think there are some people who are racist. There are, like, individuals who are. And a lot of times, I feel like those people who have, like, really strong opinions about stuff like that, they can end up being, like, really, like, smart, powerful people who make decisions. And I think it can still have an effect on the environment that they function in. Because, like, if they have strong opinions that they're trying to promote, then it can usually have an effect on other people.

EMILY: Maybe.

Rachel, unlike many of her peers who think racist people are, in the kids' words, "stupid," "live in the South," and are "hicks" or "country boys," believes that many smart and powerful people, like herself, have the potential to possess strongly held racist beliefs. She identifies the racism of privileged people as especially troubling in that she believes people in positions of power can make decisions rooted in racism that "have an effect on the environment that they function in." Rachel suggests that powerful people with racist views can spread these views more successfully because they have the resources to "promote" these views. Her sister disagrees with her, making a case for color blindness instead, though by the end of their discussion, Emily seems to be open to the possibility that perhaps her sister is onto something.

Overall, the kids talk about racism as though it exists primarily at the individual level, a clear theme in my interviews. However, there are variations between kids growing up in the context of Sheridan versus Wheaton Hills and Evergreen. The kids in Sheridan have very simplistic explanations of this phenomenon and tell me racism happens very infrequently in the United States, if at all, while the kids from Evergreen and Wheaton Hills build on these individual understandings and tell me they think racism is less of a problem than in the past but more common today than many people want to acknowledge. These kids introduce concepts such as the intersection of race and class, how language and accents relate to acts of racism, the existence of surveys that measure subjective racial bias, the existence of hate groups, and how people in positions of power who make decisions that affect lots of people can be racist just like the "country boy" living in the South or in a rural part of the state. In these ways, many kids growing up in Wheaton Hills and Evergreen understand racism as existing beyond simply the individual level.

Understandings of Institutional Racism and Racial Inequality

Children in Wheaton Hills and Evergreen also talk about racism operating at the institutional level. Specifically, these kids identify three institutions that they think are racist: the criminal justice system, government laws and policies, and the economy vis-à-vis the racial wealth gap.

Chris (11, Wheaton Hills) perceives racism to exist beyond the hurtful things white kids say to kids of color and outside of the KKK. The example that Chris brings up is the criminal justice system: "Well, I think that the white kids, since they have more power, just, in general, in society, for reasons I don't know, I think that, you know, disciplinary actions aren't brought down as hard upon them. But when it's, you know, a black kid getting in trouble with the police, . . . I think people are going to be tougher with them, because, you know, they can't really fight back as well. I think they're just punished worse for [similar behavior as white kids]." Chris openly acknowledges the power that white kids wield, particularly when it comes to discipline and punishment. While the kids in Evergreen tell me about the "no hoods up" rule that they believe is disproportionately applied to their black peers on the basis of what they observe at school, Chris tells me that he does not actually observe this kind of behavior at his own school. But he tells me that he has heard of similar things happening in the Petersfield community as kids interact with police officers. Here Chris articulates an understanding of how power is distributed to the top of our racial hierarchy in the United States through institutions such as the criminal justice system and the education system, when it comes to school discipline. He acknowledges that kids like him, kids who are white, "have more power in society," a comment with which Chris's peers in Sheridan would strongly disagree.

Andrew (12, Wheaton Hills) gives a concrete example of the point Chris makes:

> If you're black walking down the street at night with, like, a bag or something, like a really full bag, then [the police] would, compared with a white person walking down the street at night with a bag, they would probably target—if they had to choose between the two—they would probably choose the black person. . . . It kind of is just a circle. *Because* they are bringing so many blacks in jail because they're the ones [the police] choose to catch and because they catch them, there are more blacks in jail, which makes [the police] think, "Oh, the black person probably did it, rather than the white person." So they go again, and it just circles and continues, I guess.

Andrew draws on an individual-level example of a police interaction—that is, an officer choosing to target the black person over the white person, using race to inform that decision. But he does not leave this explanation at the individual level. Instead, he acknowledges that because these interactional-level choices of whom to arrest are perpetrated over and over again by the police, this leads to "circles" of who gets incarcerated and who is left alone. In his own way, Andrew talks about the police as part of an institution with the power to shape the demographics of our country's incarcerated population.

Lindsay (11, Wheaton Hills), the child who left public school because of racism, also tells me that she thinks that the color of your skin determines how people in positions of authority, such as teachers and cops, treat you as a kid. She tells me more stories about the black boys and girls at her old public school. In addition to teachers being "rude" and "racist" to her peers of color, she also saw the kids get arrested: "One time during recess, they just got taken away by the police—right in front of everybody—and then another time too, when they thought the one kid had a BB gun on them. The police just arrest them, and [the kids] don't even get a chance to say anything. It's not fair. It's like—they just think that is how it should work." Lindsay is confident that the adults at her old school were racist. But she identifies the behavior of police officers as racist and "unfair" to the black students too. From her vantage point, both the teachers and cops at her school were part of the same system of controlling the black second and third graders, meanwhile letting white kids get away with whatever they wanted. In her mind, these patterns speak to something larger than just one bad teacher or cop—and, of course, this is why her parents opted to remove her from this school. While she does not talk explicitly about policing as an institution, her comments suggest that she perceives a larger agreed-on approach that teachers and cops use to discipline black and brown kids.

William agrees that the police are unfair to black children. "I feel like sometimes police are a little more aggressive toward black people," he tells me. He then shares a story about his older brother getting picked up by the police for possession of marijuana and how his brother "did not get punished as bad, probably because he was white." William's dad happens to be nearby as we discuss this incident. He briefly joins our conversation and then returns to this later in my interview with him. He tells me how when he went before the judge with his son, he was aware of his status as the father of an affluent, white kid: "The judge was keenly aware of the fact that I was a clean-cut, upstanding-looking white professional. Um, you know. And I was there [*laughing*]. Which meant that [my son] was going to get different treatment." William's dad turns to him and tells William that he should not follow in his older brother's footsteps, before walking out of the room. William nods his head. His family talks openly with each other about the privilege involved in this particular drug incident with William's brother. William learns from observing what happened to his brother—or, rather, what did not happen—as well as from what his father says, that being white is an asset when one comes into contact with the criminal justice system. Also important to note in what William's father says, though, is the underhanded comment about fathers of black children. When he says, "And I was there," he means that unlike black kids who do not have, in his mind, fathers in their lives, he showed up as a father ought to do when his son is in trouble. In this moment, William's dad recognizes his privilege and wants his kids to do the same. William certainly does not laugh, but he observes his father act in this way, representing black men as irresponsible, absent, and ineffective at child rearing in the very same breath as articulating a recognition of differential, privileged treatment of white professionals in the justice system. In this moment, while William's dad speaks openly about the realities of racism and white privilege, he simultaneously rein-scribes through his anti-black-dad comments the very logic he says he is trying to challenge.

Charlotte tells me how she often thinks about how the police officers who patrol her neighborhood are so "friendly" and "nice" and prevent people from speeding and running over the kids who play outside in the neighborhood. But, she says, "I doubt the police are as friendly to the kids over there," pointing her hand in the direction of the black neighborhood.

Finally, Anthony tells me that he thinks the reason black kids get in trouble for drugs more than white kids do has to do with money:

If you go back really, really, like, even in the 1800s, if you have a really rich family in the 1800s, which were always white back then, and then you lead them up to now, they usually stay rich. So if there's a very wealthy family that's rich, they're probably white, which means they have more access to drugs. They are able to get it much more easily and much more kind of undercover than other people, but with black people, if they are poor—which I guess I really couldn't say because there are plenty of successful black people, obviously—but, um, if you kind of had to get into that, I guess you could kind of say they are not able to do it as secretly because they just—they don't have the money to, so they will do it for cheap, and they will do it in a bad place. Whereas someone that's white will do it from a very secluded location, and they'll get it from somebody who, like, looks like a white professional, and they do it extremely secretly. So they don't get caught, and that's because they have the money to do it. So, I guess, it might just be a money thing. But I think white people do it just like black people.

Here, Anthony connects racial disproportionality in the juvenile justice system to societal forces far outside the individual but is clear in his view that white kids do drugs just as black kids do.

In contrast, when I talk with the kids in Sheridan about this topic, many of them tell me that black kids do bad things and have bad families and bad influences in their culture, which is why the police are more involved with them. For example, Erica understands the problems of black kids to be tied to the culture in which they grow up:

Sometimes . . . kids have lots of problems. Like, in the city, where there are lots of African Americans, . . . like maybe something bad or hard is going on in their life, and then they take their anger out on other kids. . . . They could just have a cold spirit maybe even and not even care about people. . . . If they grow up around bad surroundings, they probably would look up to older kids that are bad or take drugs and steal stuff and have guns. They probably follow in their footsteps . . . if your family isn't very nice or [doesn't] care about you, . . . if you look up to bad kids. I think that happens in city schools a lot. . . . But not here.

Adam tells me that the reason black kids get in trouble so much is because "their parents raised them to be that way." Some of the kids in Sheridan go so far as to say that if there are actual differences in how kids get treated by the police, it is the white kids who have it harder. For instance, Lauren (12, Sheridan) tells me, "Personally, I think white people get in trouble more than anyone else. Like, when I hear people being called down to the principal's office, it's not necessarily [because] they're black. It's just maybe they come from, like, bad parents, or their parents have, like, drinking problems or smoking problems, so they grew up poorly. . . . So it's not necessarily always African American." Lauren attends a school that is almost exclusively white, but that is not part of her explanation here. Rather, Lauren draws on a color-blind narrative that claims that race has nothing to do with who gets in trouble at school since she observes white kids get in trouble.

Many kids in Evergreen and Wheaton Hills identify racism as operating through *laws and policies*. We talk about antipoverty policies, immigration laws, and universal health care. The kids tell me their views on ongoing debates within the Petersfield community about social issues and their views on education policies such as standardized testing and school funding.

For example, one summer evening, Conor tells me that he "loves to debate stuff" and enjoys reading the *New York Times*, which is the newspaper his family receives daily. Conor and I talk about a range of topics together, but the views about which he is most passionate are the ones he holds on race, class, and politics in the United States. "I think [racism] is a *way* bigger problem than people realize," Conor tells me. "It's nowhere near what it used to be. . . . It's just different, and white people don't realize it. . . . I think it's still there. It's just not as present, and people want to hide it. Because they are scared to talk about it." He tells me that a lot of the kids at his integrated public school want to talk about race but do not necessarily know how. He thinks part of the problem is because white kids do not pay attention to stuff happening around them as much as they should. Conor goes on to give me an example of what he believes is evidence of racism: "In Arizona, I know they passed a law that you have to . . . carry around your photo ID or something, and police, they're always stopping Latinos because they don't believe that they're Americans. They believe that they're illegal immigrants, but really they're just picking on people that are a different race. . . . I think it's really wrong and racist." I ask Conor where he learned about this law in Arizona. He tells me that he has read newspaper articles about it and had conversations about it with his dad, but also, he tells me, he has discussed it with his friends. He also mentions to me that his teacher brought it up at school, and the class had a group discussion about it.

Conor continues by telling me that he thinks it is bad that Republicans in his state are trying to cut money that goes to social services: "A lot of poor people in this area are also black and Latino, so it's pretty much racist, I think, like if they can't even eat or whatever." He continues, growing more passionate as he speaks: "And it's like *those* races.

That's just not right. I mean, really I think everyone should be able to eat. And have a home. . . . It is all so ridiculous. It just makes no sense at all." He sighs heavily and sinks back in his chair. Unlike his peers in Sheridan, Conor believes that that racism exists within the laws and policies of the government. He acknowledges that he thinks individuals can behave in racist ways, but he thinks laws and policies are even more powerful than individuals' bad behavior, such as laws that encourage racial profiling.

While Conor holds strong views, particularly about anti-immigration stances as racist, Ryan (11, Sheridan) believes that racism is no longer part of American society. Ryan also points to immigration: "I think we have moved beyond [racism]. But, like, uh—but, like, down on the Mexican and American border, I think it is wrong to let illegal immigrants come in without having a green card and steal our money. We work hard in America. They can't just come here and be lazy and take it. But for racism, yes, I think as a country we have moved beyond it." Ryan and Conor have both grown up with race and class privilege, but they have drawn very different conclusions about immigration and racism.

Kids in Sheridan believe fiercely in the American Dream. They think about the US as a land of equal opportunity. Even if you are a child who goes to a "bad" school, you can achieve your dreams as long as you work hard. In contrast, most of the kids in Evergreen and Wheaton Hills resist meritocratic ideology. Instead, these kids embrace the notion that racism shapes how wealth is passed from generation to generation, as Anthony explained earlier. Though these kids never use the word "reparations" or "racial wealth gap" or "intergenerational transmission" in their discussions, their overarching argument is that unless the government finds a way to make up for inequality of the past—and specifically, according to these kids, inequality tied to slavery—we can never hope to have racial equity in this country. For example, Andrew explains his views on racialized intergenerational transfers of wealth, using his own words: "If you're black and your ancestors were slaves back then, you *never* really got a chance to, like, like, sit upon a large sum of money. . . . I would easily say 99.9999% of the upper class are probably white." Andrew explains to me that unless somehow black Americans can access a great deal of wealth all at one time, it is likely that they will never catch up with white Americans, who have been accumulating monetary resources and passing those resources down to the next generation since the days of slavery. Some other children in Petersfield also agree with Andrew. For example, Ashley tells me that she thinks "most people that have a lot of money inherit it, the majority of the people." When I ask her what race she thinks those people who have inherited a lot of money are, she says, "Oh, white people. Definitely."

Related to the racial gaps in wealth, some of the Evergreen and Wheaton Hills kids also discuss racial gaps in wages or income, such as Caroline (13, Evergreen): "I think there is still a lot of discrimination in jobs and stuff, and there has been for a long time. And while certain people have gotten up, some have been just pushed down. Some people are not given certain opportunities that maybe someone would give white people just because they look different, which I think is kind of bogus. So then they don't have the chance to become better off because people won't—society won't let them, so they have to just stay where they are." Chris offers similar comments. He brings corporations into his discussion, talking about white CEOs of oil companies, or what he refers to as "oil tycoons," and how they not only have a great deal of economic resources but also have a great deal of power resulting from those resources: "Like, you know, if you look at the CEOs of oil companies, they're all white men. Look at the oil tycoons, they don't even, like, do anything. They just sit there and be a face. So I don't think it's [about] hard work as much as luck almost and just kind of, you know, where you start out. If you start out really high class, then you'll probably stay there. If you start out poor, you probably won't get rich. . . . Most people who start out really high class are white." The critical statement "so much of society is run by white people," coming from a white boy growing up in an affluent family, may not match traditional assumptions of how privileged white kids think (or, as some people hypothesize, do not think) about race in the United States. And certainly not all of the white kids in this research share the views of the children presented here. In fact, the responses of Sheridan children are drastically different from those of kids such as Andrew, Caroline, and Chris. As I have alluded to at various points in this book, the children growing up in the segregated context of Sheridan are likely more similar to most white kids growing up in the United States. But, indeed, there are some white kids in this research who think critically about race.

Rejecting the Prevalence of Inequality and Racism

Unlike kids in Evergreen and Wheaton Hills who recognize institutional racism and structural inequality, at least to some limited extent, Sheridan kids believe that racism in the United States is "no longer a big problem."

As quoted at the start of this book, Natalie explains to me her view on racism: "Racism is not a problem anymore. . . . Racism was a problem when all those slaves were around and that, like, bus thing and the water fountain. I mean, everything was crazy back in the olden days, all those things. But now, I mean, since Martin Luther King and, like, Eleanor Roosevelt, and how she went on the bus. And she was African American and sat on the white part. . . . But after the 1920s and all that, things changed." Presumably, Natalie is referring to the Jim Crow era of du jure segregation and the famous story of Rosa Parks. Her mom, who listens to her daughter as Natalie makes these comments, does not intervene to correct her or guide her. Rather, she nods along as her daughter speaks, agreeing with Natalie when she reaches her conclusion: "After the 1920s and all that, things changed." Natalie, as well as many other children interviewed in Sheridan, clearly has not been taught much about the history of race relations in the United States, either at school or at home. Of course, I did not attempt to quiz the kids I interviewed on history, but through our discussions, I believe they were underinformed about American history, particularly with respect to the history of race. In addition to getting major events wrong, Natalie and Erica, like many of their Sheridan peers, also tended to flatten time, lumping all of black history together—events affiliated with the 1800s and slavery and those taking place a hundred years later during the civil rights movement appear to be one and the same to many of these kids.

Much as Bonilla-Silva outlines in his work on "socially shared tales" and stories of "the past is the past,"[8] almost all of the Sheridan kids tell me, like Natalie, that racism is only a feature of the past, something that happened during "the olden days." Edward explains, "People used to treat black people really terribly and think white was, like, higher but not anymore. . . . I think as a country we have moved on [from racism]." And Carly (12, Sheridan) states cheerfully, "I think we're good. I don't really think there is many issues." And her mom agrees. "Why bring it up?" Carly's mother asks me in a separate interview. "The kids don't even think about it."

Connected to Sheridan children's narrow operational definition of racism and their limited knowledge of history, they understand the United States to be a meritocratic system in which hard work is rewarded. Almost all of the Sheridan children tell me that racism is something from "the olden days," or the past, and that political liberalism, or equal opportunity, now pervades US society. When asking these kids how rich people become rich, they all make some mention of "hard work" and meritocracy, explaining that poor people are poor because they are "lazy" or "make bad choices" or "don't save their money." While some discuss the "bad economy," they also explain to me that "anyone can get a job at McDonald's and work their way up." And Erica comments to me at one point, "Public school doesn't cost that much, does it? I think it might even be free!" as part of her argument that everyone can go to school and try their best to go to college. "Even a poor black kid could try hard and be the best they can be and move up," she tells me. Similarly, Britney tells me that black parents must "get a better job. Or even they need to get a job. Or they can stop getting things that they don't absolutely need and that they just want." Britney continues, "I don't think [black people] do all that good a job saving money." During the same interview, Britney tells me that "everything has equaled out" today when it comes to racial inequality.

Overall, children growing up in Sheridan, Evergreen, and Wheaton Hills do not all share the same perspectives on why inequality exists. This pattern is important because previous interview-based research with affluent kids about perceived causes of inequality has found that the children's views are much more aligned with the Sheridan children than the Evergreen and Wheaton Hills kids in the present study. Specifically, the sociologist Heather Beth Johnson and I conducted research in 2004 with a group of affluent children between the ages of 5 and 12 that focused on their explanations of class inequality. We found that the ideological belief in the American Dream—that if one works hard, one can achieve anything—was held strongly by the children in this study, much like the kids in Sheridan.[9] Kids in the previous study often thought of themselves as being "in the middle" of a class hierarchy and that hard work rather than good luck was what really matters for one's success in life and upward or downward social mobility. While we did not explicitly examine the broader contexts in which the children in that 2004 study were growing up, it is likely that their social environments more similarly resembled those of Sheridan kids than those growing up in Evergreen or Wheaton Hills. This is because growing up in a place like Sheridan is likely a more common experience for white, affluent kids in the United States due to well-documented patterns of residential segregation and school choice by affluent parents in the United States. As Johnson writes, "People of privileged positions, people in positions of power, are able to use the American Dream to justify and legitimize their positions and pass along a sense of entitlement to these positions to their own children. In so doing, they neglect the power of wealth in shaping the life trajectories of themselves, their own children, other people, and other people's children."[10] In addition to neglecting the power of wealth, so too do the parents in Sheridan neglect the wages of whiteness, the privileges associated with being white, the position of dominance in the United States' racial hierarchy. In short, for kids such as those growing up in Sheridan, ideologies such as that of the American Dream but also that of color blindness can be drawn on and interpreted in new ways by these kids to help them explain and justify the world around them and their position within it.

However, something different is happening in the Evergreen and Wheaton Hills families. The children growing up here do not uncritically accept meritocratic ideology as an explanation for how the world works. Instead, these kids generally draw on understandings of intergenerational transfers of wealth, the legacy of institutionalized racism in this country, and the power held by white people, such as oil CEOs or politicians. While Evergreen and Wheaton Hills children certainly still express forms of entitlement, there is a variation on this theme of "deserving" the good life despite the confluence of both race and class unearned privilege. Instead, due to kids' interactions and observations at the schools their parents send them to, the kinds of activities in which these children participate, the modeling of particular behavior on the behalf of parents, the neighborhood in which they live, the peers surrounding them, the media they consume, and so forth, these children arrive at different conclusions—conclusions that have powerful and direct connections to understandings of one's own privilege.

Understanding (or Not) One's Own Privilege

Because parents make bundled choices about neighborhoods, schools, extracurricular activities, and so forth, it is perhaps not surprising that most of the variations on themes in what the kids in this study think correspond with the city-versus-suburb divide, or Evergreen and Wheaton Hills versus Sheridan. Indeed, the kids growing up in these three distinctive racial contexts generally have three *different* sets of ideas about the concept of privilege—what it means, how it works, if and when it applies to them, and what they should do about it, if anything.

Before examining these key variations, however, it is important to point out what these white, affluent kids share in common with respect to their understandings of privilege. First, all of the kids in this research, regardless of whether they speak explicitly about privilege, truly believe that they will be successful, affluent, powerful adults when they grow up. When I ask the children about their futures, every single child tells me they "know" they will attend college, and many have concrete plans mapped out regarding their anticipated professional career or at least some ideas about what kinds of professions interest them. One child tells me that he might take some time off before college to travel but that he will "definitely go to college, eventually." These children do not believe that they will be presented with any hurdles or challenges; instead, these children expect that they will be able to accomplish whatever they dream and have whatever they want in life—and why would they not think this? After all, these are children who already have more than most children in the entire world when it comes to resources such as wealth, education, police protection, and health care.

Second, and in connection to these kids' belief that they will be successful, all of them exhibit a sense of entitlement. By this, I mean that the kids see themselves as deserving of the good life that they live, even those children who recognize unearned privilege. These kids know how to navigate interactions with adults in ways that favor them, they are not afraid to express their own opinions, and they expect to move through the world with ease. The sociologist Annette Lareau discusses entitlement in a similar way in her research with black and white middle-class children: "They acted as though they had a right to pursue their own individual preferences and to actively manage interactions in institutional settings. They appeared comfortable in these settings; they were open to sharing information and asking for attention. . . . Middle-class children also learned (by imitation and by direct training) how to make the rules work in their favor."[11] The children in this study exhibit similar characteristics, though not only are the kids in the present study affluent rather than middle-class, but they are also exclusively white. As such, their entitlement is structured not only by class privilege and the cultural repertoires associated with class but also by race and the expectations that whites often have about how the world ought to work in their favor.[12]

Third, these kids believe that they are good white people. Variations on this theme emerge with respect to whether the kids believe they have the potential to be racist, as discussed previously. But overall, most of these children view themselves as part of the solution of racial inequality rather than part of the problem.

Privilege in Sheridan: "No Such Thing"

While these three common themes link the children together, variations on these themes offer insights into how growing up in a particular racial context profoundly informs one's own ideas about what it means, or does not mean, to grow up with race and class privilege in the United States. For example, I ask Britney what her parents' jobs are. "My mom stays home, and my dad is a . . ." Britney pauses. She thinks for a second and then screams, "Hey Mom! What is Dad? Like his job?" From upstairs, Britney's mother shouts down, "Corporate executive!" Britney looks at me. "Corporate executive," she states calmly with a smile. "But I would really love to be a marine biologist or a teacher or a designer," she tells me. "What kind of designer would you want to be? Interior? Fashion?" I ask her. "Ummm, fashion?" she replies, snorting at me as if she could not believe I could possibly be asking her that. "Oh. Cool," I reply. We continue talking, and I ask her if she thinks she would have an easier time becoming a designer because she is white. She looks at me as if I am crazy. "Nuh-uh. Not now," Britney says. I ask her when she thinks her race may have mattered. "The '50s. Martin Luther King," she replies.

Erica and Natalie also have their futures mapped out in their minds. Erica plans to be an orthodontist or a plastic surgeon. Erica assures her mother that her mom can "get free plastic surgery" if Erica goes into that profession. Natalie plans to be "a neurosurgeon, a cardiothoracic surgeon, or orthopedic surgeon." I ask them how they will achieve these dreams. They immediately respond in unison, "Go to college." Erica, the future plastic surgeon, then adds, "And get a master's degree." Natalie tells me, "Work really hard and pay attention in school. And keep your grades up." I ask the girls how they will pay for college. "Oh, our parents will pay for it," Erica nonchalantly assures me. I then ask them if they have thought about people who cannot afford to go to college—what should they do to afford higher education? Natalie offers her suggestions: "What you'd have to do is, maybe, like, when you were younger, really reach out and do babysitting, mow the lawn for someone, earn money. And then you got to save all of that money or all the money that you get for presents and stuff, and save it for college or put it in, like, your savings bond. And work really hard." Natalie's perspectives make it clear that she and her sister do not have to think about the realities that many families face of whether they can afford college. Erica then offers her view on what alternative options are available to people who cannot afford "regular college":

> Like, if you want to go to a good college, like a regular college, like four years, it can be really expensive. It's like $36,000 to $40,000, like, a—like, for freshman year. But then there's always, like, the community colleges that you can go to for two years. And, like, you can get degrees there for, like, maybe culinary school or something and then go into the business of cooking. Even though it might not be your favorite, it's, like, $2,000 a year. That's pretty manageable, like, just to get a, well, job. So people can just do that.

Natalie adds, "That's apparently the price of knowledge." Their mother who is in the room at this point in the interview interjects herself into the interview. "That *is* the price of knowledge. And we will pay that price," she says matter-of-factly to her daughters. "Your job is to get the good grades."

Edward tells me that he wants to be a civil engineer. I ask him how he plans to go about having this profession. "I will go to college and work hard and get good grades," he tells me. He also tells me that his parents will pay for it. I ask him the same question I asked Natalie and Erica: can kids whose parents cannot afford to pay for college still get to go? "I think so, if they work hard," he says with a shrug. Finally, I ask him about kids who go to schools that are not as good as his—schools that he previously described to me as dilapidated and underresourced. Do they have to work harder to get to college than kids at his school? "No. Same thing," he tells me. "We all have to work hard. Doesn't matter what your school is like."

When talking with Sheridan kids about race and privilege, some of them also question moments of race consciousness. For example, Kelsey tells me that she has heard about some student unions at one of the high schools in Petersfield: "I don't know why this is. Like, this one high school has, like, the Black Student Union and the Asian Student Union. I don't really get it. Like, why do they have to be like, 'Oh, you're black, so you're in your own little union.' I mean, there's not like the White Student Union!" To Kelsey, not being racist means not talking about race or recognizing the consequences of race in society—with regard to both advantage and disadvantage. Kelsey's belief in this moment that racism is no longer a problem undermines the real challenges faced by kids of color growing up in predominantly white cities, such as Petersfield, and her claim that a white student union would be equivalent to a black student union reflects her lack of awareness about why a student union might exist in the first place.[13]

While kids growing up in Sheridan do not notice the privileges they have been given as a result of their race and wealth backgrounds, they do know that they "live where the fortunate people live" and have more than other people. They often brag to me about their vacation homes, their clothes, and their parents' occupations. Others complain to me that it is "unfair" that they do not have a pool when "everyone else on [the] block has one" or that they really "need" a new snowmobile but their dad has not yet had the time to take them to get one or that it is "annoying" when the woman who cleans their house moves their stuff and they cannot find it later. Despite the enormous class privilege that these kids have, despite the fact that their parents can and will pay for them to go to whatever college they want, despite the fact that many of these families moved to Sheridan explicitly to benefit their kids' education, despite the luxurious lifestyle that these families live, most of these kids do not see this class privilege for what it is. These kids are so accustomed to living the way they live that it is "normal" to them. Recognizing neither the ways that their own parents' wealth impacts them nor the way being white shapes their lived experiences, privilege operates profoundly in the lives of these kids, but it is invisible to them. As Lauren explains to me when I ask her if she thinks some kids get more advantages than other kids, "No. There's no such thing. Everyone gets what they deserve in life, if they work for it." Only two children in Sheridan tell me graciously how lucky they are to have parents who work so hard, demonstrating some degree of recognition about their privileges but, like Lauren, attributing their status to their parents' work ethic.

Privilege in Wheaton Hills: Recognizing Privilege

In Wheaton Hills, the kids generally recognize racism and therefore recognize their own privilege, but that is where their thinking about race comes to a standstill. They do not do anything to work against privilege, even as they recognize that it exists. Some kids are able to talk about privilege in their own personal lives. For others, such as Aaron, privilege is a more abstract concept, unconnected to one's own life. Aaron talks to me about the "upside" of being white in society: "I think [whites] just kind of have the upside, because a lot of people . . . just have the—they're a little wary of other races, because they find them too different. And since much of society is run by white people anyway, which is an upside, more white people are, you know, accepted into jobs, so they get the upside. So, yeah, I do think they have the upside." Offering a critical view on how race is tied to power in the United States, Aaron is able to clearly articulate his sense of what privilege is. He tells me that he believes "much of society is run by white people" and that whites have privileges and advantages or, in his words, "the upside." However, Aaron struggles to then apply this concept to his own life. When I ask him if he thinks being affluent and white shapes his lived experiences, he talks about other people rather than himself, such as white adults trying to get jobs or black kids facing the police. He avoids answering any of my direct questions about his own privilege. Instead, he ardently defends his private school and describes how special and smart one has to be to get into this school.

Similarly, Anthony talks about the challenges faced by President Obama as a result of being the first black president:

> President Obama is getting a lot of ratting. He's being ratted on a lot because he's black. And if it was a rich, white president that's, like, in charge, you're probably not going to get all those things, and [the president is] not going to have as much to push through. So I guess privilege is—it's just those obstacles that just come up. . . . So disadvantages and stereotypes and just bad things might result if you are black. I guess, in a way it might give me a better shot, so I guess it—it gives me an advantage, but I mean, I'm still the one that's trying to drive my own future. I mean, if you're black and you *choose* to drive yourself and your own future, then you'll be successful. You just have to push through the hard stuff. I mean, the best person is probably going to just strive through everything, and that's what makes them successful. And if there's a black person and they are the best person and they are able to strive through those things, they will be successful. I mean, sometimes it is harder for them. I guess you could say they have more obstacles. It just makes it harder. But you just have to push through.

Anthony tries to make sense of the "obstacles" black people face and the "advantages" he is given while at the same time remaining loyal to the idea of meritocracy. He talks about himself as working really hard and pushing through the hard times, just as he sees his black peers needing to do to secure their future success—maybe working even harder than he does to overcome the racism that they will face. But Anthony, like Aaron, is not involved in any activities that work against these obstacles, and the advantages that he has benefit him. Like Aaron, he loves his school, he loves traveling, and he loves all of his extracurricular activities. He offers no indication that he wants to do anything to try to change society. He recognizes that racial inequality persists, but he also buys into the ideology of meritocracy.

Kacie, who attends public middle school, explains to me that she thinks white kids are indeed racist to black kids at her school. But she also believes that the racism is initiated by the bad behavior of the black kids:

> There's racism at my school between the kids. Um, I was mostly in a group last year, and I'm not friends with any of them right now except for one,

and she's really down to earth, and so she's good to get along with. But the rest of them, they all come from very, um, high-income families, and they said racist things about the other kids. It was a very diverse [school], extremely, because then you have these other kids [of color] who are living in the apartments over there and growing up with drugs, and then the kids don't have a lot of supervision at home. I can say that because of how they were acting out in class and what they were saying, like writing swear words on papers and posting them on doors and just yelling at teachers, talking back, like, all the time, leaving class and strutting up and down the hallways—just not being respectful. But then there was a lot of racial comments from the white kids, even at that age, like because of the other kids acting out. . . . The white kids are racist and snobby, . . . and the black kids are obnoxious.

Kacie perceives the racial conflict at her school to be tied to the behaviors of both the white kids and the black kids. And while she recognizes that her white friends say racist things, she tells me she never challenged those girls because she "didn't want there to be drama" within the friendship group.

Overall, the kids in Wheaton Hills recognize that privilege and oppression exist. These kids are often critical when it comes to thinking abstractly about race. For some children, they are critical of their white peers and can think in more concrete terms about how privilege might shape their worlds. However, when it comes to their own education, their own college admission, their own imagined future, and even their own friendship groups, these kids largely embrace the privileged life around them, avoiding disruptions to the status quo. There are exceptions: Kacie distances herself from the snobby white girls, and Chris convinces his parents to send to him the public school.

Privilege in Evergreen: Doing Something

Kids in Evergreen recognize privilege and want to do something to cultivate social change. Many of these children participate in social activist work, including attending organizing meetings with their parents and/or protests, marches, and other forms of political engagement. And these kids have strongly held beliefs about political issues. For instance, when

I attend protests over state funding with some of the kids, they choose either to make their own signs prior to the event or to select a premade sign from a pile—a sign that, as one child tells me, "speaks to me." I talk with these kids about their political views. For instance, Margot tells me, "I think health care is a right. The dude that was running for president before Obama was elected? He said it was a privilege. Obama said it was a right, and I agree with Obama. Because everyone should be able to, like, if they get, like, sick or if they are in an accident or whatever, then I think they should be able to be able to pay to get health care. It is a *human right*. And if you say it is a privilege, it is a privilege that *everyone* should have!" Margot is not the only child who participates in protests or holds strong political views; almost all of the kids in Evergreen tell me about their experiences participating in social justice work. Many of these kids tell me that it is their race and class advantages that motivate them to participate in social activism. For example, William tells me, "Just like gender, you'll get an advantage just by being a white male rather than a black female." This is why, he says, he "has a responsibility" to stand up for "what is right." He participates in social activism by attending protests and takes a stand at his school through student government.

Charlotte also has much to say about privilege because her parents, as she says laughing, "*constantly* remind me of my privileges!" She goes on:

> Like, um, I recently got an iPhone. And recently they are like, "Ohhh, you're going to have to take out some of your own money." I also have to do chores too. Like, I have to empty the dishwasher and, like—yeah, they say my phone's a privilege, and I should pay some money and don't become obsessed with it [*laughing*]. All that stuff like that. Or, like, going out to dinner. Like, we go out to dinner a fair amount, and they want to make sure that I know that this is a privilege. And, like, they tell me like, "You know when you get into college or whatever, maybe you can't go out to dinner as much." And we get organic food, and maybe I won't be able to afford that when I am in college. So they make sure to show me that's a privilege. Like, "you might grow up and not have as much money as we do," they will tell me, "so you have to recognize that this is a privilege."

Charlotte tells me that she has never heard the term "white privilege." She tells me that she knows white people have advantages in the United

States, but she is skeptical about the use of this term specifically because it might be interpreted in a way that sounds like "white power," and "you just don't want to seem like you're saying it's better to be white or something like that, even if white people do have it easier."

Unlike most Sheridan kids, who do not recognize privilege, and unlike most Wheaton Hills kids, who recognize privilege but do not care or know how to do anything positive with it, kids in Evergreen recognize their privilege and want to (and expect to be able to) use their privilege to change the world into whatever they want it to be. These children are largely optimistic about the future, they join their parents in political protests and activist organizations, and they tend to have more interracial friendships than the other kids in this study do.

These kids feel empowered by their privilege. And this empowerment can be interpreted in two contradictory ways. On the one hand, these kids have very good intentions: they want to fight against injustice as they see it and speak out on topics important to them, such as factory farming or women's rights or the murder of Trayvon Martin or the policy positions of certain politicians. They recognize their privileged position and want to use that status to make a difference. Certainly, these children are thinking about privilege in a more critical light than their peers in Wheaton Hills and Sheridan are.

On the other hand, rarely do any of these children think seriously about ways to reduce their own privilege or consider strategies for challenging white racial power. Instead, these kids genuinely believe that as white, affluent people they can and will save the world for everyone else. Simply put, this empowerment is a variant form of the entitlement shared by all the kids in this study. Although these kids are involved in a number of protests and school clubs focused on the issues they care about, these actions rarely lead to actual social change. These actions are in an important sense self-serving, helping privileged white kids feel good about themselves and removing any feelings of guilt that they may experience as a result of the privileged lives they lead. These kids are rarely critical of the many unearned advantages they receive in their day-to-day lives. In fact, most of the social justice work they do now and into their high school years will likely help them get into elite and predominantly white colleges. After all, despite their social activism and good intentions, these are people who are situated within the social structure such that they will inevitably go to prestigious universities likely paid for by their parents. They will inevitably receive intergenerational transfers of wealth in youth and in adulthood. And, no matter what they do, no matter that they are "good" white people, they will still inevitably receive the wages of whiteness as long as the United States continues to be a country organized structurally by race.

Conclusion

Four Years Later

During the summer of 2015, four years after I first began this project, I returned to Petersfield and conducted follow-up interviews with one-third of the families in the initial study, including the parents and (now) teenagers. When I reinterviewed the young people, I found a striking pattern: these kids' views on race had grown more confident and more polarized.[1]

Jessica (16), a Wheaton Hills child who previously attended private Catholic school, tells me about her high school experiences. She starts by telling me how she purposefully avoids particular hallway routes at Wheaton Hills High when she switches classes in order to avoid groups of black teenagers. "I keep my eyes down," she says. She tells me that it is "definitely important" to have black teachers at the school, explaining how black teachers and security guards do a better job "dealing with" black students, especially when there is conflict. She tells me story after story about black kids at her school smoking weed, swearing, and talking about sex. She says she never tells the teacher about these instances for fear of "getting on the wrong side" of the black students, especially the black girls.

I ask Jessica about her initial observations when she first arrived at the school after leaving her predominantly white Catholic elementary and middle school:

My first day, I thought it was so bizarre. Everyone in my class, we were all Caucasian. We were all saying, "Wow, that's strange 'cause we thought this school was supposed to be more than half minority, yet we're sitting here in an honors class and there's no African Americans." I feel like that was just bizarre because, I mean, you don't have to pay anything [to be in this class]. All you have to do is put in a little bit of extra effort, like read another book. . . . If you people [black kids] aren't even bothering to apply yourselves, to just read an extra book, then you're on the track of being a kid who just doesn't care.

In Jessica's mind, students of color are not in advanced courses as she is because they are unwilling to try.

Jessica and teenagers such as Kelsey (17), who lives in Sheridan, tell me that even though their high school experience is more diverse than in middle school, their friendship groups remain racially homogeneous. As Kelsey says, "My friends are all white. Well, I was cheer captain, and we had a little diversity on the team. But my friends are all white." Nate (16), who still lives in Sheridan, tells me the same is true for his friend-ship group.

I also talk with the teenagers about a tragedy that happened in the Petersfield area a few months prior to my second round of interviews: a black teenager was shot and killed by a white police officer. This spurred large protests and school walkouts as well as a great deal of controversy in the local community. A couple of months after the shooting, it was announced that the officer would not face any charges and that his use of deadly force was lawful.

Given the devastating nature of this tragedy as well as the degree of controversy and unrest in the community in response to it, most of the kids bring it up to me during our interviews before I can. Jessica, though, does not. When I finally ask her about it directly, she reluctantly tells me that her parents talked to her about it, and they agreed as a fam-ily that the police did nothing wrong. She proceeds to tell me about a private conversation she had with her friend about it, mentioning that while she tried to make this point in a class discussion, she was met with contention by peers who did not approve of what she describes as her "conservative views."

My friend and I, we never really like took a very strong opinion because we had no horse in the race. I mean, we were still trying to figure it out still and just talked through the different ideas, but it's ultimately like, "We're not the police. We don't know what happened." And then I said to her, "What do you think about everyone saying that cops are just murderers?" And she said, "No, that's really not right. I've got a cousin who's a cop, and he's like a really good guy." And then I said, "Yeah, and I mean they go through intense training, and that's the thing the cops-are-murderers people are forgetting. . . . And I don't think race necessarily needed to play such a strong card. . . . I think the African American people at my school weren't even bothering to look at, like, the facts and deeper ideas. I don't think it was about race."

I ask her what she thought about the student protests and walkouts at the schools in Petersfield that followed the shooting.

> Yeah. Um, that happened a few times. . . . Um, it always happened at the same time of day. And so I'd be looking at the clock and then, like, looking around, mainly to see if any white kids in my class would walk out. No one would walk out. There was like one girl I knew who did, but she just wanted to put it on Snapchat and be like, "Look at me, I'm supporting a cause you all should be fighting for. Look at me, looking all strong, protesting." She was just doing it for attention. I don't know anyone who participated who actually believed in any of it.

Similarly, Nate tells me that in talking about police violence and race at Sheridan High with friends, a consensus was shared: "Cops don't shoot people 'cause they're black. They shoot them because people attack them. If you actually look at the facts, when black people get shot, it is because they fucked up." Kelsey tells me that when she tried to stand up for the police in a class discussion about the shooting, she was "crucified" by her teacher and some of the other white kids. She also rolls her eyes condescendingly when talking about #BlackLivesMatter and offers her view that all lives matter and that black people "need to stop talking so much about race." Overall, the kids who previously believed that racism was not an issue in US society continue to believe that racism does not exist, but they add that race has become "a big thing" due to people of color making it so. All of these young people have grown up in color-blind contexts of childhood.

Alternatively, kids who in middle school had told me that racism was a problem in the United States now tell me how angry they are about racism. They share stories about the racist things they notice at their school and other schools when traveling for sports or graduations, they speak passionately about current events involving race and politics, and they share with me examples of action they had recently taken to work for racial justice in their own ways. They, too, are more self-assured in their views.

Margot (16), who attends Evergreen High School, tells me about her observations of racial patterns in her school, returning to the concept of "prejudice" that she had told me about when she was younger:

> We talked about [tracking] in my English class last year. Some people were saying, like, maybe it was 'cause [students of color], like, their friends weren't doing it, so they didn't feel like they should do it. . . . But I think it's more like, there might—there's a little bit of this idea that black students wouldn't be able to, like, do as much. Like, I think it's just engrained in, you know, popular thought. [*Sighs*] I . . . I don't know. I have this belief that, like, everybody's kind of racist 'cause of, like, we grow up in these institutions that are racist and then co-grow up with, like, these messages being told to us and these, um, ideas and these, um, like— [*pause*] I'm blanking on the word. You know, prejudices. It's like even if you're not, like, a horrible, like, an outright racist person like me—like, I wouldn't be racist intentionally, ever. But I think we all have, like, these little things that are, like, in the back of our mind, and we all have, you know, you have these prejudices about people. Just from living and growing up in this country and the institutions. Like, the education system is really racist I feel like. . . . And the teachers are *pretty* white.

Margot, who takes exclusively honors classes, notices the same racial pattern that Jessica articulates about her school. However, Margot's explanation for these patterns calls into question broader structural issues and underlying racist assumptions made by all white people.

William (16), who attends Evergreen High along with Margot, shares his perspective on this topic.

> A lot of black people are growing up in poorer places where, like, education isn't something that is held as something important. It's not, like, put on a pedestal the way it is for me, or it was for me when I was growing up. You can even link it all the way back to slavery and then when there was segregation in the towns and how mainly black people in those towns

never had that much money and they continued to just not have that much money. And, um, that just results in less time for trying to, like, educate your kids and less money to buy books for them and that kind of stuff.

William weaves together individual-, cultural-, and structural-level explanations for the patterns he observes, but his idea of how to fix this problem centers entirely on the individual level.

There's this statistic in Petersfield that shows that the third grade is when you start seeing a literacy difference between white and black kids. And for African Americans, that means they're worse off for the rest of their school career. And my friends and I, we just think that if we can—we can get some role models that are very, like, relatable to them and show them things that, um, will inspire them to just read more, and do it in a way that's from high schoolers who have—I mean, if you—if you think about life as a whole, we were in their position pretty recently, I think it could maybe help.

William's ideas of how to address the results of racism in the system of education are rooted in good intentions and a recognition that something is not right. His position is certainly different from that of Jessica, and that is important to note. Nonetheless, his belief that black kids need better role models and that white kids can help fix the problems of black kids by serving as such is still part of the problem of white supremacy. As Matthew Hughey demonstrates, these ideas are quite popular and are held even by white racial justice activist groups. These ideas about how to fix the problem reflect white savior ideals, particular understandings of how race works, and a commitment to debunked notions of why these patterns exist in the first place.[2] Nevertheless, unlike kids such as Jessica, Kelsey, and Nate, William recognizes there is a problem and wants to try to be part of the solution the best way he knows how.

I also talk to William about police violence and race. He shares his reaction to the death of Eric Garner, a black man in Staten Island, New York, who was strangled to death in 2014 by police officers: "I think that the Eric Garner case, I found that even more ridiculous than ones with guns. It was just mind-boggling! . . . To get down on the ground and strangle a man to death is just—it's *so* brutal. Like, you—you're—it's *so* . . . personal. Yeah. That video really got to me. That one struck me as a lot more eye-opening than some of the other cases—I mean, they were both equally important and tragic—but wow. It makes me so angry." William talks openly and passionately about this act of police violence. Similarly, within the first few moments of my interview with Charlotte (16), on her own, she brings up the local shooting: "Right after [the teenager] was shot, before there was a lot of information out, my parents wanted me to think about the other side. Like, they definitely weren't siding with the police, but my dad did say, 'We want you to at least consider this from the perspective of the police.' And that was, like, *very* hard for me to do. That was really hard because I have a lot of friends who were dealing with this, and it was in my community, and I was and am still *really angry* about it, so that was very hard." Charlotte expresses to me that not only did her parents try to shape how she thought about the shooting, but she, too, tried to shape how they thought about it, pushing back against their desires for her to be open-minded. This is a good example of how kids also participate in the racial socialization of their parents.

Charlotte and I talk some more about how her family processed this event and how angry and frustrated she and her black and white friends were and still are. "I mean, look at this instance!" she tells me, her voice rising, other people in the restaurant in which we are sitting glancing over at us. "And lots of other instances just like it! It should all be stopped. There is actually a problem and a *system* that allowed this to happen. . . . Technically, legally, what that officer did was 'okay'?! It's like, well, maybe *that's* the problem. Maybe killing black people shouldn't be legally 'okay,' you know?!" She also tells me with pride how she and her peers "blocked off" a major road in Petersfield as part of a protest of the police. "In the front of the line, 'cause, you know, it was a wide thing as we walked down the street [holding a long banner]. In the front were mainly people of other ethnicities. I stayed at the back. And that was kind of like—I didn't want to be in front because I think some of the white kids, we kind of felt like, 'This is of course important to us, but it is mainly affecting our other friends. So we want to be here and be supportive, but they want to lead. So we will follow.'" Charlotte also speaks passionately about the problem of racism in the criminal justice system when it comes to kids doing drugs. "I think about how you see a white kid walking down the street smoking weed, which happens in my neighborhood basically *all* the time. But people aren't worried about it. But I feel like people would be threatened and call the cops if it was black kids, which is obviously ridiculous, but that definitely happens."

Evergreen teenagers, as well as a few in Wheaton Hills, talk to me about their own participation in protests related to the recent police shooting. While the kids have different perspectives on what should have happened to the police officer and different views on whether "Fuck the police" is appropriate to chant at protests, they all speak fervently about their involvement and why they participate and continue to do so. Conor (15) explains his reasoning for joining the protest:

> I did it to raise awareness on the overall problem of African Americans getting shot by police. A lot of people jump to the conclusion "Oh, it was a white policeman and a black person," and they jump right to "Oh, he's guilty, and it's a hate crime." I think that a lot of the shootings are definitely that, but I think instead of, like, focusing on one officer, we need to raise awareness on how the *entire* system is messed up. You gotta, like, look at the big picture and the whole criminal justice system, not just one individual case.

Unlike kids such as William who are more hopeful about the future, Charlotte is less convinced that she can find a good way to help solve the problem, especially since she, like Conor, recognizes the structural components of racism:

> You can someday vote, and you can protest, but you know, if you're a white liberal, yes, some things the government is doing can affect you—jobwise and stuff—but racially you're not really that affected. You can be empathetic and you can say your opinion, but I think when it really comes down to it, you need to *do* something. It is your responsibility to *do* something. . . . That's why I thought it was good to go protest. But besides protesting, I haven't really done that much. . . . It's hard to know the best thing you can do as a white person to help fix things and not just make them worse.

Charlotte recognizes the complexity of her own position in advocating for social change and the reality that sometimes white people make things worse even when they do not mean to do so. "I am still trying to figure all of this out," she tells me.

While the responses from the teenagers growing up in color-conscious contexts of childhood vary in some important and meaningful ways, none of the kids with whom I spoke have changed their mind about the significance of race in US society; rather, their views from middle childhood are now more strongly held and are articulated with more confidence and conviction. When looking across all of the young people I reinterviewed, regardless of their perspectives, it is clear that the views of this set of youth have also become more polarized.

Shifting Contexts

While certainly age brings more lived experiences and learning opportunities that may help to inform one's views and perhaps lead one to feel more self-assured when expressing opinions, I do not think developmental explanations alone can explain the pattern I found. As I have argued throughout this book, the racial context surrounding a young person informs how she or he makes sense of race. In the case of the kids in my study, the past four years have included heightened public discourse surrounding race and youth in the United States. The media's coverage of the 2012 murder of 17-year-old Trayvon Martin and the court trial that followed took place while these children were finishing middle school. The past few years have included more visible public debate about police killings of young people such as 7-year-old Aiyana Stanley-Jones, 12-year-old Tamir Rice, 15-year-old Jordan Edwards, 18-year-old Michael Brown, and 19-year-old Tony Robinson.[3] So too has more attention been given to the police shootings of mothers while they are with their young children, such as Miriam Carey, Meagan Hockaday, and Korryn Gaines.[4] The social movement #BlackLivesMatter as well as initiatives such as #SayHerName and #BlackGirlsMatter have emerged. Youth focused and led organizations such as the Black Youth Project 100 (BYP 100) have grown. Young protesters have been pepper sprayed as they stand in the street demanding basic human rights. Discussions between young people and adults regularly take place on social media about girls such as 14-year-old Dajerria Becton, who was sat on by a white police officer with his drawn weapon at a pool party, about boys such as 14-year-old Ahmed Mohamed, who was arrested for bringing a "bomb" to school that was really a clock, and about youth such as 15-year-old Shakara Rutherford being physically abused in their schools by adults in positions of authority.[5] The headlines are filled with this sort of news involving children and race.

These and many other current moments involving young people—both as victims and as white perpetrators of racial violence—are nothing new in the United States. This is a country with a long history of racial violence, racial divides, and systematic racial discrimination. As such, these are not so much isolated moments of new racialized animosity as they are evidence of a society that has always been racialized. For instance, more than 50 years ago, on September 15, 1963, four innocent black children, 11-year-old Carol Denise McNair, 14-year-old Carole Robertson, 14-year-old Addie Mae Collins, and 14-year-old Cynthia Wesley, were murdered in their church in Birmingham, Alabama, by the Ku Klux Klan. Later that afternoon, two black boys were also murdered: 16-year-old Johnny Robinson was shot in the back by a white police officer, and 13-year-old Virgil Ware was shot by two white teenagers. The parallels between the horrific events of that day and those occurring within the contemporary United States make it clear that this violence is nothing new. And certainly conversations between parents and children of color about racial violence are also nothing new.

But the call for conversations about racism between white children and white parents *is* new and appears to be growing in popularity. For example, reminiscent of the 16th Street Church bombing in 1963, on the evening of June 17, 2015, nine black people were killed at the Emanuel African Methodist Episcopal Church in Charleston, South Carolina, by a 21-year-old white man committing racist hate crimes. In the days following the Charleston church shooting, a flurry of headlines appeared in the news about how to talk to children about what had happened. Headlines on parenting blogs and in the opinion pages of major newspapers read, "How Silence Can Breed Prejudice" and "Here's How You Talk to Your Kids about the Tragedy in Charleston" and "We Need to Deal with Our Discomfort and Talk to Our Kids about Racism."[6] Although many of these articles offered ideas about how to talk about this tragedy with kids of all races, over the past few years, I have seen a number of headlines such as "Talking about Racism with White Kids" and "How White Parents Should Talk to Their Young White Kids about Race."[7] Typically these articles aimed at white parents are published following a racist hate crime. Racial violence has persisted in this country, but suddenly, over the past few years, there appears to be a newly perceived need for white parents to talk about race with their white children. I think it is important that white parents talk to their children about racial divides in the United States, but it is even more important that parents think about the larger social environment that they construct for their child, thinking about what they *do* in addition to what they *say*. Choices about homes, schools, vacations, social networks, extracurricular activities, media, language, and so forth play a key role in shaping young people's racial views. And these actions matter all the time, not just in the aftermath of a racialized tragedy.

Rethinking "Good" White Parenting

I am often asked for parenting advice by white friends, colleagues, and students who want to know what I have learned from my research that might help them raise their own children of privilege. Sometimes these questions are rooted in a sense of guilt and paralysis: "I want to give my future child as many opportunities as I can, but I know if I do, I will be complicit in reproducing unfair advantages. What do I do?" Sometimes these questions are rooted in a sense of frustration and hopelessness: "No matter what I do, I know I am part of the problem. Why should I even try?" Sometimes the questions are more practical: "My daughter said something I think is racist. How should I respond?" or "I'm concerned about the lack of diversity in my child's life, but I live in a white community. What can I do?" These are important questions, and I appreciate the concern shown by those who ask them. It is clear that white people need to confront honestly all the very personal ways that racism is reproduced—intentionally and unintentionally, overtly and subtly, through big decisions and everyday choices—in the private sphere of their own *families*. I think some of this work can begin through asking self-reflexive questions.

But I do not have easy answers to offer. I am not an expert on parenting; I am not even a parent myself. I am a sociologist, and thinking sociologically about our lives often includes recognizing our complicity in the reproduction of all kinds of injustices that we say we otherwise reject. American families are located within a society structured at its most fundamental core by intersecting forms of inequality, and parents of race- and class-privileged children are faced with a difficult paradox: in order to be a "good parent," they must provide their children as many opportunities and advantages as possible; in order to be a "good citizen," they must resist evoking structural privileges in ways that disadvantage others. Decisions about navigating this paradox are part of a complex, ongoing, everyday process of parenting, a process that is filled with many other challenges, day-to-day trials, and unintentional missteps. This is not easy work, and it also may never be possible to solve structural problems entirely through individual acts. As long as structural inequality persists, affluent, white parents who are willing to evaluate their own culpability in the reproduction of inequality will continue to be challenged to navigate the conundrum of privilege.[8] Although the work of figuring out how to be a "good parent" while also being a "good citizen" is not easy, one cannot give up hope and stop trying. After all, at the very same time that white parents contemplate how to raise kids with structural privilege, parents of children of color strategize how to raise children in a society that does not value their lives. They do not have the luxury of giving up.

What I do have to offer is empirical evidence about what goes on in the everyday lives of these white, affluent families. The young people in this study make sense of race, racism, inequality, and privilege by interpreting aspects of their racial contexts of childhood, contexts designed and informed by their parents' choices. And these children do not reach the same conclusions. They do not share the same racial common sense with each other, even as they all are the recipients of race and class privilege. And, as it turns out, this is true not only in middle childhood but also as these young people become teenagers.

Certainly, there is more than one way to approach parenting an affluent, white child. Parents' choices are shaped by what they think is best for their child, what they think is ethically right, and what they think matters in life. These ideas, at least in part, are shaped by prevailing ideologies. For some parents in this study, what it ultimately means to raise a "good" white child is shaped by a color-conscious racial ideology and a desire to raise a child who is informed about the realities of social inequality, who values civic engagement, and who identifies as antiracist. For other parents, raising a child who will be accepted to the most competitive and prestigious university such that they can compete in the global economy is the absolute top priority. For other parents, raising a child who is hardworking and entrepreneurial and motivated by financial profit is most important. It is clear that racial ideologies as well as capitalist ideologies and ideologies of childhood help define common understandings of what it means to be a "good parent."

Despite these different parenting priorities, however, none of the parents in this book tell me that they hope to raise a racist or bigoted child. Indeed, all of these parents believe they are doing their best to raise what they perceive to be "good" kids. Differences in the choices they make, then, are due largely to differences in how these affluent whites understand inequality in the world around them. These understandings may seem very personal and individual, but they are ultimately influenced by much-larger social structures. Ideologies are powerful not only in how they motivate people to behave in certain ways but also in how they motivate others to judge people who do not follow along or in how they pressure us all to conform. All the parents in this study, for instance, believe that part of being a "good" parent means pushing for more resources for their own child, even if those resources are the result of the historical legacy of white supremacy in the United States. And when parents do *not* push for more—when they, for instance, pull their child from a private school or an honors class—they are questioned by other parents (and kids) as to whether that is the right choice, whether they are doing what is in the best interest of their child. As a result, there is a great deal of pressure on these kids to pursue a lifestyle of continued privilege into adulthood. Ideologies about race, economic relationships, and the role of children in a society intersect with agreed-on belief systems about what it means to be a "good" parent raising a "good" child and thereby shape approaches to parenting. These different approaches to parenting lead to the construction of different racial contexts of childhood, which in turn shape how youth produce understandings about race.

Raising Good Citizens

Overall, from my point of view, this has not been a particularly hopeful book. In many ways, the white families depicted here do as much to perpetuate racial inequality as they do to challenge it. But what we can learn from these children, however, especially kids such as Charlotte and Chris and Conor, is that whites can and do play a role in subverting white supremacy. White families can be a space for this radical work. White parents who set up their children's lives such that their kids are equipped with both the language to directly name racial injustice and the experience to actively resist it can play a powerful role in making our society more equal. When confronted with the realities of racial injustice, white parents who are willing to forgo some of their own structural advantages can help shift the course of their families and society itself. But white parents and young people must also resist centering themselves in this work or viewing themselves as white saviors or performing a disingenuous version of "antiracism" for purposes of feeling morally superior to other whites; those who are willing to hear and believe people of color can better understand the barriers to racial justice in their communities and use their own positions of power and influence in more strategic and collaborative ways for the collective rather than the individual good. Whites can learn to shift their own ways of thinking and acting in the world if they allow themselves to face the discomfort that inevitably comes with honest confrontations with race in the United States, to listen and make mistakes and admit that they are not always right, and to accept that the potential collective benefits of challenging forms of racism in private white spaces ultimately outweigh any perceived personal, emotional costs.

Most importantly, white parents can play an important role in challenging the perpetuation of racism and racial inequality in the United States *only if* they are willing to give up some of their own white racial power by rejecting the idea that their own child is more innocent and special and deserving than other people's children are.[9] Indeed, placing value on children collectively rather than individually is the most important way white parents can challenge ideologies of parenting that are deeply entwined with the legacy of white supremacy in the United States. What it means to be a "good" parent must be about more than securing various forms of resources for one's own child; being a "good" parent must become intertwined with notions of good citizenship—which means living according to the social, ethical, and moral principles that many of the parents in this research already profess.

My hope is that parents such as the ones described in this book accept the radical notion that the happiness, success, health, and well-being of other children is as important as that of their own. My hope is that parents commit to caring about how young people as a whole are treated or mistreated, educated or miseducated, supported or marginalized, treated with dignity or criminalized, heard or silenced. And my hope is that parents make a decision to act in ways that align with these principles. Collectively, the challenge ahead is to rethink taken-for-granted assumptions about what constitutes a "good" school or a "good" neighborhood or even a "good" kid and to decide instead that being a "good" parent means being—and actively raising—a good citizen.

ACKNOWLEDGMENTS

This book builds on the empirical insights and critical thought of a long-standing community of scholarly thinkers devoted to understanding and resisting racism in the United States. My own work would not be possible without the work of this larger community, both past and present, and for that, I am appreciative.

This book would also not be possible without the parents who generously opened their worlds to me, welcomed me into their homes, invited me to soccer games and birthday parties, and shared with me their honest perspectives on personal and controversial topics. I am grateful for their willingness to participate in this research, and I acknowledge fully the courage it takes to let a researcher like me into the private life of one's family. I also thank the young people in this book for teaching me so many things that I did not know, for sharing their ideas and questions, and for taking this project so seriously. While I believe a critical race analysis of the worlds of white families in general is necessary, I also care deeply for these specific families and am thankful for the meaningful relationships and bonds I developed as a result of this research.

Ilene Kalish understood my passion behind this project, patiently and enthusiastically guided me through the process of writing my first book, and has undoubtedly made this work stronger. I sincerely thank her as well as Maryam Arain and the editorial staff at New York University Press for their help. Thanks as well to the series editors of the Critical Perspectives on Youth series, Amy Best, Lorena Garcia, and Jessica Taft, and to the reviewers who provided helpful feedback.

Amanda Lewis is an exceptional and generous mentor who supported this project and me every step of the way. Amanda is an incredibly talented teacher and researcher, and she provided me with many opportunities to explore and develop my interests. To this day, she pushes me to make my work better and offers concrete suggestions of how to do so. Amanda always had faith in me that I could actually take on this project, even in moments when I was not so sure myself. She has helped me find my way professionally and intellectually, and I will always be sincerely grateful for everything she has done for me. I also thank Tyrone Forman, who supported this project from the very early stages and who furthered my interest in conducting research on racism with young people. Tyrone always knew the best book or article to recommend and offered excellent advice, and this work is enriched by his thoughtfulness. In addition, I sincerely thank both Amanda and Tyrone for all the laughter, all the dinners, all the wine, and the warm sense of community that they cultivate and share with their students and friends. I am so fortunate for their mentorship.

I thank William Corsaro for teaching me about children's agency, for encouraging me to conduct this research, and for reading early drafts of this work. I also thank Irene Browne for her help with coding and for reading my work and offering helpful suggestions for improvement. Two scholars from disciplines outside sociology also greatly influenced this project, and I am fortunate to have been able to learn from their own expertise: I thank Maisha Winn and Barbara Woodhouse for sharing their knowledge and helping my intellectual work grow in new directions.

I was able to collect the bulk of the data for this project thanks to generous funding from the Race and Difference Initiative, the Laney Graduate School, and the Department of Sociology at Emory University. I am grateful to my Emory colleagues for their help along the way. I thank Isabella Alexander, Kendra Freeman, Kim Hall, Celeste Lee, Tiffany Pogue, Chelsea Jackson Roberts, Roselyn Thomas, and Adria Welcher. And I thank especially Liz Alexander and Michelle Manno for their constant feedback and help with this project from beginning to end, for our long-distance writing-group meetings, and for their camaraderie. I know this work is better and more critical because of their input.

The big questions that inform this research began in an undergraduate sociology class I took with Heather Beth Johnson at Lehigh University titled "Race and Class in America." The child-centered methodological techniques used in this project, in addition to the larger questions I pose, are influenced directly by her. I thank Heather for being such a supportive mentor and great friend, for encouraging me and so many others to pursue the question of "how can this be?," for reading my work over the past 15 years, for pushing scholars to critically think through the sociology of privilege, for sharing her amazing family with me and for embracing my own, and most of all, for changing my life by teaching me to think sociologically.

I also thank my classmates and friends from Lehigh for all that I learned from them, especially Kaloma Cardwell, Jessica De Pinto, Neil Hurley, Teniece Johnson, Jill Fitzpatrick, Samina Luthfa, Jennifer McCarthy, Xóchitl Mota, Greg Palmer, Lavar Pope, and Carlos Tavares. I thank my English and sociology professors at Lehigh for teaching me what it means to be a scholar, especially Beth Dolan, Mary-Jo Haronian, Dawn Keetley, Jackie Krasas, Judy Lasker, and Ziad Munson. Many thanks also to those who helped me develop ideas for this project during my brief yet intellectually significant time at the University of Illinois, Chicago, especially Amy Brainer, Sharon Collins, Georgiann Davis, Nilda Flores, Mosi Ifatunji, Maria Krysan, Barbara Risman, María Victoria Badillo Rodríguez, and Patrick Washington.

The second round of interviews in 2015 was generously supported by Mississippi State University. I thank my colleagues in the Department of Sociology for their help with aspects of this book, especially Rachel Allison, Dustin Brown, Adele Crudden, Leslie Hossfeld, Kimberly Kelly, Braden Leap, and Ashley Perry. Special thanks to Nicole Rader for being my faculty mentor and friend and to Rick Travis for his consistent encouragement and words of wisdom. Many thanks also to graduate students Courtney Heath and Izzy Pellegrine for their assistance. I also thank my former students for sharing their insights with me about their own racial socialization experiences. I thank Tommy Anderson, Marsha Barrett, Courtney Carter, Mike Roche, Donald Shaffer, Chris Snyder, Ashley Vancil-Leap, and Danielle Wylie for being such supportive colleagues and friends. And many thanks to my archeologist friend Shane Miller for helping me with the map.

I have been fortunate to meet a number of scholars who have kindly offered me their time and advice. I especially acknowledge the help of Erin Winkler, who is one of smartest and nicest people I know, who pushes us all to think more carefully about how kids learn about race, and whose own work has greatly influenced and guided this research. I am also grateful for the encouragement and mentorship of Matthew Hughey, who has provided feedback on many of the ideas in this book, whose research informs my own, and who has generously offered his advice and assistance at various stages of this process. I thank Antonia Randolph for our brief yet incredibly helpful conversation at the 2016 Southern Sociological Society conference. Many thanks to David Embrick for helping me think through the organization of this book.

I thank my friends who have each directly contributed to the completion of this project in their own meaningful way. While I cannot name them all, I thank Mondi Basmenji, Laurel Bastian, Suzanne Blackamore, Kevin Boettcher, Keith Borden, Julia Dauer, Devin Garofalo, Vanessa Lauber, Kerri Matthews, Hassan Pasha, Jessie Reeder, Steel Wagstaff, Stephanie Youngblood, and Erica Zurawski. Special thanks to Emily Clark for everything she did to help me with this research. And thanks to Julie, whom I look up to tremendously, for helping me with this project in so many ways and for serving as such an important mentor to me, whether she knows it or not. I will always be appreciative.

I thank my family, especially my parents, Jean Maloney Hagerman and Doug Hagerman, for always having a positive outlook, for supporting me in every way imaginable, and for consistently modeling the importance of standing up for what you believe is right and speaking the truth, even if it is unpopular. I thank Gail and David McKay for their enthusiasm about this book. I thank Melissa McKay, Mike Sondel, and Laura and Matt Vaughn for their encouragement. And I thank my brother, James Hagerman, for technical assistance along the way. I could not have completed this project without the practical advice, unique perspective, and emotional support of Mikyla Smith, my best friend. I also thank my grandmother JoAnne Sinden Hagerman, who received her first graduate degree in 1948 and who inspires me. I thank her for sharing her stories and knowledge with me, for taking such an interest in my research, and for serving as such strong example of the kind of person I strive to be.

I am grateful to have a partner who earnestly supports me and my ambitions, who endlessly listens to me talk about my research, who helps me find just the right words to express complex ideas simply, who continually teaches me new things and reads me old things, who encourages me to work harder, and who read this manuscript more times than he probably wanted to. Thank you Eric Vivier for being outraged and outspoken about the things that really matter in the world, for reminding me to laugh at the things that do not, and for continuing to walk to the library with me.

Methodology

Given that scholars studying white racial subjects have often found whites to experience and discuss race in ways that are contradictory and elusive, ethnography is a particularly useful method for exploring how race is discussed and lived.[1] From January 2011 to December 2012, I conducted ethnographic research with 30 affluent families in a midwestern metropolitan area who self-identified as white. The ethnographic approach I utilized allowed me to access what Amanda Lewis describes as the "'everydayness' of whiteness" within the institution of the white family.[2]

Because this research included work with kids, child-centered approaches to data production were used. Critical youth studies call for methods that are innovative and lead to accurate depictions of children's viewpoints rather than adult memories of what it was like to be a child.[3] Additionally, child-centered research recognizes the power dynamics between children and adults and seeks to reduce this power as much as possible.

Overall, my research is based on data gathered through (1) ethnographic observations of 30 white families in their everyday lives in Petersfield and (2) semistructured, in-depth, child-centered interviews with 36 white kids between the ages of 10 and 13 and their parents.

INCLUSION CRITERIA

While many scholars debate how to best measure class, in this study, families were characterized as affluent if at least one parent (though oftentimes both parents) (1) holds a graduate or professional degree, (2) has a career as a lawyer, medical doctor, engineer, university professor, business CEO/manager, scientific researcher, or similar occupation, *and* (3) owns a home. While occupation and education have often been used to measure class in sociological research, I also included home ownership to account for measures of wealth.[4]

The ages of the child participants in this study fall in the second half of middle childhood, or ages 10 to 13. Middle childhood is a developmental stage in which moral principles such as "justice, fairness, compassionate caring, and feelings of responsibility for one's fellow human beings" emerge.[5] This developmental stage is also when children are in the midst of developing a social and ideological perspective of the world.[6] Thus, middle childhood is a crucial developmental stage for the formation of racial ideologies.

SELECTING A RESEARCH SITE AND IDENTIFYING NEIGHBORHOODS

I selected Petersfield as my research site because this community is large enough for variation across groups of affluent whites but small enough that understandings about the community are locally shared. Suburbs surrounding Petersfield are almost exclusively white, and a sizable affluent population lives in the Petersfield area due to various industries, a major university, and government-related activities. Additionally, members of this metropolitan area occupy political positions at extreme ends of the political spectrum, though I did not know about the extent of the political segregation of this community or the impact that politics would have on this project initially.

In order to describe and interpret the everyday meanings of race in the lives of white, affluent kids and their parents, I immersed myself as an actor into the Petersfield community. From the outset, I appreciated that it would be my interactions with members of this community that would help me generate my data. After moving to this city, I spent approximately three months figuring out the lay of the land. Through an inductive process in which I spent most of my time in public places talking to strangers and building relationships, I was able to identify different neighborhoods within the metropolitan area that were literally and symbolically distinct. Rather than entering the field with preconceived notions about what I would find, I selected the neighborhoods of Sheridan, Evergreen, and Wheaton Hills after learning more about what was actually happening in this particular environment. Drawing on grounded theory, I made theoretical sampling decisions after learning more about the community under study.[7] Of note, before entering the field, I considered sampling from a different suburb than the one I ultimately included in my study. However, as I learned more about how people in Petersfield constructed local meanings around place and race, the suburb I ended up including emerged as a better comparison group during the middle stages of my data-collection process. This choice was also shaped by the difficulty I experienced gaining access to families in this alternative suburb. This is evidence of the utility of grounded theory, or the idea that "simultaneous involvement in data collection and analysis . . . [leads] the researcher subsequently to collect more data around emerging themes and questions," as well as of practical issues of access that present themselves in ethnographic work.[8]

RECRUITMENT OF PARTICIPANTS AND THE IRB

After selecting the neighborhoods, I used a structured snowball sampling method to recruit participants. My snowball sample began with multiple nodes—individuals I met through seeking child-care positions, people to whom I was introduced by friends, and people I met through spending time in coffee shops, yoga studios, and gyms. Through building personal relationships in this community, I was able to recruit families to participate. A few of the mothers in different parts of the city helped with recruitment efforts in substantial ways through drawing on their own social networks and connections to private school communities and youth athletics. Almost every family helped me find additional families, including some parents sending emails to their friends introducing them to me. To these parents, I presented myself as both an "insider" (white, educated at prestigious institutions, grew up in a similar family and community as theirs) and an outsider (knowing "nothing" about the community, asking them for their explanations of various dynamics and observations). I always talked about my work in this initial recruitment stage as "a project on how parents talk to their kids about social issues" or a project on "families with middle school kids" rather than using the word "race" up front for fear that they may not be willing to participate because of the controversial nature of race relations in the United States. However, my consent and assent materials were more straightforward. Only two families declined to participate after initially learning of my project, and both indicated it was due to their busy schedules, one of the biggest challenges in this study overall.

Researchers studying children often cite the IRB process as a major roadblock to gathering information directly from children about their everyday lives, including how they think about and make sense of the world around them. I actively sought to construct an IRB application that paid particular attention to the power dynamics implicated in an adult-research and child-participant interview model. I wrote the child-assent form in language that was child friendly, asking a child within the age range to look over an early draft of the document. In my IRB proposal, I included a discussion of why these elements of the child-assent form were so important to safeguarding against the possibility of a child feeling unwanted pressure to participate in my project but also to establish rapport with the kids from the onset of the interview process. I also discussed the importance of child-centered research methods and implemented best practices for these methods in my research design.

PARTICIPANT OBSERVATION

In order to facilitate the collection of my ethnographic data, and especially during the first year of data collection, I spent significant amounts of time in public places observing the interactions, behaviors, and language of white families. Spending an extended period of time in public places allowed me to acquire a sense of the larger social geography of race and the cultural milieu of the Petersfield metropolitan area.

Public places were not the only places in which I gathered my data. I was also able to successfully form relationships with families that provided me access to the private places where affluent kids spend a lot of time. Through these relationships, I was also able to access spaces that are designated for children and authorized adults. Because affluent children spend so much time in private spaces, the observations I made in these places were especially important for my research. I also spent informal time in the private homes or out in public with most of the families in the study. In some families, I spent multiple afternoons a week with the kids for long stretches of the data-collection period. In other families, I spent only a few hours with the family. Most of these more personal in-home experiences were with children with whom I formed relationships, as a friend of the family, as their babysitter, or through the process of asking if I could observe a home for a few hours following an interview session. Because children talk about race sometimes in very spontaneous, unpredictable moments, the observational component to this project was key.

INTERVIEWS WITH KIDS

In an attempt to include children in the research process from the very beginning, I sought the help of kids within the appropriate age range in developing an activity in which I compiled photos of popular celebrities of different races that I could use as part of my interview. Drawing on this activity as well as techniques outlined in various methodological texts, I established rapport with the children by talking to them about topics that mattered to them, by making them feel as if they were the experts rather than I, by reinforcing the point that I was not testing them or that there was a "right" answer to my questions, and by connecting with them in ways that made the interview process fun and interesting to them.[9] I asked kids questions in terms that I thought they would understand, I encouraged them to ask me questions throughout the process, and I repeated their language back to them rather than insisting on using sociological jargon. I also encouraged the children to laugh, as well as to be serious, and I was always careful not to push them to answer questions that appeared to make them feel unreasonably uncomfortable. A few children were very shy, but the majority of them appeared to be very comfortable and reported enjoying the experience and telling me that they thought it was important that adults hear their voices.[10]

Child interviews generally lasted between 30 and 60 minutes. I usually conducted these interviews at the child's home in the living or dining room. Occasionally, I interviewed children at a coffee shop or restaurant. In total, 36 children were interviewed. Gender representation of the children was a relatively equal split between girls (20) and boys (16).

INTERVIEWS WITH PARENTS

I also conducted more traditional, semistructured interviews with the parents of the children in the sample. Parents were interviewed separately from kids in all but one case. In the other cases, parents were frequently nearby, sometimes drifting in and out of the room in which the interview was being conducted. Most parent interviews lasted 75–90 minutes. In seven families, mothers and fathers were interviewed separately. In three families, both parents were interviewed together at the same time. In only one family, the father was the only parent interviewed, while the other 29 families included interviews with mothers. Parents generally shared similar views, which helped reduce concerns that this gender imbalance would distort my findings. All of the children in this study have heterosexual parents, most of whom were married at the time of data collection. These interviews often took place in the family home, though occasionally parents invited me to their work office or a restaurant to conduct the interview.

DATA ANALYSIS

After transcribing interview recordings and typing up field notes as well as changing all identifying details to protect the confidentiality of my participants, I used MAXQDA to code my data in multiple ways. First, I coded "categories that make sense in terms of . . . relevant interests, commitments, literatures, and/or perspectives," otherwise known as "initial coding" or "open" coding.[11] Drawing on "qualitative grounded theory coding" as described by sociologist Kathy Charmaz, data were then recoded.[12] Here, the objective was to develop theoretical categories from the data on the basis of what participants told me and what I observed about how they constructed ideas about race, racism, inequality, privilege, and so forth, to generate theory about racial socialization processes.[13] I coded my data while still collecting data, which allowed me to conduct an inductive analysis of my data and develop further questions to ask participants or next directions for my ethnographic data collection on the basis of emergent themes.

RESEARCHER STANDPOINT

My own social position as a white woman in my mid- to late 20s shaped not only the data I produced but also my interpretations of it in more ways than I can possible state here. In short, I was able to access private white, family-centered spaces given my own whiteness, gender, and age without anyone questioning who I was or why I was there. Numerous times, parent and child respondents told me that they only felt comfortable talking to me or that they only answered my questions the way they did because I was white. Parents trusted me with their children and even asked me for advice about college and other topics given my own educational background, which I offered when appropriate. Parents also assumed due to my age and gender that one day I would want to have kids and as such were happy to talk to me at length about parenting. Finally, I was familiar with many of the aspects of these families' lives given my own experiences growing up in a similar community, and I drew on this knowledge to gain insider access to this particular social world.

APPENDIX B

Child Participants

Child	Age	Gender	Neighborhood	School
Emily Anderson	13	Girl	Wheaton Hills	Progressive, then Talented and Gifted (TAG) school
Rachel Anderson	12	Girl	Wheaton Hills	Progressive, then TAG school
Simon Anderson	11	Boy	Wheaton Hills	Progressive, then TAG school
Edward Avery	12	Boy	Sheridan	Sheridan Middle
Lauren Avery	12	Girl	Sheridan	Sheridan Middle
Jessica Boone	11	Girl	Wheaton Hills	Saint Anne's
Ashley Carter	10	Girl	Evergreen	Evergreen Middle
Meredith Chablis	12	Girl	Sheridan	Sheridan Middle
Adam Church	11	Boy	Sheridan	Saint Anne's, then Sheridan Middle
William Green	12	Boy	Evergreen	Evergreen Middle
Anthony Hall	12	Boy	Evergreen	Evergreen Middle
Aaron Hayes	11	Boy	Wheaton Hills	TAG school
Elizabeth Jones	11	Girl	Evergreen	Evergreen Middle
Lindsay Kerner	11	Girl	Wheaton Hills	Wheaton Hills Elementary, then Progressive
Charlotte Lacey	13	Girl	Evergreen	Evergreen Middle
Kacie Martin	12	Girl	Wheaton Hills	Saint Anne's, then Wheaton Hills Middle
Ryan Morris	11	Boy	Sheridan	Sheridan Middle
Robert Norbrook	12	Boy	Wheaton Hills	Wheaton Hills Middle
Conor Norton-Smith	11	Boy	Evergreen	Evergreen Middle
Chris Palmer-Ross	11	Boy	Wheaton Hills	Saint Anne's, then Wheaton Hills Middle
Caroline Parker	13	Girl	Evergreen	Evergreen Middle
Margot Patterson	12	Girl	Evergreen	Evergreen Middle
Tyler Patterson	10	Boy	Evergreen	Evergreen Middle

Child	Age	Gender	Neighborhood	School
Nate Reed	12	Boy	Sheridan	Sheridan Middle
Bethany Roberts	12	Girl	Evergreen	Evergreen Middle
Carly Robinson	12	Girl	Sheridan	Saint Anne's
Erica Schultz	13	Girl	Sheridan	Saint Anne's, then Sheridan Middle
Natalie Schultz	11	Girl	Sheridan	Saint Anne's, then Sheridan Middle
Danny Silber	12	Boy	Evergreen	Evergreen Middle
Britney Smith	11	Girl	Sheridan	Sheridan Middle
Rosie Stewart	10	Girl	Sheridan	Saint Anne's
Andrew Taylor	12	Boy	Wheaton Hills	Progressive, then TAG school
Matthew Tucker	12	Boy	Wheaton Hills	Progressive, then Wheaton Hills Middle
Logan Wells	13	Boy	Wheaton Hills	Wheaton Hills Middle
Jamie Younker	10	Girl	Sheridan	Saint Anne's
Kelsey Younker	13	Girl	Sheridan	Saint Anne's

NOTES

INTRODUCTION

1. All names and identifying details of people and places are changed.
2. Du Bois 1998, 700.
3. Bonilla-Silva 1997, 474.
4. Cornell and Hartmann 2006; Haney López 1996.
5. Bonilla-Silva 2018, 2; Krysan and Lewis 2006.
6. Delpit 2006; Frankenberg and Orfield 2012; Kozol 2012; Lewis and Diamond 2015; Lewis and Manno 2011; Noguera 2009; Oakes 2005; Posey-Maddox 2014.
7. Fenning and Rose 2007; Flavin 2008; Gregory, Skiba, and Noguera 2010; Kupchik 2007; Meiners 2007; Nicholson-Crotty, Birchmeier, and Valentine 2009; Skiba et al. 2011; Winn 2011.
8. Alexander 2010; Poehlmann et al. 2010; D. Roberts 2002; Travis and Waul 2004; Wakefield and Wildeman 2016.
9. Billingsley 1972; D. Roberts 2002.
10. Bridges 2011; Flavin 2008.
11. Goyal et al. 2015.
12. Garcia 2012; Solinger 2002.
13. Oliver and Shapiro 2006; Turner and Wienk 1993.
14. Quadagno 1996; D. Roberts 2002.
15. Johnson 2014; Oliver and Shapiro 2006.
16. Zinn 1993.
17. M. Anderson 2003.
18. Roediger 2007; Kimmel 2015. Referring to the 19th century, Roediger (2007) writes, "Whiteness was a way in which white workers responded to a fear of dependency on wage labor and to the necessities of capitalist work discipline. . . . The white working class constructed an image of the black population as other—as embodying the preindustrial, erotic, careless style of life the white worker hated and longed for" (13–14).
19. Kefalas 2003, 8. Both Kefalas and the sociologist Monica McDermott (2006) have shown that these working-class white understandings of race are often locally situated and context dependent.
20. Bonilla-Silva 2018, 143.
21. Van Ausdale and Feagin 2001.
22. L. Hughes 2001; Meece 2002.

23. For examples of research that does examine socialization processes along the lines of gender, sexuality, and race, see Bettie 2014; Garcia 2012; Kenny 2000; and Pascoe 2011.
24. Bonilla-Silva 2018, 9.
25. Goff et al. 2014.
26. See Alexander 2010, 261, for a long list of national reports on drug use, race, and youth, documenting lower drug-usage rates by black kids than white kids.
27. Barber and Torney-Purta 2008; Carman 2011; Lewis and Manno 2011.
28. Du Bois 1998, 700; Lipsitz 2009; McIntosh 1989; Roediger 2007.

CHAPTER 1. "RACE REALLY DOESN'T MATTER ANYMORE"

1. Best 2007; Corsaro 2014; Frønes 1994; Hagerman 2010; Handel 2006; Johnson 2001; Parsons and Bales 1956.
2. Corsaro 2014, 4.
3. Winkler 2012, 4.
4. Hughes and Johnson 2001, 981.
5. Rollins and Hunter 2013, 141.
6. Winkler 2012.
7. Winkler 2012, 7.
8. Bonilla-Silva 1997; Du Bois 1994.
9. Bonilla-Silva 1997, 469
10. Bonilla-Silva 1997, 469.
11. D. Roberts 2011, 4.
12. D. Roberts 2011, 5.
13. Omi and Winant 2014.
14. Haney López 1996.
15. Cornell and Hartmann 2006.
16. Bonilla-Silva 1997; Haney López 1996.
17. Almaguer 2008; Takaki 1998; R. Thornton 1990.
18. D. Roberts 2011, 25.
19. Johnson 2014, 4.
20. Lewis 2004, 632.
21. Hall 1996, 444.
22. Forman 2004, 58.
23. For further elaboration on the theoretical nuances of this point, see Hagerman 2016.
24. Constantine and Blackmon 2002, 324. See also Bowman and Howard 1985; Peters 2002; Knight et al. 1993; Phinney and Chavira 1995; Brega and Coleman 1999.
25. Thomas and Blackmon 2015.
26. Brown et al. 2007; D. Hughes 2003; Hughes et al. 2006; Hughes and Chen 1997; Ou and McAdoo 1993; Winkler 2010.
27. Lacy 2007; Peters 2002; Scottham and Smalls 2009; M. Thornton 1997; Winkler 2008.

28. Brown et al. 2007; Coles and Green 2009; D. Hughes 2003; Lacy and Harris 2010; McAdoo 2006; M. Thornton 1997; Winkler 2008, 2012.

29. Lacy 2007; Lacy and Harris 2010.

30. Hughes et al. 2006; Peters 2002; Scottham and Smalls 2009; Winkler 2008.

31. Thomas and Blackmon 2015; Threlfall 2016.

32. See review pieces by Brown et al. 2007; Hughes et al. 2006; and Winkler 2012, 5.

33. D. Hughes 2003, 16.

34. Brega and Coleman 1999; Douglass and Umaña-Taylor 2015; Gartner, Kiang, and Supple 2014; D. Hughes 2003; Orbe 1999; Phinney and Chavira 1995; Quintana and Vera 1999; Rivas-Drake 2010; Rockquemore and Laszloffy 2005; Rollins and Hunter 2013.

35. Burton et al. 2010, 453.

36. Burton et al. 2010, 453.

37. Hamm 2001.

38. Derman-Sparks, Phillips, and Hilliard 1997.

39. Underhill 2017. For research on "antiracist" white parenting, see also Matlock and DiAngelo 2015; and Hagerman 2017b.

40. Feagin and O'Brien 2004, 30.

41. Bourdieu 1977.

42. Bonilla-Silva 2018, 121.

43. Bonilla-Silva, Goar, and Embrick 2006, 233.

44. Hagerman 2016.

45. Kinder and Sanders 1996, 110.

46. Sears and Henry 2003, 260.

47. Bonilla-Silva 2018; Doane 1997; Forman and Lewis 2006; Gallagher 2008; Hughey 2012; Lewis 2004; McDermott and Samson 2005.

48. Hughes et al. 2006; Rollins and Hunter 2013.

49. Lewis 2004, 634, citing Rasmussen et al. 2001. See also Hartigan 1999; Kenny 2000.

50. As the sociologists Monica McDermott and Frank Samson (2005) state, "Navigating between the long-term staying power of white privilege and the multifarious manifestations of the experience of whiteness remains the task of the next era of research on white racial and ethnic identity" (256).

51. Lewis 2004, 637.

52. Emerson 2001, 30.

53. Winkler 2012, 1.

54. For methodological detail, see appendix A.

55. Bronfenbrenner 1979, 3.

56. Bobo 2004, 15.

CHAPTER 2. "THE PERFECT PLACE TO LIVE"

1. In 2010, the United States as a whole was 72.4% white, 12.6% black, 4.8% Asian, 0.9% American Indian, and 16.3% Latinx, according to the Census Bureau. The

median household income in the United States was $53,482, with a 14.8% poverty rate. The median value of owner-occupied homes was $175,700.

2. Bobo and Zubrinsky 1996; Charles 2003; Farley and Frey 1994; Krysan et al. 2009.
3. Crowder and Krysan 2016, 18.
4. Massey and Denton 1993; Meyer 2001; Oliver and Shapiro 2006; Sugrue 2005.
5. LaVeist et al. 2011; Polednak 1991.
6. Frankenberg and Orfield 2012; Kozol 2012; Orfield, Kucsera, and Siegel-Hawley 2012.
7. Crowder and Downey 2010.
8. Krysan et al. 2009.
9. Bobo 1989; Krysan et al. 2009.
10. Bishop 2009; Lareau and Goyette 2014.
11. Zamal, Liu, and Ruths 2012.
12. Walks 2006, 20.
13. Desilver 2014.
14. Winkler 2012, 180.
15. Lewis and Diamond 2015; Noguera 2009; Oakes 2005.
16. Johnson 2014; Holme 2002; Lareau and Goyette 2014; Schneider 2001.
17. Shapiro and Johnson 2005.
18. Johnson 2014, 56.
19. Johnson 2014, 41.
20. Lewis and Diamond 2015, 156.
21. Johnson 2014; Cookson and Persell 1987.
22. Informant interview with school social worker.
23. Lewis and Diamond 2015, 43–44.
24. Johnson 2014; Holme 2002; Lareau and Goyette 2014; Schneider 2001.
25. Bonilla-Silva 2018; Bonilla-Silva and Forman 2000; Carr 1997; Crenshaw 1997; Forman 2004; Forman and Lewis 2006; Gallagher 2003.
26. Lewis and Hagerman 2016, 158.
27. Lewis and Hagerman 2016, 159; Bonilla-Silva 2018; Crenshaw 1997; Forman and Lewis 2006; Gallagher 2003.
28. Ball 1997; Betts and Fairlie 2001; Buddin, Cordes, and Kirby 1998; Lareau and Goyette 2014; Cookson and Persell 1987.
29. M. Anderson 1999.
30. Halley, Eshleman, and Vijaya 2011.
31. Bartky 2002.
32. Perry and Shotwell 2009, 34.
33. Posey-Maddox 2013.
34. Lewis and Diamond 2015, 134.
35. Lareau 2011.
36. Calarco 2011.
37. Lewis 2003; Noguera 2009; Posey-Maddox 2013; Posey 2012.
38. Cucchiara 2013.
39. Delpit 2006.

CHAPTER 3. "WE'RE NOT A RACIAL SCHOOL"

1. Different families in these communities do experience differing degrees of wealth privilege, but they are all affluent.
2. Goyette and Lareau 2014, xxii.
3. Goyette and Lareau 2014, xxii.
4. Gallagher (2003) speaks to the "hypervisibility of blacks by whites" in a context of high levels of racial segregation (383). Similarly, Alba, Rumbaut, and Marotz (2005) and others studying racial innumeracy find that whites often engage in a "numerical inflation" of the size of the nonwhite population in the United States. This designation of the school as "diverse" seems to be because of the presence of only a few students of color. Saporito (2003) also examines patterns of white families removing children from schools as the proportion of black students increases. Billingham and Hunt (2016) illustrate that the racial composition of schools influences white parents' school choices.
5. Saporito and Hanley (2014) find that white private school enrollment is correlated with the racial composition of the community. For further discussion, see Zhang 2008; Saporito 2003; and Li 2009.
6. Despite the strong philosophical commitment to fairness of these parents, they are also regularly pushing hard to provide their children with the best opportunities and advantages, but they do not leave the public schools entirely.
7. Much of his anxiety about college resonates with the work of the journalist Alexandra Robbins (2007) and her insights into "driven kids" as they participate in "overachiever" culture and engage in practices of fierce capitalism-driven competition with one another for admission to selective universities, often with negative consequences for self-worth, anxiety, stress, and so forth.
8. Roda and Wells 2013.
9. Roda 2015, 2–3.
10. Oakes 2005, 22.
11. Oakes 2005, 3.
12. Oakes 2005, 4.
13. Carman 2011.
14. Barber and Torney-Purta 2008, 412.
15. Lewis and Manno 2011.
16. The Moynihan Report, published in 1965 by the secretary of labor, Daniel P. Moynihan, "contained the thesis that weaknesses in the black family are at the heart of the deterioration of the black community" (Johnson and Staples 2004, 46). Moynihan and his team reported that high rates of "dissolved" or unstable marriages, "illegitimate" children, and female-headed households in the black community were the cause of "the failure of youth," measured by black children's school performance, work ethic, IQ scores, and delinquency rates. Overall, as Jewell (2003) writes, "perceptions of African American families as structurally

and functionally dysfunctional have been at the basis of both conservative and liberal social policy" (12).

17. D. Roberts 2002, 65.
18. Roda 2015, 83.
19. Roda 2015, 83.
20. Forman and Lewis 2006, 178, quoting Sue 2005, 108.
21. The term "opportunity hoarding" originates from Charles Tilly (1999). Scholars have built on his term, particularly with respect to education, arguing that goods are regulated by groups in positions of power subsequently monopolizing the use of these goods.
22. Tyson 2011, 9.
23. E. Anderson 2013.
24. Oakes 2005.
25. Bartky 2002.
26. Goyette and Lareau 2014, xiii.
27. These schools range from a few thousand dollars a year to nearly $15,000 per year.
28. Forman 2004.
29. "The specialness of white kids" is a phrase used by Antonia Randolph during conference proceedings at the 2016 Southern Sociological Society annual meeting, used with her permission.
30. As Amanda Lewis and John Diamond (2015) find in a school-based ethnographic study involving similar types of parents, "Parents are not just advocating for their own children. They are also advocating for the maintenance of the structures of inequality that facilitate their advantage" (156)—structures that are maintained in part by dominant ideologies across generations as young people adopt, reject, or transform them.

CHAPTER 4. "THAT'S SO RACIST!"

1. Myers 2005; Picca and Feagin 2007.
2. Bonilla-Silva, Goar, and Embrick 2006, 233.
3. Hagerman 2016.
4. For a discussion of the history of "after-school activities" and the various forms these activities take, see Adler and Adler 1998, 98–114.
5. For a discussion about the long history and current manifestations of race and science in the United States, see Davis 1983, 202–221; and D. Roberts 2011.
6. This is why ethnographic methods were necessary for this research.
7. For a discussion of verbal routines and games, see Corsaro 2014.
8. For more theoretical depth on this topic, see Hagerman 2016.
9. Connections can be drawn here between the policing of whiteness and the policing of masculinity found in Pascoe's (2011) research with high school boys.
10. Robert's use of "light" and "dark" skin was somewhat unique across the kids in this study, although many of their parents told me that when the children were younger, this is how they would talk about kids at school.

11. For a discussion of how scholars are only beginning to consider racial socialization as a "transactional process—how parents' racial socialization is influenced by children's experiences," see Hughes and Johnson 2001 (981).

12. Perry and Shotwell 2009, 34, 40.

13. Allport 1954; Feagin and O'Brien 2004; Pettigrew 1998.

14. Although the shooting of Trayvon Martin happened during the period of data collection, this episode occurred prior to that.

15. Perry and Shotwell (2009) distinguish their notion of "antiracist praxis" from the term "antiracism" because "antiracism" "implies a reactive politics that is not always true of successful practices for social justice." They argue that three specific types of knowledge must combine with a relational understanding of self and one's group position in order for "antiracist consciousness and practice" to emerge (34).

16. Adler and Adler 1998, 206.

17. Corsaro 2014, 20 (emphasis added).

CHAPTER 5. "EVERYBODY IS WHITE"

1. Winkler 2012, 178.

2. Winkler 2012, 52. When children leave Detroit, they compare places and produce ideas about race and about behavior of people of particular racial groups (Winkler 2012, 66).

3. Urry 1990.

4. Hughey's (2012) research finds evidence of "antiracist" whites drawing on a paternalistic white savior complex, informing how they view themselves as white allies.

5. Lasker's (2016) research explores related debates in the realm of global health volunteering.

6. Hagerman 2017b, 69.

7. Whyte, Selinger, and Outterson 2011, 337.

8. Steinbrink 2012, 232.

9. Whyte, Selinger, and Outterson 2011, 337.

10. Steinbrink 2012, 213.

CHAPTER 6. "SHAKING THOSE GHETTO BOOTIES"

1. Association of Black Women Historians 2011.

2. Hughey 2014, 15.

3. Dubrofsky 2013, 83.

4. Dubrofsky 2013, 98.

5. Greenberg 1972.

6. Van Evra 2004.

7. See, e.g., Berry 1998; Guidotti-Hernández 2007; Moran 2007; and E. Roberts 2004.

8. Bernstein 2011.

9. Thomas and Blackmon 2015.

10. Adler and Adler 1998; Lareau 2011.

11. Rodriquez 2006, 645. For further debates about the relationship between hip hop, whiteness, and cultural appropriation, see also Kitwana 2005; and Eberhardt and Freeman 2015.

12. For a historical analysis of race, class, and youth soccer, see Andrews et al. 1997.

13. Much as existing research shows, fathers frequently hold leadership positions in the context of youth sports. See Gottzén and Kremer-Sadlik 2012; and Messner 2009.

14. Hamm (2001) illustrates how white parents tend to passively hope for interracial "exposure" through institutions, whereas black parents tend to actively encourage individual interracial contact outside of places such as school. Here, Seth actively works to build a racially diverse environment, which is a deviation from Hamm's findings and also stands out within my own findings.

CHAPTER 7. "IT WAS RACISM"

1. Bell and Hartmann 2007; Doane 1997; Lewis 2004.

2. Bonilla-Silva 2018, 70.

3. DiAngelo 2011, 57.

4. Bonilla-Silva 2018, 91.

5. Goffman 1959, 113.

6. DiAngelo 2011, 61.

7. In these kids' individualized understanding of racism, they are in line with the views of many white Americans. But as the writer Chimamanda Ngozi Adichie (2016) has recently remarked, "no racism story is a 'simple' racism story, in which grinning evil people wearing white burn crosses in yards." Sociologists such as Eduardo Bonilla-Silva (1997) have suggested that a structural framework rather than an individual one is required to understand racism.

8. Bonilla-Silva 2018, 98.

9. Johnson 2014, 27–73.

10. Johnson 2014, 201.

11. Lareau 2011, 6.

12. While it is beyond the scope of this book to examine how kids engage with privilege and disadvantage due to gender or sexuality, some of the children I interviewed did mention the additional privileges that come with being a man or being straight in their interviews. Other scholars have examined gender socialization and male, heterosexual privilege in young people (Thorne 1993; Pascoe 2011).

13. Interestingly, in other moments, Kelsey is more willing to recognize that racism exists, such as when she references the *That's So Raven* episode. This shows that these kids are in the process of figuring out what they think and that, to some extent, their racial common sense is either inconsistent or still forming.

CONCLUSION

1. This research is in progress and will be described in more detail in future publications.
2. For more on this topic, see Hughey 2012.
3. Hackman 2015; Dewan and Oppel 2015; Graham 2017; Democracy Now 2017; Sullivan 2015.
4. Democracy Now 2015; Scholl 2015; Lowery 2016.
5. Pearce 2015; Fernandez and Hauser 2015; Jarvie 2015.
6. Vittrup 2015; Vawter 2015; Leahy 2015.
7. Dell'Antonia 2014; Moyer 2014.
8. Bartky 2002.
9. For more on this topic, see Bernstein 2011.

APPENDIX A

1. Zuberi and Bonilla-Silva 2008.
2. Lewis 2004, 637.
3. Biklen 2007.
4. Lamont 1992; Oliver and Shapiro 2006.
5. L. Hughes 2001, 515.
6. Meece 2002, 443.
7. Charmaz 2001.
8. Charmaz 2001, 336.
9. Barker and Weller 2003; Biklen 2007; Fraser et al. 2003; Freeman and Mathiston 2008; Hagerman 2010.
10. For more about the use of photographs of celebrities, see Hagerman 2017a.
11. Lofland et al. 2005, 201.
12. Charmaz 2001.
13. Emerson 2001.

REFERENCES

Adichie, Chimamanda Ngozi. 2016. "Now Is the Time to Talk about What We Are Actually Talking About." *New Yorker*, 2 December. www.newyorker.com.

Adler, Peter, and Patricia Adler. 1998. *Peer Power: Preadolescent Culture and Identity*. New Brunswick, NJ: Rutgers University Press.

Alba, Richard, Rubén G. Rumbaut, and Karen Marotz. 2005. "A Distorted Nation: Perceptions of Racial/Ethnic Group Sizes and Attitudes toward Immigrants and Other Minorities." *Social Forces* 84 (2): 901–19.

Alexander, Michelle. 2010. *The New Jim Crow: Mass Incarceration in the Age of Colorblindness*. New York: New Press.

Allport, Gordon W. 1954. *The Nature of Prejudice*. Boston: Addison-Wesley.

Almaguer, Tomas. 2008. *Racial Fault Lines: The Historical Origins of White Supremacy in California*. Berkeley: University of California Press.

Anderson, Elizabeth. 2013. *The Imperative of Integration*. Princeton, NJ: Princeton University Press.

Anderson, Margaret L. 1999. "The Fiction of 'Diversity without Oppression.'" In *Critical Ethnicity: Countering the Waves of Identity Politics*, by Robert H. Tai and Mary L. Kenyatta, 5–20. Lanham, MD: Rowman and Littlefield.

———. 2003. "Whitewashing Race: A Critical Perspective on Whiteness." In *White Out: The Continuing Significance of Racism*, edited by Ashley W. Doane and Eduardo Bonilla-Silva, 21–34. East Sussex, UK: Psychology Press.

Andrews, David L., Robert Pitter, Detley Zwick, and Darren Ambrose. 1997. "Soccer's Racial Frontier: Sport and the Suburbanization of Contemporary America." In *Entering the Field: New Perspectives on World Football*, edited by Gary Armstrong and Richard Giulianotti, 261–81. Oxford, UK: Berg.

Association of Black Women Historians. 2011. "An Open Statement to the Fans of The Help." 12 August. www.abwh.org.

Ball, Stephen J. 1997. "On the Cusp: Parents Choosing between State and Private Schools in the UK: Action within an Economy of Symbolic Goods." *International Journal of Inclusive Education* 1 (1): 1–17.

Barber, Carolyn, and Judith Torney-Purta. 2008. "The Relation of High-Achieving Adolescents' Social Perceptions and Motivation to Teachers' Nominations for Advanced Programs." *Journal of Advanced Academics* 19 (3): 412–43.

Barker, John, and Susie Weller. 2003. "Is It Fun? Developing Children Centred Research Methods." *International Journal of Sociology and Social Policy* 23 (1–2): 33–58.

Bartky, Sandra Lee. 2002. *Sympathy and Solidarity: And Other Essays*. Lanham, MD: Rowman and Littlefield.

Bell, Joyce M., and Douglas Hartmann. 2007. "Diversity in Everyday Discourse: The Cultural Ambiguities and Consequences of 'Happy Talk.'" *American Sociological Review* 72 (6): 895–914.

Bernstein, Robin. 2011. *Racial Innocence: Performing American Childhood from Slavery to Civil Rights*. New York: NYU Press.

Berry, Gordon L. 1998. "Black Family Life on Television and the Socialization of the African American Child: Images of Marginality." *Journal of Comparative Family Studies* 29 (2): 233–42.

Best, Amy L., ed. 2007. *Representing Youth: Methodological Issues in Critical Youth Studies*. New York: NYU Press.

Bettie, Julie. 2014. *Women without Class: Girls, Race, and Identity*. Berkeley: University of California Press.

Betts, Julian R., and Robert W. Fairlie. 2001. "Explaining Ethnic, Racial, and Immigrant Differences in Private School Attendance." *Journal of Urban Economics* 50 (1): 26–51.

Biklen, Sari Knopp. 2007. "Trouble on Memory Lane: Adults and Self-Retrospection in Researching Youth." In *Representing Youth: Methodological Issues in Critical Youth Studies*, edited by Amy L. Best, 251–68. New York: NYU Press.

Billingham, Chase M., and Matthew O. Hunt. 2016. "School Racial Composition and Parental Choice: New Evidence on the Preferences of White Parents in the United States." *Sociology of Education* 89 (2): 99–117.

Billingsley, Andrew. 1972. *Children of the Storm: Black Children and American Child Welfare*. New York: Harcourt College.

Bishop, Bill. 2009. *The Big Sort: Why the Clustering of Like-Minded America Is Tearing Us Apart*. Boston: Mariner Books.

Bobo, Lawrence. 1989. "Keeping the Linchpin in Place: Testing the Multiple Sources of Opposition to Residential Integration." *International Review of Social Psychology* 2 (3): 305–23.

———. 2004. "Inequalities That Endure? Racial Ideology, American Politics, and the Peculiar Role of the Social Sciences." In *The Changing Terrain of Race and Ethnicity*, edited by Maria Krysan and Amanda E. Lewis, 13–42. New York: Russell Sage Foundation.

Bobo, Lawrence, and Camille L. Zubrinsky. 1996. "Attitudes on Residential Integration: Perceived Status Differences, Mere In-Group Preference, or Racial Prejudice?" *Social Forces* 74 (3): 883–909.

Bonilla-Silva, Eduardo. 1997. "Rethinking Racism: Toward a Structural Interpretation." *American Sociological Review* 62 (3): 465–80.

———. 2018. *Racism without Racists: Color-Blind Racism and the Persistence of Racial Inequality in America*. 5th ed. Lanham, MD: Rowman and Littlefield.

Bonilla-Silva, Eduardo, and Tyrone A. Forman. 2000. "'I Am Not a Racist But . . .': Mapping White College Students' Racial Ideology in the USA." *Discourse & Society* 11 (1): 50–85.

Bonilla-Silva, Eduardo, Carla Goar, and David G. Embrick. 2006. "When Whites Flock Together: The Social Psychology of White Habitus." *Critical Sociology* 32 (2–3): 229–53.

Bourdieu, Pierre. 1977. *Outline of a Theory of Practice.* Translated by Richard Nice. New York: Cambridge University Press.

Bowman, Phillip J., and Cleopatra Howard. 1985. "Race-Related Socialization, Motivation, and Academic Achievement: A Study of Black Youths in Three-Generation Families." *Journal of the American Academy of Child Psychiatry* 24 (2): 134–41.

Brega, Angela G., and Lerita M. Coleman. 1999. "Effects of Religiosity and Racial Socialization on Subjective Stigmatization in African-American Adolescents." *Journal of Adolescence* 22 (2): 223–42.

Bridges, Khiara M. 2011. *Reproducing Race: An Ethnography of Pregnancy as a Site of Racialization.* Berkeley: University of California Press.

Bronfenbrenner, Urie. 1979. *The Ecology of Human Development: Experiments by Nature and Design.* Cambridge, MA: Harvard University Press.

Brown, Tony N., Emily E. Tanner-Smith, Chase L. Lesane-Brown, and Michael E. Ezell. 2007. "Child, Parent, and Situational Correlates of Familial Ethnic/Race Socialization." *Journal of Marriage and Family* 69 (1): 14–25.

Buddin, Richard J., Joseph J. Cordes, and Sheila Nataraj Kirby. 1998. "School Choice in California: Who Chooses Private Schools?" *Journal of Urban Economics* 44 (1): 110–34.

Burton, Linda M., Eduardo Bonilla-Silva, Victor Ray, Rose Buckelew, and Elizabeth Hordge Freeman. 2010. "Critical Race Theories, Colorism, and the Decade's Research on Families of Color." *Journal of Marriage and Family* 72 (3): 440–59.

Calarco, Jessica McCrory. 2011. "'I Need Help!' Social Class and Children's Help-Seeking in Elementary School." *American Sociological Review* 76 (6): 862–82.

Carman, Carol A. 2011. "Adding Personality to Gifted Identification: Relationships among Traditional and Personality-Based Constructs." *Journal of Advanced Academics* 22 (3): 412–46.

Carr, Leslie G. 1997. *"Color-Blind" Racism.* Thousand Oaks, CA: Sage.

Charles, Camille Zubrinsky. 2003. "The Dynamics of Racial Residential Segregation." *Annual Review of Sociology* 29:167–207.

Charmaz, Kathy. 2001. "Grounded Theory." In *Contemporary Field Research: Perspectives and Formulations*, 2nd ed., edited by Robert M. Emerson, 335–52. Prospect Heights, IL: Waveland.

Coles, Roberta, and Charles Green, eds. 2009. *The Myth of the Missing Black Father.* New York: Columbia University Press.

Constantine, Madonna G., and Sha'Kema M. Blackmon. 2002. "Black Adolescents' Racial Socialization Experiences Their Relations to Home, School, and Peer Self-Esteem." *Journal of Black Studies* 32 (3): 322–35.

Cookson, Peter W., and Caroline Hodges Persell. 1987. *Preparing for Power: America's Elite Boarding Schools.* New York: Basic Books.

Cornell, Stephen E., and Douglas Hartmann. 2006. *Ethnicity and Race: Making Identities in a Changing World*. 2nd ed. Thousand Oaks, CA: Pine Forge.

Corsaro, William A. 2014. *The Sociology of Childhood*. 4th ed. Los Angeles: Sage.

Crenshaw, Kimberlé. 1997. "Color-Blind Dreams and Racial Nightmares: Reconfiguring Racism in the Post–Civil Rights Era." In *Birth of a Nation'hood: Gaze, Script, and Spectacle in the O. J. Simpson Case*, edited by Toni Morrison and C. B. Lacour, 97–168. New York: Pantheon.

Crowder, Kyle, and Liam Downey. 2010. "Inter-neighborhood Migration, Race, and Environmental Hazards: Modeling Micro-level Processes of Environmental Inequality." *AJS: American Journal of Sociology* 115 (4): 1110–49.

Crowder, Kyle, and Maria Krysan. 2016. "Moving beyond the Big Three: A Call for New Approaches to Studying Racial Residential Segregation." *City & Community* 15 (1): 18–22.

Cucchiara, Maia Bloomfield. 2013. *Marketing Schools, Marketing Cities: Who Wins and Who Loses When Schools Become Urban Amenities*. Chicago: University of Chicago Press.

Davis, Angela Y. 1983. *Women, Race, and Class*. New York: Vintage Books.

Dell'Antonia, K. J. 2014. "Talking about Racism with White Kids." *Motherlode* (blog), *New York Times*, 25 November. www.parenting.blogs.nytimes.com.

Delpit, Lisa. 2006. *Other People's Children: Cultural Conflict in the Classroom*. New York: New Press.

Democracy Now. 2015. "A Deadly U-Turn: Did Miriam Carey Need to Die after Wrong Car Move at White House Checkpoint?" 17 March. www.democracynow.org.

———. 2017. "Michael Brown." 13 March. www.democracynow.org.

Derman-Sparks, Louise, Carol Brunson Phillips, and Asa G. Hilliard. 1997. *Teaching/Learning Anti-Racism: A Developmental Approach*. 2nd ed. New York: Teachers College Press.

Desilver, Drew. 2014. "How the Most Ideologically Polarized Americans Live Different Lives." Pew Research Center. 13 June. www.pewresearch.org.

Dewan, Shaila, and Richard A. Oppel Jr. 2015. "In Tamir Rice Case, Many Errors by Cleveland Police, Then a Fatal One." *New York Times*, 22 January. www.nytimes.com.

DiAngelo, Robin. 2011. "White Fragility." *International Journal of Critical Pedagogy* 3 (3) 54–70. www.libjournal.uncg.edu.

Doane, Ashley W. 1997. "Dominant Group Ethnic Identity in the United States:" *Sociological Quarterly* 38 (3): 375–97.

Douglass, Sara, and Adriana J. Umaña-Taylor. 2015. "Development of Ethnic-Racial Identity among Latino Adolescents and the Role of Family." *Journal of Applied Developmental Psychology* 41 (November): 90–98.

Du Bois, W. E. B. 1994. *The Souls of Black Folk*. Chicago: Knopf.

———. 1998. *Black Reconstruction in America, 1860–1880*. New York: Free Press. First published 1935.

Dubrofsky, Rachel E. 2013. "Jewishness, Whiteness, and Blackness on *Glee*: Singing to the Tune of Postracism." *Communication, Culture & Critique* 6 (1): 82–102.

Eberhardt, Maeve, and Kara Freeman. 2015. "'First Things First, I'm the Realest': Linguistic Appropriation, White Privilege, and the Hip-Hop Persona of Iggy Azalea." *Journal of Sociolinguistics* 19 (3): 303–27.

Emerson, Robert M. 2001. *Contemporary Field Research: Perspectives and Formulations.* 2nd ed. Prospect Heights, IL: Waveland.

Farley, Reynolds, and William H. Frey. 1994. "Changes in the Segregation of Whites from Blacks during the 1980s: Small Steps toward a More Integrated Society." *American Sociological Review* 59 (1): 23–45.

Feagin, Joe R., and Eileen O'Brien. 2004. *White Men on Race: Power, Privilege, and the Shaping of Cultural Consciousness.* Boston: Beacon.

Fenning, Pamela, and Jennifer Rose. 2007. "Overrepresentation of African American Students in Exclusionary Discipline: The Role of School Policy." *Urban Education* 42 (6): 536–59.

Fernandez, Manney, and Christine Hauser. 2015. "Handcuffed for Making Clock, Ahmed Mohamed, 14, Wins Time with Obama." *New York Times.* 16 September. www.nytimes.com.

Flavin, Jeanne. 2008. *Our Bodies, Our Crimes: The Policing of Women's Reproduction in America.* New York: NYU Press.

Forman, Tyrone A. 2004. "Color-Blind Racism and Racial Indifference: The Role of Racial Apathy in Facilitating Enduring Inequalities." In *The Changing Terrain of Race and Ethnicity*, edited by Maria Krysan and Amanda E. Lewis, 43–66. New York: Russell Sage Foundation.

Forman, Tyrone A., and Amanda E. Lewis. 2006. "Racial Apathy and Hurricane Katrina: The Social Anatomy of Prejudice in the Post–Civil Rights Era." *Du Bois Review: Social Science Research on Race* 3 (1): 175–202.

Frankenberg, Erica, and Gary Orfield, eds. 2012. *The Resegregation of Suburban Schools: A Hidden Crisis in American Education.* Cambridge, MA: Harvard Education Press.

Fraser, Sandy, Vicky Lewis, Sharon Ding, Mary Kellett, and Chris Robinson, eds. 2003. *Doing Research with Children and Young People.* Thousand Oaks, CA: Sage.

Freeman, Melissa, and Sandra Mathiston. 2008. *Researching Children's Experiences.* New York: Guilford.

Frønes, Ivar. 1994. "Dimensions of Childhood." In *Childhood Matters: Social Theory, Practice and Politics*, edited by Jens Qvortrup, Marjatta Bardy, Giovanni Sgritta, and Helmut Wintersberger, 145–64. Aldershot, UK: Avebury.

Gallagher, Charles A. 2003. "Color-Blind Privilege: The Social and Political Functions of Erasing the Color Line in Post-Race America." *Race, Gender & Class* 10 (4): 22–37.

———. 2008. "'The End of Racism' as the New Doxa: New Strategies from Researching Race." In *White Logic, White Methods: Racism and Methodology*, edited by Tukufu Zuberi and Eduardo Bonilla-Silva, 163–78. Lanham, MD: Rowman and Littlefield.

Garcia, Lorena. 2012. *Respect Yourself, Protect Yourself: Latina Girls and Sexual Identity*. New York: NYU Press.

Gartner, Meaghan, Lisa Kiang, and Andrew Supple. 2014. "Prospective Links between Ethnic Socialization, Ethnic and American Identity, and Well-Being among Asian-American Adolescents." *Journal of Youth and Adolescence* 43 (10): 1715–27.

Goff, Phillip Atiba, Matthew Christian Jackson, Brooke Allison Lewis Di Leone, Carmen Marie Culotta, and Natalie Ann DiTomasso. 2014. "The Essence of Innocence: Consequences of Dehumanizing Black Children." *Journal of Personality and Social Psychology* 106 (4): 526–45.

Goffman, Erving. 1959. *The Presentation of Self in Everyday Life*. New York: Anchor Books.

Gottzén, Lucas, and Tamar Kremer-Sadlik. 2012. "Fatherhood and Youth Sports: A Balancing Act between Care and Expectations." *Gender & Society* 26 (4): 639–64.

Goyal, Monika K., Nathan Kuppermann, Sean D. Cleary, Stephen J. Teach, and James M. Chamberlain. 2015. "Racial Disparities in Pain Management of Children with Appendicitis in Emergency Departments." *JAMA Pediatrics* 169 (11): 996–1002.

Goyette, Kimberly, and Annette Lareau. 2014. Preface to *Choosing Homes, Choosing Schools*, edited by Annette Lareau and Kimberly Goyette, xi–xxiii. New York: Russell Sage Foundation.

Graham, David A. 2017. "The Shooting of Jordan Edwards." *Atlantic*. 2 May. www.theatlantic.com.

Greenberg, Bradley S. 1972. "Children's Reactions to T.V. Blacks." *Journalism Quarterly* 49 (1): 5–14.

Gregory, Anne, Russell J. Skiba, and Pedro A. Noguera. 2010. "The Achievement Gap and the Discipline Gap Two Sides of the Same Coin?" *Educational Researcher* 39 (1): 59–68.

Guidotti-Hernández, Nicole M. 2007. "*Dora the Explorer*, Constructing 'Latinidades' and the Politics of Global Citizenship." *Latino Studies* 5 (2): 209–32.

Hackman, Rose. 2015. "'She Was Only a Baby': Last Charge Dropped in Police Raid That Killed Sleeping Detroit Child." *Guardian*. 31 January. www.theguardian.com.

Hagerman, Margaret Ann. 2010. "I Like Being Intervieeeeeeewed!: Children's Perspectives on Participating in Social Research." In *Children and Youth Speak for Themselves*, vol. 13, edited by Heather Beth Johnson 61–105. Sociological Studies of Children and Youth. Bingley, UK: Emerald.

———. 2016. "Reproducing and Reworking Colorblind Racial Ideology: Acknowledging Children's Agency in the White Habitus." *Sociology of Race and Ethnicity* 2 (1): 58–71.

———. 2017a. "'The Celebrity Thing': Using Photographs of Celebrities in Child-Centered, Ethnographic Interviews with White Kids about Race." In *Researching Children and Youth: Methodological Issues, Strategies, and Innovations*, Sociological Studies of Children and Youth 22, edited by Ingrid E. Castro, Melissa Swauger, and Brent Harger, 303–24. Bingley, UK: Emerald.

———. 2017b. "White Racial Socialization: Progressive Fathers on Raising 'Antiracist' Children." *Journal of Marriage and Family* 79 (1): 60–74.

Hall, Stuart. 1996. "New Ethnicities." In *Stuart Hall: Critical Dialogues in Cultural Studies*, edited by David Morley and Kuan-Hsing Chen, 442–52. New York: Routledge.

Halley, Jean, Amy Eshleman, and Ramya Mahadevan Vijaya. 2011. *Seeing White: An Introduction to White Privilege and Race*. Lanham, MD: Rowman and Littlefield.

Hamm, Jill V. 2001. "Barriers and Bridges to Positive Cross-Ethnic Relations African American and White Parent Socialization Beliefs and Practices." *Youth & Society* 33 (1): 62–98.

Handel, Gerald. 2006. *Childhood Socialization*. London: Transaction.

Haney López, Ian. 1996. *White by Law: The Legal Construction of Race*. New York: NYU Press.

Hartigan, John. 1999. *Racial Situations: Class Predicaments of Whiteness in Detroit*. Princeton, NJ: Princeton University Press.

Holme, Jennifer Jellison. 2002. "Buying Homes, Buying Schools: School Choice and the Social Construction of School Quality." *Harvard Educational Review* 72 (2): 177–206.

Hughes, Diane. 2003. "Correlates of African American and Latino Parents' Messages to Children about Ethnicity and Race: A Comparative Study of Racial Socialization." *American Journal of Community Psychology* 31 (1–2): 15–33.

Hughes, Diane, and Lisa Chen. 1997. "When and What Parents Tell Children about Race: An Examination of Race-Related Socialization among African American Families." *Applied Developmental Science* 1 (4): 200–214.

Hughes, Diane, and Deborah Johnson. 2001. "Correlates in Children's Experiences of Parents' Racial Socialization Behaviors." *Journal of Marriage and Family* 63 (4): 981–95.

Hughes, Diane, James Rodriguez, Emilie P. Smith, Deborah J. Johnson, Howard C. Stevenson, and Paul Spicer. 2006. "Parents' Ethnic-Racial Socialization Practices: A Review of Research and Directions for Future Study." *Developmental Psychology* 42 (5): 747–70.

Hughes, Laurel E. 2001. *Paving Pathways: Child and Adolescent Development*. Belmont, CA: Wadsworth.

Hughey, Matthew. 2012. *White Bound: Nationalists, Antiracists, and the Shared Meanings of Race*. Stanford, CA: Stanford University Press.

———. 2014. *The White Savior Film: Content, Critics, and Consumption*. Philadelphia: Temple University Press.

Jarvie, Jenny. 2015. "Girl Thrown from Desk Didn't Obey Because the Punishment Was Unfair, Attorney Says." *Los Angeles Times*. 29 October. www.latimes.com.

Jewell, Karen S. 2003. *Survival of the African American Family: The Institutional Impact of U.S. Social Policy*. Westport, CT: Praeger.

Johnson, Heather Beth. 2001. "From the Chicago School to the New Sociology of Children: The Sociology of Children and Childhood in the United States, 1900–1999." In *Advances in Life Course Research*, vol. 6, *Children at the*

Millennium: Where Have We Come From, Where Are We Going?, edited by Timothy Joseph Owens and Sandra L. Hofferth, 53–93. Greenwich, CT: JAI.

———. 2014. *The American Dream and the Power of Wealth: Choosing Schools and Inheriting Inequality in the Land of Opportunity.* 2nd ed. New York: Routledge.

Johnson, Leanor Boulin, and Robert Staples. 2004. *Black Families at the Crossroads: Challenges and Prospects.* Rev. ed. San Francisco: Jossey-Bass.

Kefalas, Maria J. 2003. *Working-Class Heroes: Protecting Home, Community, and Nation in a Chicago Neighborhood.* Berkeley: University of California Press.

Kenny, Lorraine, ed. 2000. *Daughters of Suburbia: Growing Up White, Middle Class, and Female.* New Brunswick, NJ: Rutgers University Press.

Kimmel, Michael. 2015. *Angry White Men: American Masculinity at the End of an Era.* New York: Nation Books.

Kinder, Donald R., and Lynn M. Sanders. 1996. *Divided by Color: Racial Politics and Democratic Ideals.* Chicago: University of Chicago Press.

Kitwana, Bakari. 2005. *Why White Kids Love Hip-Hop: Wankstas, Wiggers, Wannabes, and the New Reality of Race in America.* New York: Basic Books.

Knight, George P., Martha E. Bernal, Camille A. Garza, Marya K. Cota, and Katheryn A. Ocampo. 1993. "Family Socialization and the Ethnic Identity of Mexican-American Children." *Journal of Cross-Cultural Psychology* 24 (1): 99–114.

Kozol, Jonathan. 2012. *Savage Inequalities: Children in America's Schools.* New York: Broadway Books.

Krysan, Maria, Mick P. Couper, Reynolds Farley, and Tyrone A. Forman. 2009. "Does Race Matter in Neighborhood Preferences? Results from a Video Experiment." *American Journal of Sociology* 115 (2): 527–59.

Krysan, Maria, and Amanda E. Lewis, eds. 2006. *The Changing Terrain of Race and Ethnicity.* New York: Russell Sage Foundation.

Kupchik, Aaron. 2007. *Judging Juveniles: Prosecuting Adolescents in Adult and Juvenile Courts.* New York: NYU Press.

Lacy, Karyn R. 2007. *Blue-Chip Black: Race, Class, and Status in the New Black Middle Class.* Berkeley: University of California Press.

Lacy, Karen R., and Angel L. Harris. 2010. "Breaking the Class Monolith: Understanding Class Differences in Black Adolescents' Attachment to Racial Identity." In *Social Class: How Does It Work?*, edited by Annette Lareau and Dalton Conley, 152–78. New York: Russell Sage Foundation.

Lamont, Michèle. 1992. *Money, Morals, and Manners: The Culture of the French and the American Upper-Middle Class.* Chicago: University of Chicago Press.

Lareau, Annette. 2011. *Unequal Childhoods: Class, Race, and Family Life.* 2nd ed. Berkeley: University of California Press.

Lareau, Annette, and Kimberly Goyette, eds. 2014. *Choosing Homes, Choosing Schools.* New York: Russell Sage Foundation.

Lasker, Judith N. 2016. *Hoping to Help: The Promises and Pitfalls of Global Health Volunteering.* Ithaca, NY: Cornell University Press.

LaVeist, Thomas, Keshia Pollack, Roland Thorpe, Ruth Fesahazion, and Darrell Gaskin. 2011. "Place, Not Race: Disparities Dissipate in Southwest Baltimore When Blacks and Whites Live under Similar Conditions." *Health Affairs* 30 (10): 1880–87.

Leahy, Meghan. 2015. "We Need to Deal with Our Discomfort and Talk to Our Kids about Racism." *Washington Post*, 1 July. www.washingtonpost.com.

Lewis, Amanda E. 2003. *Race in the Schoolyard: Negotiating the Color Line in Classrooms and Communities*. New Brunswick, NJ: Rutgers University Press.

———. 2004. "'What Group?' Studying Whites and Whiteness in the Era of 'Color-Blindness.'" *Sociological Theory* 22 (4): 623–46.

Lewis, Amanda E., and John B. Diamond. 2015. *Despite the Best Intentions: How Racial Inequality Thrives in Good Schools*. New York: Oxford University Press.

Lewis, Amanda E., and Margaret Ann Hagerman. 2016. "Using Ethnography and Interviews to Study Color-Blind Racial Ideology." In *The Myth of Racial Color Blindness: Manifestations, Dynamics, and Impact*, edited by H. A. Neville, M. E. Gallardo, and D. W. Sue, 157–71. Washington, DC: American Psychological Association.

Lewis, Amanda E., and Michelle J. Manno. 2011. "The Best Education for Some: Race and Schooling in the United States Today." In *State of White Supremacy: Racism, Governance, and the United States*, edited by Moon-Kie Jung, João Costa Vargas, and Eduardo Bonilla-Silva, 93–109. Stanford, CA: Stanford University Press.

Li, Mingliang. 2009. "Is There 'White Flight' into Private Schools? New Evidence from High School and Beyond." *Economics of Education Review* 28 (3): 382–92.

Lipsitz, George. 2009. *The Possessive Investment in Whiteness: How White People Profit from Identity Politics, Revised and Expanded Edition*. Philadelphia: Temple University Press.

Lofland, John, David A. Snow, Leon Anderson, and Lyn H. Lofland. 2005. *Analyzing Social Settings: A Guide to Qualitative Observation and Analysis*. 4th ed. Belmont, CA: Cengage Learning.

Lowery, Wesley. 2016. "Korryn Gaines, Cradling a Child and Shotgun, Is Fatally Shot by Police." *Washington Post*, 2 August. www.washingtonpost.com.

Massey, Douglas S., and Nancy A. Denton. 1993. *American Apartheid: Segregation and the Making of the Underclass*. Cambridge, MA: Harvard University Press.

Matlock, Sarah A., and Robin DiAngelo. 2015. "'We Put It in Terms of Not-Nice': White Antiracists and Parenting." *Journal of Progressive Human Services* 26 (1): 67–92.

McAdoo, Harriette Pipes, ed. 2006. *Black Families*. 4th ed. Thousand Oaks, CA: Sage.

McDermott, Monica. 2006. *Working-Class White: The Making and Unmaking of Race Relations*. Berkeley: University of California Press.

McDermott, Monica, and Frank L. Samson. 2005. "White Racial and Ethnic Identity in the United States." *Annual Review of Sociology* 31:245–61.

McIntosh, Peggy. 1989. "White Privilege: Unpacking the Invisible Knapsack." *Peace and Freedom Magazine*, July–August.

Meece, Judith. 2002. *Child and Adolescent Development for Educators*. 3rd ed. New York: McGraw-Hill.

Meiners, Erica R. 2007. *Right to Be Hostile: Schools, Prisons, and the Making of Public Enemies*. New York: Routledge.

Messner, Michael A. 2009. *It's All for the Kids: Gender, Families, and Youth Sports*. Berkeley: University of California Press.

Meyer, Stephen Grant. 2001. *As Long as They Don't Move Next Door: Segregation and Racial Conflict in American Neighborhoods*. Lanham, MD: Rowman and Littlefield.

Moran, Kristin C. 2007. "The Growth of Spanish-Language and Latino-Themed Television Programs for Children in the United States." *Journal of Children and Media* 1 (3): 294–300.

Moyer, Melinda Wenner. 2014. "Teaching Tolerance." *Slate*, 30 March. www.slate.com.

Myers, Kristen A. 2005. *Racetalk: Racism Hiding in Plain Sight*. Lanham, MD: Rowman and Littlefield.

Nicholson-Crotty, Sean, Zachary Birchmeier, and David Valentine. 2009. "Exploring the Impact of School Discipline on Racial Disproportion in the Juvenile Justice System." *Social Science Quarterly* 90 (4): 1003–18.

Noguera, Pedro A. 2009. *The Trouble with Black Boys: . . . And Other Reflections on Race, Equity, and the Future of Public Education*. San Francisco: Jossey-Bass.

Oakes, Jeannie. 2005. *Keeping Track: How Schools Structure Inequality*. 2nd rev. ed. New Haven, CT: Yale University Press.

Oliver, Melvin, and Thomas M. Shapiro, eds. 2006. *Black Wealth / White Wealth: A New Perspective on Racial Inequality*. 2nd ed. New York: Routledge.

Omi, Michael, and Howard Winant. 2014. *Racial Formation in the United States*. 3rd ed. New York: Routledge.

Orbe, M. P. 1999. "Communicating about 'Race' in Interracial Families." In *Communication, Race, and Family: Exploring Communication in Black, White, and Biracial Families*, edited by Thomas J. Socha and Rhunette C. Diggs, 167–80. Mahwah, NJ: Erlbaum.

Orfield, Gary, John Kucsera, and Genevieve Siegel-Hawley. 2012. "E Pluribus . . . Separation: Deepening Double Segregation for More Students." Civil Rights Project / Proyecto Derechos Civiles. www.civilrightsproject.ucla.edu.

Ou, Young-shi, and Harriette Pipes McAdoo. 1993. "Socialization of Chinese American Children." In *Family Ethnicity: Strength in Diversity*, edited by Harriette Pipes McAdoo, 245–70. Thousand Oaks, CA: Sage.

Parsons, Talcott, and R. F. Bales. 1956. *Family, Socialization and Interaction Process*. London: Routledge and Kegan Paul.

Pascoe, C. J. 2011. *Dude, You're a Fag: Masculinity and Sexuality in High School*. 2nd ed. Berkeley: University of California Press.

Pearce, Matt. 2015. "Texas Officer Suspended after Aggressively Confronting Teens at Pool Party." *Los Angeles Times*, 8 June. www.latimes.com.

Perry, Pamela, and Alexis Shotwell. 2009. "Relational Understanding and White Antiracist Praxis." *Sociological Theory* 27 (1): 33–50.

Peters, Marie F. 2002. "Racial Socialization of Young Black Children." In *Black Children: Social, Educational, and Parental Environments*, edited by Harriette Pipes McAdoo, 57–72. Thousand Oaks, CA: Sage.

Pettigrew, Thomas F. 1998. "Intergroup Contact Theory." *Annual Review of Psychology* 49 (1): 65–85.

Phinney, Jean S., and Victor Chavira. 1995. "Parental Ethnic Socialization and Adolescent Coping with Problems Related to Ethnicity." *Journal of Research on Adolescence* 5 (1): 31–53.

Picca, Leslie, and Joe Feagin. 2007. *Two-Faced Racism: Whites in the Backstage and Frontstage*. New York: Routledge.

Poehlmann, Julie, Danielle Dallaire, Ann Booker Loper, and Leslie D. Shear. 2010. "Children's Contact with Their Incarcerated Parents: Research Findings and Recommendations." *American Psychologist* 65 (6): 575–98.

Polednak, A P. 1991. "Black-White Differences in Infant Mortality in 38 Standard Metropolitan Statistical Areas." *American Journal of Public Health* 81 (11): 1480–82.

Posey, Linn. 2012. "Middle- and Upper-Middle-Class Parent Action for Urban Public Schools: Promise or Paradox?" *Teachers College Record* 114 (1): 122–64.

Posey-Maddox, Linn. 2013. "Professionalizing the PTO: Race, Class, and Shifting Norms of Parental Engagement in a City Public School." *American Journal of Education* 119 (2): 235–60.

———. 2014. *When Middle-Class Parents Choose Urban Schools: Class, Race, and the Challenge of Equity in Public Education*. Chicago: University of Chicago Press.

Quadagno, Jill. 1996. *The Color of Welfare: How Racism Undermined the War on Poverty*. New York: Oxford University Press.

Quintana, Stephen M., and Elizabeth M. Vera. 1999. "Mexican American Children's Ethnic Identity, Understanding of Ethnic Prejudice, and Parental Ethnic Socialization." *Hispanic Journal of Behavioral Sciences* 21 (4): 387–404.

Rasmussen, Birgit Brander, Irene J. Nexica, Eric Klinenberg, and Matt Wray. 2001. *The Making and Unmaking of Whiteness*. Durham, NC: Duke University Press.

Rivas-Drake, Deborah. 2010. "Ethnic-Racial Socialization and Adjustment among Latino College Students: The Mediating Roles of Ethnic Centrality, Public Regard, and Perceived Barriers to Opportunity." *Journal of Youth and Adolescence* 40 (5): 606–19.

Robbins, Alexandra. 2007. *The Overachievers: The Secret Lives of Driven Kids*. New York: Hachette Books.

Roberts, Dorothy. 2002. *Shattered Bonds: The Color of Child Welfare*. New York: Basic Civitas Books.

———. 2011. *Fatal Invention: How Science, Politics, and Big Business Re-create Race in the Twenty-First Century*. New York: New Press.

Roberts, Ebony M. 2004. "Through the Eyes of a Child: Representations of Blackness in Children's Television Programming." *Race, Gender & Class* 11 (2): 130–39.

Rockquemore, Kerry Ann, and Tracey A. Laszloffy. 2005. *Raising Biracial Children*. Lanham, MD: AltaMira.

Roda, Allison. 2015. *Inequality in Gifted and Talented Programs: Parental Choices about Status, School Opportunity, and Second-Generation Segregation*. New York: Springer.

Roda, Allison, and Amy Stuart Wells. 2013. "School Choice Policies and Racial Segregation: Where White Parents' Good Intentions, Anxiety, and Privilege Collide." *American Journal of Education* 119 (2): 261–93.

Rodriquez, Jason. 2006. "Color-Blind Ideology and the Cultural Appropriation of Hip-Hop." *Journal of Contemporary Ethnography* 35 (6): 645–68.

Roediger, David R. 2007. *The Wages of Whiteness: Race and the Making of the American Working Class*. New York: Verso.

Rollins, Alethea, and Andrea G. Hunter. 2013. "Racial Socialization of Biracial Youth: Maternal Messages and Approaches to Address Discrimination." *Family Relations* 62 (1): 140–53.

Saporito, Salvatore. 2003. "Private Choices, Public Consequences: Magnet School Choice and Segregation by Race and Poverty." *Social Problems* 50 (2): 181–203.

Saporito, Salvatore, and Caroline Hanley. 2014. "Declining Significance of Race?" In *Choosing Homes, Choosing Schools*, edited by Annette Lareau and Kimberly A Goyette, 64–96. New York: Russell Sage Foundation.

Schneider, Mark. 2001. "Information and Choice in Educational Privatization." In *Privatizing Education: Can the School Marketplace Deliver Freedom of Choice, Efficiency, Equity, and Social Cohesion?*, edited by Henry Levin, 72–102. Boulder, CO: Westview.

Scholl, Claire. 2015. "Woman Killed in Oxnard Officer-Involved Shooting." KEYT.com, 30 March 2015.

Scottham, Krista Maywalt, and Ciara P. Smalls. 2009. "Unpacking Racial Socialization: Considering Female African American Primary Caregivers' Racial Identity." *Journal of Marriage and Family* 71 (4): 807–18.

Sears, David O., and P. J. Henry. 2003. "The Origins of Symbolic Racism." *Journal of Personality and Social Psychology* 85 (2): 259–75.

Shapiro, Thomas M., and Heather Beth Johnson. 2005. "Family Assets and School Access: Race and Class in the Structuring of Educational Opportunity." In *Inclusion in the American Dream: Assets, Poverty, and Public Policy*, edited by Michael Sherraden, 112–27. New York: Oxford University Press.

Skiba, Russell J., Robert H. Horner, Choong-Geun Chung, M. Karega Rausch, Seth L. May, and Tary Tobin. 2011. "Race Is Not Neutral: A National Investigation of African American and Latino Disproportionality in School Discipline." *School Psychology Review* 40 (1): 85–107.

Solinger, Rickie. 2002. *Beggars and Choosers: How the Politics of Choice Shapes Adoption, Abortion, and Welfare in the United States*. New York: Hill and Wang.

Steinbrink, Malte. 2012. " 'We Did the Slum!'—Urban Poverty Tourism in Historical Perspective." *Tourism Geographies* 14 (2): 213–34.

Sue, Derald Wing. 2005. "Racism and the Conspiracy of Silence: Presidential Address." *Counseling Psychologist* 33 (1): 100–114.

Sugrue, Thomas J. 2005. *The Origins of the Urban Crisis: Race and Inequality in Postwar Detroit.* Princeton, NJ: Princeton University Press.

Sullivan, Zoe. 2015. "Tony Robinson's Mother Files Civil Rights Lawsuit over Fatal Police Shooting of Son." *Guardian*, 13 August. www.theguardian.com.

Takaki, Ronald. 1998. *Strangers from a Different Shore: A History of Asian Americans.* Rev. ed. Boston: Little, Brown.

Thomas, Anita Jones, and Sha'Kema M. Blackmon. 2015. "The Influence of the Trayvon Martin Shooting on Racial Socialization Practices of African American Parents." *Journal of Black Psychology* 41 (1): 75–89.

Thorne, Barrie. 1993. *Gender Play: Girls and Boys in School.* New Brunswick, NJ: Rutgers University Press.

Thornton, Michael C. 1997. "Strategies of Racial Socialization Among Black Parents: Mainstream, Minority and Cultural Messages." In *Family Life in Black America*, edited by Robert Joseph Taylor, James S. Jackson, and Linda Marie Chatters, 201–15. Thousand Oaks, CA: Sage.

Thornton, Russell. 1990. *American Indian Holocaust and Survival: A Population History since 1492.* Norman: University of Oklahoma Press.

Threlfall, Jennifer Mary. 2016. "Parenting in the Shadow of Ferguson: Racial Socialization Practices in Context." *Youth and Society*, September. OnlineFirst: dx.doi.org.

Tilly, Charles. 1999. *Durable Inequality.* Rev. ed. Berkeley: University of California Press.

Travis, Jeremy, and Michelle Waul. 2004. *Prisoners Once Removed: The Impact of Incarceration and Reentry on Children, Families, and Communities.* Washington, DC: Urban Institute Press.

Turner, Margery Austin, and Ron Wienk. 1993. "The Persistence of Segregation in Urban Areas: Contributing Causes." In *Housing Markets and Residential Mobility*, edited by G. Thomas Kingsley and Margery Austin Turner. Washington, DC: Urban Institute Press.

Tyson, Karolyn. 2011. *Integration Interrupted: Tracking, Black Students, and Acting White after Brown.* New York: Oxford University Press.

Underhill, Megan R. 2017. "Parenting during Ferguson: Making Sense of White Parents' Silence." *Ethnic and Racial Studies*, 1–18.

Urry, John. 1990. *The Tourist Gaze: Leisure and Travel in Contemporary Societies.* Newbury Park, CA: Sage.

Van Ausdale, Debra, and Joe R. Feagin. 2001. *The First R: How Children Learn Race and Racism.* Lanham, MD: Rowman and Littlefield.

Van Evra, Judith Van. 2004. *Television and Child Development.* 3rd ed. Mahwah, NJ: Erlbaum.

Vawter, Eve. 2015. "Here's How You Talk to Your Kids about the Tragedy in Charleston." *SheKnows*, 19 June. www.sheknows.com.

Vittrup, Brigitte. 2015. "How Silence Can Breed Prejudice: A Child Development Professor Explains How and Why to Talk to Kids about Race." *Washington Post*, 6 July. www.washingtonpost.com.

Wakefield, Sara, and Christopher Wildeman. 2016. *Children of the Prison Boom: Mass Incarceration and the Future of American Inequality.* New York: Oxford University Press.

Walks, R. Alan. 2006. "The Causes of City-Suburban Political Polarization? A Canadian Case Study." *Annals of the Association of American Geographers* 96 (2): 390–414.

Whyte, Kyle Powys, Evan Selinger, and Kevin Outterson. 2011. "Poverty Tourism and the Problem of Consent." *Journal of Global Ethics* 7 (3): 337–48.

Winkler, Erin N. 2008. "'It's Like Arming Them': African American Mothers' Views on Racial Socialization." In *The Changing Landscape of Work and Family in the American Middle Class: Reports from the Field*, edited by Elizabeth Rudd and Lara Descartes, 211–41. Lanham, MD: Lexington Books.

———. 2010. "'I Learn Being Black from Everywhere I Go': Color Blindness, Travel, and the Formation of Racial Attitudes among African American Adolescents." In *Children and Youth Speak for Themselves*, vol. 13 edited by Heather Beth Johnson, 423–53. Bingley, UK: Emerald.

———. 2012. *Learning Race, Learning Place: Shaping Racial Identities and Ideas in African American Childhoods.* New Brunswick, NJ: Rutgers University Press.

Winn, Maisha T. 2011. *Girl Time: Literacy, Justice, and School-to-Prison Pipeline.* New York: Teachers College Press.

Zamal, Faiyaz, Wendy Liu, and Derek Ruths. 2012. "Homophily and Latent Attribute Inference: Inferring Latent Attributes of Twitter Users from Neighbors." Conference Proceedings, Sixth International AAAI Conference on Weblogs and Social Media. www.aaai.org.

Zhang, Haifeng. 2008. "White Flight in the Context of Education: Evidence from South Carolina." *Journal of Geography* 107 (6): 236–45.

Zinn, Maxine Baca. 1993. "Feminist Rethinking from Racial-Ethnic Families." In *Women of Color in U.S. Society*, edited by Maxine Baca Zinn and Bonnie Thornton Dill, 303–11. Philadelphia: Temple University Press.

Zuberi, Tukufu, and Eduardo Bonilla-Silva. 2008. "'The End of Racism' as the New Doxa: New Strategies for Researching Race." In *White Logic, White Methods: Racism and Methodology*, edited by Tukufu Zuberi and Eduardo Bonilla-Silva, 163–78. Lanham, MD: Rowman and Littlefield.

INDEX

ABOUT THE AUTHOR

Margaret A. Hagerman is Assistant Professor of Sociology at Mississippi State University.